The Merchant Prince
of Poverty Row

The Merchant Prince of Poverty Row

Harry Cohn of Columbia Pictures

BERNARD F. DICK

THE UNIVERSITY PRESS OF KENTUCKY

For William N. Graf and Paul N. Lazarus

Frontispiece: Harry Cohn sporting a bow tie and looking uncharacteristically benevolent. Library of Congress.

Copyright © 1993 by The University Press of Kentucky

Scholarly publisher for the Commonwealth,
serving Bellarmine College, Berea College, Centre
College of Kentucky, Eastern Kentucky University,
The Filson Club, Georgetown College, Kentucky
Historical Society, Kentucky State University,
Morehead State University, Murray State University,
Northern Kentucky University, Transylvania University,
University of Kentucky, University of Louisville,
and Western Kentucky University.

Editorial and Sales Offices: Lexington, Kentucky 40508-4008

Library of Congress Cataloging-in-Publication Data

Dick, Bernard F.
    The Merchant Prince of Poverty Row : Harry Cohn of Columbia
Pictures / Bernard F. Dick.

    p.   cm.
    Includes bibliographical references (p.   ) and index.
    ISBN 0-8131-1841-7
    1. Cohn, Harry, 1891-1958. 2. Columbia Pictures Corporation—
History. 3. Motion picture producers and directors—United States
—Biography. I. Title.
PN1998.3.C665D53   1993
791.43'0232'092—dc20   93-3348
[B]

Contents

[Illustrations follow pages 26 and 122]

Acknowledgments

My deepest gratitude is expressed in the dedication; had the late Lou Harris not put me in touch with William N. Graf, who then told me about Paul N. Lazarus, this book could never have taken the form it did. I must also acknowledge my usual indebtedness to my wife, Katherine M. Restaino, dean of St. Peter's College at Englewood Cliffs, New Jersey, for accompanying me on these voyages into the unknown; the archivists Ned Comstock and Sam Gill for making the unknown knowable; Fairleigh Dickinson University reference librarians Judy Katz and Laila Rogers, and periodicals librarian Mary MacMahon, for making the unknown available. And finally, my thanks go to Robert Blees, Vanessa Brown, Emmett D. Chisum, Robert Cohn, Betty Garrett, Anthony Greco, William Humphrey, Evelyn Keyes, Kristine Krueger, Lynne Larsen, Terrance McCluskey, Martin Nocente, Kim Novak, Alan Press, Ron Randell, Daniel Taradash, and Malvin Wald.

The two appendixes are courtesy of William N. Graf, Harry's former secretary, and Kristine Krueger of the National Film Information Service, respectively.

Introduction

Of all the studio heads of Hollywood's Golden Age, Harry Cohn (1891-1958) was the least typical. Compared to MGM's Louis Mayer, Harry was a late convert to film. He was almost thirty when he began to take the medium seriously; by the time he became president of Columbia in 1932, he was forty and had been in the business for thirteen years. By contrast, Louis Mayer bought his first movie house in 1907, when he was twenty-two, opened a second four years later, became secretary of Metro Pictures at thirty, and at thirty-nine gave his surname to Metro-Goldwyn, becoming vice-president of the "Tiffany" of studios, Metro-Goldwyn-Mayer.

True, Mayer was born in 1885, six years before Harry. Yet while Harry was leading sing-alongs in nickelodeons at the dawn of the movie palace era, Mayer was already planning to move from exhibition to distribution, later acquiring the New England rights to *The Birth of a Nation* (1915). One assumes that Harry saw D.W. Griffith's epic; but if he did, it did not convince him that film was the century's newest art form. In 1915, Broadway was Harry's beat and Tin Pan Alley was his milieu. If Harry envisioned himself as anything, it was as a Broadway impressario or a partner in a music publishing company.

Except for Darryl Zanuck, born in 1902 (and, if a year matters, Jack Warner, born in 1892), Harry Cohn was the youngest of the legendary moguls. Carl Laemmle was born in 1867, Adolph Zukor in 1873, Joseph Schenck in 1878, his brother Nicholas in 1881, William Fox in 1879, Sam Goldwyn probably in 1879 (and certainly not 1882, as he always claimed[1]), and Cecil B. De Mille in 1881. And Zanuck, who was almost ten years younger than Harry, was writing scripts at Warners at twenty-two; at that age, Harry, who could easily have been working in the movies, was doing a vaudeville act with Harry Ruby.

The story of Harry's entrance into the movies is not material for an American Dream scenario. He did not, like Mayer, buy a theater to get out of the junk business; nor did he go into exhibition when refused a raise, as Laemmle did. He started neither in the pulps like Zanuck nor in penny arcades like Zukor. Harry Cohn went into film primarily for one reason:

to rival his brother Jack, who was a respected editor at Universal when Harry was plugging songs in five-and-ten-cent stores.

Harry's animosity toward his brother was common knowledge in Hollywood. Friction between siblings is not unusual in the entertainment industry, which to a great extent is familial in both theory and practice. Not only were the studios extensions of the family, with a patriarchal head and surrogate children, but in some cases they were family-controlled (Warners) or nepotistic (Carl Laemmle's handing Universal over to his son, who was hardly up to the demands of production, much less at the beginning of the Great Depression; Republic's Herbert J. Yates's insistence on making his wife, Vera Hruba Ralston, a regular attraction in his films despite her limited acting ability).

While the brothers Warner (also Jack and Harry) were more like Romulus and Remus than Castor and Pollux, the brothers Cohn seem to have stepped out of a 1930s movie melodrama—the fraternal equivalent of *A Star Is Born* (1937), in which the more famous brother (Jack) recedes into the shadows as the newcomer (Harry) emerges to go on to even greater heights. But perhaps the most significant difference between the Warner brothers and Harry and Jack Cohn is that Jack Warner truly detested his brother, while Harry Cohn did not feel hatred toward Jack— he only wanted to punish him for reasons that will become clear in the early chapters. While a call from Harry left Jack shaking, Jack Cohn never returned his brother's hostility. Harry's need to surpass Jack resulted in estrangement but not mutual hatred.

Their story, and that of their studio, Columbia Pictures, can be corroborated by the coast-to-coast teletypes. The studio's story could be better documented if production files on the order of MGM's, Fox's, Warners', Paramount's, and Universal's (which are available, if not complete) existed. While one can consult the Paramount Collection at the Margaret Herrick Library of the Academy of Motion Picture Arts and Sciences or the Fox collection at UCLA, no library houses a Columbia collection.

Columbia started showing an interest in film preservation in the 1980s, but striking fresh prints or restoring lost footage is not the same as establishing a studio collection. Thomas Schatz's *The Genius of the System* has demonstrated the need for studying production files to understand a film's genesis and analyzing budgets to appreciate the economics of moviemaking.[2] Unfortunately, Columbia favored its films over its files— an understandable preference given the cavalier attitude Hollywood took toward its art. The movie's the thing; everything else is print or preproduction.

In Columbia's case, the situation was exacerbated by an event that occurred when Columbia moved from Gower Street to Burbank in 1972, joining Warners to form the Burbank Studios. Sam Gill, the archivist at the Margaret Herrick, "had the opportunity of talking with several individuals who were eyewitnesses to a massive amount of destruction of Columbia records which apparently took place at the old Columbia studios in Hollywood at Sunset and Gower during the 1970s. It appears that the bulk of production records and office files were destroyed at that time."[3]

Since there is no Columbia collection at this writing, juxtaposing the life of Harry Cohn with the evolution of his studio has required the use of other sources—the trade magazines, collections of individuals associated with Columbia (such as Frank Capra, George Stevens, Jerry Wald, and Irene Dunne), and the teletypes. The last have proved invaluable.

The story of the Columbia teletypes has yet to be told. The 6 December 1985 *Daily Variety* advertised the sale of "chronologically filed daily teletypes containing the personal and corporate conversations of HARRY & JACK COHN," along with "inter-office memos, telegrams, messages, personal notes & signatures," all of which were part of "the most turbulent & triumphant years of Columbia history." The asking price was $10,000.

Although few ads deliver what they promise, this one was at least partly true. It is easy to understand why Gene M. Gressley, then director of the American Heritage Center at the University of Wyoming, was eager to add the teletypes to the Center's holdings, which already comprised several important film collections.[4] Whether the Columbia collection was complete when Wyoming purchased it is unknown; it was not complete in June 1989 when I examined it. But this is not unusual; what often seems to be missing may be in someone's personal library. Besides, the teletypes cannot tell everything; since they were intended to be filed, they can hardly be a "look into the highly guarded daily life" of Harry Cohn, as the *Daily Variety* ad claims. While they tell us much about Harry's executive style and the daily operations of the studio, there were occasions when a conversation reached a point at which the parties decided to continue it on their private phones.

As of this writing, the teletypes are uninventoried. While most of the boxes are dated accurately, some are a chronological jumble, containing material from different years. One assumes that eventually the teletypes will be catalogued so that citation can be by box and year. But I am citing the teletypes as I found them in June 1989—by date and place of origin (Los Angeles or New York); when it is impossible to identify parties by name, they are designated by city.

The standard biography of a studio head (such as Bosley Crowther's life of Mayer, *Hollywood Rajah,* or Mel Gussow's life of Zanuck, *Don't Say Yes until I Finish Talking*) is straight biography. The standard studio history (Crowther's history of MGM, *The Lion's Share,* Tino Balio's *United Artists,* Charles Higham's *Warner Brothers*) is a chronological account of the studio's evolution that is historical, biographical, and often anecdotal. In between is film criticism.

The Merchant Prince of Row combines all three approaches for one main reason: unlike Mayer and Zanuck or, for that matter, the other Golden Age moguls, Harry was both president and head of production. He *was* his studio; hence the interweaving of Harry's life and Columbia's history. But the man was also his movies. Quality of product, to use a favorite industry expression, determined studio status. Harry was committed to making Columbia a major studio but could do so only with movies that ranked with those of the majors.

While detailed film analysis does not fall within the scope of this study, critical assessment does, particularly of Columbia's films of the 1930s, the decade when the studio shed its Poverty Row image. It is impossible to write about Columbia without reaching some conclusion about Frank Capra's role in the studio's rise to prominence in the 1930s. Although much has been written about Capra at Columbia, including his own account and Joseph McBride's response to it, there has been no attempt to gauge Capra's impact on other Columbia films of that decade, probably because the other films are so rarely shown. While Capra's major Columbia films and a few others (*The Criminal Code, Twentieth Century, The Awful Truth*) are well known, most Columbia films of the period are not. Yet if one looks at such Columbia releases as *Virtue, No More Orchids, The Captain Hates the Sea, Cocktail Hour, Party Wire, Whirlpool,* and *If You Could Only Cook,* it becomes apparent that Capra's "melting pot" formula of combining genres, so that the film is an amalgam rather than a pure strain, became studio policy during the decade. This is surprising when one considers that Columbia, unlike other studios, did not distinguish between president and production head: Harry was both. Yet Capra's concept of a movie coincided so perfectly with Harry's that, during Capra's twelve years at Columbia (1927-39), that concept was reflected in a surprisingly large number of films. Capra's were not the only movies that were "Capraesque."

Some information is never obtainable. In response to my inquiry about the grade school Harry attended, H. Carl McCall, president, Board of Education of the City of New York, replied that that Board "does not maintain a registry of former students" (7 January 1993). Although Kenneth R. Cobb of the New York City Department of Records and Information Services searched in vain for the information, he has at least been able to suggest possibilities: P.S. 30 at 230 E. 88th St. or P.S. 66 at 419–29

E. 88th St., each of which would have been a block away from Harry's home.

I admit to having enjoyed Bob Thomas's *King Cohn*, which I occasionally cite. Having been denied access to the interviews Thomas conducted for the book, which are in the Bob Thomas Collection at UCLA, I was unable to verify some of the statements made in *King Cohn*. I am sure much of what Thomas has written is accurate, especially since some who worked at Columbia under Harry (Paul N. Lazarus, William N. Graf) felt that *King Cohn* rang true. Yet certain details—the absence of documentation, especially regarding conversations, a chronological vagueness about Harry's early life, and a reference to his being drafted *before* America entered World War I—have prompted me to adhere, first, to what is demonstrably accurate, then, to what can be assumed to be accurate on the basis of interviews, inference, and personal judgment.

1 _____

Two Persons in One God

An eminent screenwriter and longtime associate of Harry Cohn admits to never having heard him speak obscenely around women. Another writer and an equally reliable source remembers how Harry, in the presence of some male executives, asked a young actress if, to put it euphemistically (which Harry did not), her reputation as Hollywood's foremost exponent of fellatio was based on fact. What disturbed the writer about an incident that happened in the 1940s was the intentional combination of gaucheness and perversity. The remark was supposed to be both cruel and shocking; it was directed at a woman, or, as Harry would have said, a broad.

Louis B. Mayer, who once struck Charlie Chaplin for showing disrespect for women, would probably not have done the same to Harry, although the sight of two moguls pummeling each other would have made Hollywood history. Nevertheless, Mayer would have reprimanded Harry. Mayer, who regarded women as avatars of his mother, was less of a philanderer than Harry; in Mayer's case, infidelity was a form of sexual release and quite distinct from adoration. One could respect the female sex and at the same time sleep with selected members of it. Harry did not respect the female sex; he respected certain females who transcended their gender by becoming ladies in the classic sense (Loretta Young, Rosalind Russell, Irene Dunne) or love goddesses (Rita Hayworth, Kim Novak). Each was an extreme and was worthy of awe. In between were mothers and broads—the former for breeding, the latter for sex.

There are probably more stories about Harry Cohn than about any other studio head except Sam Goldwyn. Exaggerations they may be, if not untruths, but they all seem to fit: Harry's secret passageway to a star's dressing room, the visitor's chair electrified by the press of a buzzer, a Herod-like Christmas present to a secretary allowing her to choose someone to be fired.[1]

One should look at Harry Cohn as one would at a rocky crag or a swollen river: while they may be considered examples of nature's capriciousness or prodigality, they are nonetheless *there*, impervious to change by human means. Harry Cohn was also *there*—at Columbia Pictures on Gower Street in Hollywood, the studio he co-founded in 1924 and of which he was president from 1932 to his death in 1958. The other moguls may have resembled dinosaurs, but Harry was more like a Stonehenge slab: a sculptor's nightmare but an archaeologist's dream.

Yet the man who enjoyed speaking crudely to a certain type of woman commanded the respect of Loretta Young and Rosalind Russell, two of Hollywood's Roman Catholic elite, a small circle that usually attended Sunday mass at the Church of the Good Shepherd in Beverly Hills—"Our Lady of the Cadillacs," as Rosalind Russell dubbed it. That these women attended his funeral is significant; equally significant was the presence of another well-known Hollywood Catholic, Danny Thomas, who recited the Twenty-third Psalm. The most unusual feature of the funeral, however, was the total absence of anything Jewish; and yet, according to Neal Gabler, Harry Cohn was one of the Jews who invented Hollywood.[2]

The paradoxes continue. Harry Cohn, or "White Fang," as Ben Hecht called him—ex–pool hall hustler, trolleycar conductor, songplugger, model for the "uncouth" Harry Brock in *Born Yesterday* (the film version of which Cohn produced)—once offered to pace the floor with an expectant father, a man he later fired and then rehired.

The expectant father was Oscar Saul, who came to Columbia as a screenwriter shortly after World War II. Unlike the Harry Cohn who pursued Budd Schulberg's wife, Geraldine Brooks, around the desk, tearing at her clothes,[3] Saul's Harry is much more complex:

Cohn fired me one day, and he had a right to fire me. I was out of line. I was producing a picture—*Let's Do It Again* (1953), the remake of *The Awful Truth* (1937). The writer was Richard Sale. Richard also thought he would be directing as well, but Jane Wyman, the star, wanted Alexander Hall. Richard was depressed and just wanted to get away from the studio. Anyway, he asked me if he could go down to Palm Springs to work on the script. I said, "Sure." Cohn called me into his office—there were other executives there, Ben Kahane and Irving Briskin—and said, "Sale wasn't in the studio yesterday. How about that!" I said, "Well, Mr. Cohn, he was so disappointed about not being director that he asked if he could go to Palm Springs and work there." Cohn said, "I don't care if he's disappointed; he's still getting paid." Then I said, "He's also a human being."

Cohn didn't like that. I heard later that Kahane was outraged. If no one else had been in the room, we would have been all right. But you can't put Cohn down in the presence of others. He was a very strong man, and like all strong men, he had his insecurities. He liked to get close to people, but no one likes to get too close. He always picked on his favorites, and the minute you became a favorite, you were in trouble because his expectations were impossible. He was very contradictory, especially under pressure. He once dismissed a director from a picture. It's bad enough to do it to a writer, yet it happens all the time to writers. But when it happens to a director, it gets around town.

A few months later, I was sitting in the projection room in Cohn's house, and he said to me, "Are you a friend of Phil's?" [Phil Karlson, who directed such Columbia films as *Ladies of the Chorus* (1949), *Lorna Doone* (1951), *Scandal Sheet* (1952), and *Tight Spot* (1955)]. I said, "Yes; we're pretty close." Cohn said, "You know, I did a terrible thing to that boy." Here was this hard-boiled guy, feeling guilty. But much of that hard-boiled stuff was a facade. I once had a meeting with Samuel Arkoff [co-founder of American-International Pictures, which specialized in horror and motorcycle gang movies]. He spoke like one of the Medici, a merchant prince, yet he made movies like a mug. Harry Cohn acted like a mug, but he made movies like a merchant prince. He once said to me, "If you don't learn anything else from me, learn this: Always let the other fellow think he's smarter than you." That talk about Cohn's being illiterate—it was an act.

It was also a myth about his not reading scripts. He would call me at 2:00 A.M. sometimes and just say, "Page 48." I said, "I'll go in the study and get my script." Cohn said, "Why isn't your script by your bed? Page 48. Did I approve that line?" I said, "Yes." "Well, I don't like it," he answered. "I'll change it," I said.

It wasn't just that he'd think nothing of calling at any hour in the morning. He'd also call you at other people's homes. I was at a dinner party, and Cohn called and asked me if I would have dinner with him. I told him I couldn't and asked for a raincheck. He did the same thing a few weeks later when I was at someone else's house. He was a very lonely man. When my wife was in the hospital, about to give birth, he said he'd come over to the hospital and walk the floor with me. I told him I'd arranged to stay at a friend's house until I got a call from the hospital. He was terribly hurt. I think the key to Cohn's personality was his belief that he didn't just make movies; somehow he created them. He once told me, in strict confidence when we were the only two people in the room, that I was in the presence of America's greatest dramatist. And he wasn't kidding.[4]

"Make" is one of the most common verbs in film. Everyone in the industry uses it, but in different ways. When an actor claims to have made a movie, he or she means something quite different from the producer or director, who will also speak of having *made* a movie. It is clear what an actor means by making a movie. It is at least understood what a director means: that he or she was responsible for the script's realization, which, depending on the director, can reflect a personal vision. A producer means something else: that he or she was responsible for the film's inception. Sam Goldwyn thought of *Wuthering Heights* (1939) as *his* movie; William Wyler was only the director. David O. Selznick felt the same about *Gone with the Wind* (1939) and, in fact, about every film he produced. Hal Wallis also spoke of "his" films. Probably all producers and studio heads think similarly.

Harry phrased it differently: he considered himself a dramatist, America's greatest. Like Goldwyn, Harry respected writers, knowing that without them there could be no film. Even at story conferences, when an executive would try to monopolize the meeting, Harry would interrupt and say, "Let the writer talk."[5] Harry thought of himself not as the surrogate parent of his films but as something greater—as their procreator, who did not so much provide as produce the seed from which they grew. He could look back at his films—his dramas—and take pride in knowing that many were among the greatest of the American screen: *Platinum Blonde, It Happened One Night, Twentieth Century, Mr. Smith Goes to Washington, The Jolson Story, All the King's Men, From Here to Eternity.* Without him, they could not have been made; if another had made them, they would not be the films we know today. If they were Harry's dramas, he was their dramatist.

Journalism, with its assumptions about studio heads, has prejudged Harry; psychology, with its emphasis on duality (conscious/unconscious, self/anti-self), encourages one to imagine a dichotomous figure. Thus one can approach Harry in terms of the eternal correlatives: "on the one hand, on the other." On the one hand, he was a bastard; on the other, America's greatest dramatist.

If it were as simple as that, Harry—along with Mayer, the brothers Warner, Zanuck, Selznick, and Goldwyn—would be a case history of a man who, by living the Pygmalion myth, transformed not only mortals into stars but also himself into a god. The moguls—to use the term with which they will forever be associated—are better explained in terms of myth and literature than in those of psychology. The irony is that they probably never read the myths or the literature that explains them. While Harry was known to use abusive language to women, Daniel Taradash, one of the industry's finest screenwriters and author of several Columbia screenplays (*Golden Boy, Knock on Any Door, From Here to Eternity, Picnic,* and others), claims he never heard him do so. Yet there is evidence that he did. Similarly, Hamlet could behave outrageously to Ophelia, not to mention his own mother, whom he lectured on the inappropriateness of middle-age adultery. "On the other hand," Hamlet's love for Gertrude was never in doubt, nor can one deny that he felt, if not love, then at least affection for Ophelia. Raskolnikov in *Crime and Punishment* could torment Sonia, conjuring up visions of the penury awaiting a St. Petersburg prostitute, but he could also fall to his knees and beg her forgiveness.

While Harry never genuflected before a woman, he would have had no difficulty understanding those who did. When human beings shed their nature and assume the mantle of myth, the result is divinity. Sonia is virgin/whore, Madonna/Magdalene. Sonia the streetwalker is vilified; Sonia the transcendent anima is glorified.

If Harry had been a Catholic like his second wife, Joan Perry, he would have understood the difference between beatification and canonization. If offered the choice, he would have gone all the way: why settle for "Blessed" when one can be "Saint?" When one reads the lives of the moguls, it is hard to envision them as anything other than Promethean. Mortlings they were not. Their larger-than-life stature explains why, long after Hollywood's Golden Age has ended and the moguls themselves have departed the scene (leaving a succession of replacements no more familiar to the public than the faceless heads of corporations), they still fascinate us.

One reason is that the inconsistencies present in human nature, which frustrate our attempts at self-understanding, vanish in mythology, whose characters refuse to be confined within something so limiting as a species. The contradictory behavior of mythological figures is understandable once we regard them as self-transcending, self-dramatizing, and self-perpetuating creations in whom all tensions and polarities are resolved. Achilles can remain a hero although he behaves like an adolescent, sulking in his tent when his mistress is taken from him and given to Agamemnon. Homer's point is lost unless Achilles is considered an adolescent (which he must have been); yet he is not an ordinary adolescent, but rather one who comes to a profound realization of the nature of evil—something few adolescents (or adults, for that matter) achieve in real life. Achilles could also be both tender and savage: he could drag Hector's corpse around the walls of Troy and later commiserate with Hector's father.

Harry could be obscene yet win the respect of Rosalind Russell, who was so concerned about the racy dialogue in *Auntie Mame* that, before agreeing to do the play, she went over the script with her confessor. While Harry could say that the best way to judge a movie's quality was by the number of times he shifted in his seat (thus equating a successful film with the state of his behind), he also understood the nature of producing better than most studio heads. When he told Oscar Saul he was "America's greatest dramatist," he was expressing a philosophy and a mission. Knowing what screen drama was, he applied the philosophy; by creating screen drama, he achieved his mission.

That the moguls behaved as they did is understandable if one views a studio as a patriarchy continually expanding to accommodate new members, not all of whom were males. Although men had the power, women to a great extent made it possible for them to retain it. When one speaks of sex symbols and icons, the names that come to mind first are not men's.

The moguls were ambivalent about women, but they would not have thought so; nor would they have seen anything contradictory about compromising women (stopping short of *le droit de seigneur*) and idealizing them on the screen. Women are made for veneration—at least in the movies. But when a god takes an interest in a real woman, she should be honored to receive him. Should she prove evasive, the god will pursue her, as Apollo pursued Daphne when she resisted his advances, as Harry pursued Geraldine Brooks when she resisted his.

To Harry, Geraldine Brooks was a property—one of the most commonly used words in the industry. A script is a property; a novel bought for the screen is a property. Why should it be any different with actors? While it may not be flattering to be thought of as real estate, neither does it hurt a career; it certainly did not hurt Kim Novak's.

Once Harry decided to groom Novak for stardom after her Columbia debut in *Pushover* (1954), he had no intention of allowing gossip to interfere with his plans. Thus, in 1956 when Dorothy Kilgallen's column hinted at a romance between Novak and Sammy Davis, Jr., Harry reacted like a property owner: he wanted whatever existed between them to end. The mere suggestion of an interracial romance in an industry that avoided dramatizing the subject gave rise to rumors ranging from Harry's hiring a Las Vegas mobster to threaten Davis with the loss of his right eye (he had lost the left one in a 1954 accident) to Harry's taking out a contract with the Chicago Mafia to deprive Davis not of his eye but of his legs![6] Or was it the Los Angeles Mafia, as a friend of Davis's intimated?[7]

Studio heads were masters of intimidation. Louis Mayer, for one, was noted for playing actors against each other, pitting June Allyson against Judy Garland by telling each that the other was up for the same role. MGM's patriarch also thought nothing of doubling as matchmaker. Once he decided Ilona Massey could be another Jeanette MacDonald, Mayer began monitoring Massey's private life. Learning that she was dating Alan Curtis, whose home studio was Universal, Mayer informed her that MGM stars do not go slumming. When she continued seeing Curtis and eventually married him, Massey found herself working at lesser studios, returning to MGM for only one film, *Holiday in Mexico* (1946).

Threats are simple; for one thing, there is rarely any evidence. Threats also reinforce the image of the blackmailing mogul. A Mafia contract is another matter. For Harry to involve himself in a scheme to disable one of the most popular entertainers of the period (and an African-American, to boot) would require a level of hybris that he would have condemned in others.

The Davis-Novak affair was tabloid material; the Davis-Novak relationship was a case of mutual attraction—Davis to Novak's aura, she to his talent. And when Harry imposed his interdiction, Novak and Davis became co-conspirators in their attempt to defy it.[8] That their defiance was short-lived was due not so much to Harry as to their realization that playacting at being lovers instead of rebels would jeopardize both of their careers.

Just as Mafia contracts seemed characteristic of Harry Cohn the mogul, so did billing Columbia for maintenance of his yacht, home repairs, a projection room, and New Year's parties. These accusations too were unfounded, but that did not stop some stockholders from making them in 1950, causing Harry to avoid New York until the matter was settled two years later. The stockholders' suit was heard in the Superior Court of the State of New York, and the decision handed down on 8 July 1952 was a victory for Harry: there was no evidence of his appropriating studio funds for yacht or home; the parties were good for studio morale; the projection room was a necessity. If Harry bought studio clothes at cost plus 10 percent, he also paid for the material and the labor. He was, according to the Court, "a very valuable asset to the corporation."[9]

Unlike Goldwyn, Harry never felt the need for psychotherapy. He had no reason to; his behavior was erratic only in human terms. But Harry could not be measured by human terms. The integration of the twin selves that all of us possess (but few can harmonize) had occurred. What one saw in Harry were manifestations of a unified personality capable of extreme forms of behavior that never seemed anything less than plausible. It was the mean that Harry avoided; the middle-of-the-road position and the state of equanimity that he shunned. That was for normal folk, and Harry was of another race.

And so, in 1946, it did not bother Harry to fire his publicity director, Whitney Bolton (who later became drama critic for the *Morning Telegraph*), for doing something that would ordinarily have merited commendation. Bolton spoke up for Harry during an argument with a producer who had criticized Harry's apathy toward striking studio workers. Harry overheard Bolton's apologia; he then sought Bolton out, lecturing him on the inappropriateness of his action and insisting that he neither asked nor wanted to be defended. Since Bolton had put Harry in a position in which gratitude was expected, Harry fired him. But the incident gave Harry guilt pangs. Unbeknownst to Bolton, Harry tried to find him a job at another studio.[10]

During World War II, Columbia, like all studios, was besieged with requests from organizations to sponsor movie premieres for the war effort. When one such group approached Harry, he berated it for trying to "wheedle" films out of the studios. He then asked how much the organization would clear from the event. Learning that it would be $10,000, Harry gave the group his personal check for that amount. To Harry, the difference between feeling obligated to sponsor a screening and making a charitable contribution was a question of coercion versus freedom of choice. Harry would not be coerced.

Despite rumors of mob connections, Harry knew the difference between frequenting Las Vegas's Sands Hotel, whose manager, Jack Entratter, was hardly above reproach, and financing mob operations. In the movie business, friendships that would otherwise have been impossible not only existed but thrived. Just as Harry felt as much at home with Frank Costello as he did with Moss Hart, so did Rosalind Russell with Francis Cardinal Spellman and Frank Sinatra, who probably knew more unsavory characters than Harry. Yet when Rosalind Russell and her husband, Frederick Brisson, celebrated their twenty-fifth wedding anniversary in 1966, Sinatra arranged a weekend of festivities at the Sands; ten years later at Rosalind Russell's funeral, he was one of the pallbearers.

In 1943, Willie Bioff, a corrupt Hollywood labor leader serving a ten-year sentence at Alcatraz for blackmailing the studios into paying him money to prevent strikes, agreed to name names; the industry wondered if Harry would be implicated, especially since the Hearst papers implied that he already was. The answer came in a letter from Harry to Hearst, quoted in the *Los Angeles Examiner* (11 November 1943), stating that, unlike the heads of MGM, Warners, Fox, and Paramount, "I am a person who refused to pay any money to Bioff and his gang."

Harry was an enigma lodged inside a paradox. If he was "the man you stood in line to hate," as Hedda Hopper used to say, he was also the man whose eulogy was composed by a major American playwright, Clifford Odets, and delivered by an actor whose name is synonymous with humanitarianism, Danny Kaye.

What, then, was Harry Cohn? Simply, the man who helped create an empire called Columbia Pictures, born in a dingy room at 1600 Broadway and raised on Poverty Row in West Hollywood where fly-by-night independents ground out their flicks. Through a series of rebirths and resurrections, Columbia progressed from the studio that gave the world the Three Stooges to the studio that never won an Academy Award until 1935, when, in one evening, it won seven—five for a single movie, *It Happened One Night.*

Who, then, was Harry Cohn? That is more difficult. Psychography, as Joyce Carol Oates calls the approach to the subject's life that relies more on unconscious motivation than on documentation, does not work in Harry's case. If Harry did not need psychotherapy, he would hardly benefit from psychography. Besides, there is enough primary material (story conference notes, teletypes) to create a reasonably clear picture of Harry and his studio without resorting to the unverifiable. Like any subject, Harry will not give up all his secrets to biographers any more than his studio will yield all of its to historians. But what exists at present allows for considerably more than a sketch.

At least Harry and his studio can be demythologized. Whether or not Harry, if asked to spell Columbia, would spell it with a second "o" instead of a "u" is of interest only to those who revel in a president's inability to spell his company's name. Similarly, Sam Goldwyn was known for his malapropisms, yet some of them may not even have been his. Whether Harry was a poor speller or Goldwyn a twister of phrases (if he was, he probably knew what he was twisting), their origins and backgrounds have encouraged the public to regard them as vulgarians who exposed their ignorance whenever they had to discuss anything other than box office receipts.

Harry may not have attended high school, yet he had a command of the language that would delight any high school English teacher. He did not always reveal that facility, and in fact usually downplayed it, preferring to sound like a typical studio boss. But in a teletype to Moss Hart (8 November 1954), whom he often saw when he was in New York, Harry sounds almost like an academic as he sets forth his ideas for a movie about band leader–pianist Eddy Duchin:

We know that we must dramatize the basic internal conflict within Duchin—what did he want as a young man and how did he relate his private and personal dreams to the actual world in which he lived. . . . First we must know his purpose, ambition and to what lengths he would go to achieve them. . . . Although he became successful externally, internally he had many doubts and fears about himself. . . . We don't see this as a musical, but rather as a drama with music. We believe that this should be the story of a man with the capacity to rise to the peaks of unselfishness, courage, wisdom, and heroism.

Harry was unlike any of the other moguls. He had never had to go on junkets to find scrap metal to sell, as Mayer did; he had never walked from Warsaw to Hamburg, as Goldwyn had; he never had to change his name, as Goldwyn did, from Schumuel Gelbfisz to Samuel Goldfish to, finally, Samuel Goldwyn; he never felt the need to add a middle initial to sound important, as Mayer and Selznick did with their "B" and "O," respectively. And, despite obituaries that spoke of Harry's Lower East Side boyhood, he was actually born on the Upper East Side, to a household in which German, not Yiddish, was spoken.

Since Harry was not a typical mogul, Columbia was not a typical studio. While the other studios were easy to categorize (Warners = social consciousness and headline-fresh movies, MGM = family fare, Universal = low-budget horror and comedy, Fox = highbrow, Paramount = white-telephone sophistication), Columbia was an anomaly. Its movies ranged from Three Stooges shorts and the Blondie series to *All the King's Men* and *From Here to Eternity*. It made its first Technicolor film in 1943, seven years after Fox and Paramount began using the process. Its contract players were far fewer than MGM's or Warners'. Unlike the Big Five (MGM, Fox, Warners, RKO, and Paramount), Columbia did not have a theater chain. Except for Frank Capra, Columbia's directors lacked the prestige of Billy Wilder (Paramount), Joseph L. Mankiewicz (Fox), and Raoul Walsh (Warners). Columbia's idea of a series was Boston Blackie; MGM's was Andy Hardy and Dr. Kildare.

And yet Harry was never deposed, as Mayer was. His studio did not cease production, as RKO did in 1957. While Columbia Pictures Corporation (1924-67) underwent some name changes (Columbia Pictures Industries, 1968-87; Columbia Pictures Entertainment, 1987-89; and, as of 1992, Columbia Pictures, a part of Sony Pictures Entertainment), there is still a Columbia. At least it never went through the convulsions that wracked MGM, which was merged, bought, sold, bid on, resold, and renamed.

Columbia still stands, with the same logo—the lady with the torch, looking more resplendent in color than she did in black and white. The reason for Columbia's longevity and its appeal to such diverse buyers as Coca-Cola, which owned the studio from 1982 to 1989, and Sony, which purchased Columbia Pictures Entertainment in 1989, can be expressed in two words: Harry Cohn.

2

From Yorkville to Broadway

On the northwest corner of East 88th Street and First Avenue in New York stands a five-story apartment house built in the 1880s. Today the roof is crowned with a television antenna, but the building is still a walk-up; and its Queen Anne exterior—red brick with sandstone window-sills—has been preserved, along with such other characteristic features as shaped gables and a combination of straight and round-arched windows. In 1891 it was probably not an address the upwardly mobile coveted, but eight years later the street received an impressive addition: the Church of the Holy Trinity, built in the French Gothic style. Social climbers would have considered East 88th Street and First Avenue superior to Stanton Street on the Lower East Side, where William Fox (whose Fox Film Corporation helped spawn Twentieth Century-Fox) was raised; but if they were going to live on East 88th, they would have preferred to be closer to Fifth Avenue. 355 East 88th Street was below Lexington Avenue, which marked the beginning of the immigrant section; it was in Yorkville—historically, the area east of Third Avenue from East 64th Street to East 99th Street, yet far enough from Stanton, Delancey, and Hester streets to offer its residents cultural diversity.

While peddlers could be spotted on the streets of Yorkville, they did not create the congestion they did on the Lower East Side, nor was the air filled with the sound of Yiddish. Yorkville was home to several classes of immigrants, including German Jews who preferred to distance themselves from their unassimilated coreligionists downtown and who prided themselves on speaking the mother tongue, not the vernacular. It was also home to Irish and Czechs. Since the Irish favored Third Avenue, the area around Second and First became a Central and Eastern European enclave and less parochial than the lower East Side. By early November, store windows were decorated for Christmas, and pushcarts on First Avenue were festooned with holly and fir.[1]

355 East 88th Street was convenient to transportation. The elevated ran along Second and Third avenues, and there was also the electric trolley. One could take advantage of the bargains at Rosenberg's Dry

Goods at First and 83rd, and the pastries at Fleischman's Vienna Bakery at York and 81st. At the corner of 81st and Second was a Hungarian grocery store, Paprika Weiss, and a block down on First was Goodman's Drug Store, which sold everything from herbal tea to arthritis cures. And if one enjoyed the aroma of beer, a stroll past the Hell Gate Brewery on 90th and Third would at least gratify the olfactory nerve until the taste buds could be satisfied at any of the numerous cafes, beer halls, and social clubs around 86th Street.

But 355 East 88th Street does not seem the right address for the future head of a movie studio—at least not in the industry's infancy. The Lower East Side would have been more appropriate, an Eastern European *stetl* better yet. Both figure prominently in Hollywood lore, along with tales of impoverishment and misfortune. To have lived in a Lower East Side tenement as Fox, Marcus Loew, and Adolph Zukor did; in a St. John, New Brunswick, harbor slum as Louis Mayer did; or in a sleepy village in Southwest Germany as Carl Laemmle did would have been more characteristic of "the Jews who invented Hollywood." And if not in such surroundings, then one should at least have a father who sent his nine-year-old son out on the streets to sell homemade stove polish, as Michael Fox did to William; or one, like Ben Warner, who dealt with failure by relocating and thus exposing the future Warner brothers to a cross-section of the population for whom they would be making movies.

But Joseph Cohn was not an itinerant father. He was a local tailor who had a shop a block from his home. What Harry felt for his father was midway between the Warner brothers' respect for Ben Warner and Louis Mayer's detestation of Jacob Mayer. And while Harry loved his mother, Bella, he did not venerate her, as Louis did Sarah Mayer, which may explain why Columbia never developed a reputation for the idealized family movie, as MGM did.

Harry found school a chore, but not to the extent that he left after the fourth grade as Jack Warner did. Harry at least finished grade school. To use the titles of two popular biographies, Harry was "King Cohn" while Jack Warner was the "Clown Prince of Hollywood."[2]

Had Harry worked in his father's tailor shop on Second Avenue and entered the garment trade, film historians would have placed him in the tradition of Sam Goldwyn, the glove salesman, and Adolph Zukor, the furrier. Harry, an elegant dresser, did not learn fashion from clothiers but from songwriters and vaudevillians. He did not fit into a familiar mold: on the basis of his background, he would have been named least likely to succeed in Hollywood but most likely in New York. The opposite was the case.

A mogul's funeral was fairly standard. A rabbi generally officiated, and the services were usually at a temple (New York's Temple Emmanu-El for

William Fox and Jack Cohn, Los Angeles' Wilshire Boulevard Temple for Irving Thalberg and Louis Mayer). Harry's took place on a Columbia soundstage. For a Jew, the service had distinctly Catholic overtones, especially the singing of the Our Father. Joan Perry Cohn, who had made a total commitment to Catholicism, wanted to make sure she and her husband would be reunited in heaven. She therefore had his corpse baptized; few cadavers have been baptized, but then, Harry's was not just any cadaver.

Yet for the first thirty years of his life, there was little about Harry that was exceptional. If anyone had told Bella Cohn on 23 July 1891 as she went into labor in a sweltering Yorkville apartment, where she had given birth twice before, that her third son would grow up to be a movie tycoon, she would have smiled uncomprehendingly. Russian-born and more devout than her husband, Bella would have preferred that Harry observe the Sabbath, which he rarely did: "Religion was not important to Harry . . . in any way." [3]

What was important to Harry was making it—"it" being whatever commodity he was hawking or idea he was pitching. The streets of New York were his training ground, and, if there was one major difference between Harry and the other studio heads, it was that he stayed longest in New York, absorbing its ways and assimilating its rhythms. Later, when he could, he hired former New Yorkers who had not lost the urban beat.

Harry did not enter the movies until his late twenties; he did not become involved with features until his early thirties. It was Jack Cohn (born Jacob, 27 October 1889) who first understood that movies would be the new mass medium and prepared himself accordingly, by taking a job at Carl Laemmle's IMP (Independent Motion Picture Company, later Universal) when he was barely nineteen.

While Harry would never admit it, there was a time, from about 1913 through the 1920s, when the only Cohn known to the industry was Jack, a respected newsreel editor long before Harry gave any thought to the flickers. They were his brother's turf; his was Broadway, Baghdad on the Hudson, with its high rollers, flimflam men, touts, and purse-swinging hookers. Had he stayed a Gothamite, one could imagine him in the company of Damon Runyon's Nicely Nicely and Sky Masterson, eating cheesecake at Mindy's and ogling Miss Adelaide at the Hot Box.

The apartment on East 88th Street was too confining for the Cohn brothers, who had discovered there was life outside Yorkville. But they also knew that if they wanted to frequent the tenderloin or catch Nora Bayes at the Palace, they needed money, which was not to be made by staying in school. Jack and Harry, who were two years apart, both left school at about thirteen. But Jack, the older and more responsible

brother, found what his parents would have considered gainful employment, while Harry merely drifted.

In 1902, Jack landed a $4-a-week job at the Hampton Advertising
Agency on 22nd Street, west of Fifth Avenue and a block away from the
Flatiron district. It was another world compared to Yorkville. Although
his lack of education restricted him to the status of errand boy and clerk,
Jack was able to strike up an acquaintance with Joseph Brandt, who had
come to the city from Troy in upstate New York and was pursuing a law
degree at New York University, an institution that would figure prominently in the history of Columbia Pictures, furnishing the studio with
many of its personnel as late as 1989, when Sony bought Columbia and
made Peter Guber head of the studio.[4]

Working at Hampton paid for Brandt's tuition. Although he was
admitted to the bar in 1906, he never practiced law. From the moment he
came to New York, he was drawn to the entertainment world. After
receiving his law degree, Brandt did advertising for *Billboard* and the *New
York Daily Mirror*, which took movie reviewing seriously, unlike many of
the trades that often simply reprinted studio releases.

Brandt would eventually team up with Jack, who, by 1908, had had
his fill of Hampton. Still, the experience had a profound effect on Jack's
future: it was impossible to work for an ad agency and be unaware of the
impact movies were having on Americans. Jack was determined to find a
place for himself in the new medium and encouraged Brandt to join him.
Brandt was intrigued but not enough to start at the bottom like Jack, who
took a job at IMP as assistant to the lab manager, C.A. "Doc" Willat—the
same Willat who later built his own studio across the Hudson in Fort Lee,
New Jersey.

Even before Jack discovered he had an affinity for film, Harry found
he had a talent that, while not major, was at least marketable: he could
sing as well as entertain, and he never lost the ability to do both. Once in
Columbia's executive dining room, Harry explained why he had never
made a movie about the American Revolution: it reminded him of Archi-
bald M. Willard's painting *Spirit of '76*. He then proceeded to hobble
around the room, imitating the fife player with the bandaged head and
whistling "Yankee Doodle Dandy."[5] Even in the late 1940s, when this
incident occurred, Harry had lost neither his theatrical flair nor his sense
of pitch.

As a child, Harry had a good enough tenor to qualify for a part in
Theodore Kremer's melodrama *The Fatal Wedding*, which Al Woods presented at the Grand Opera House on Eighth Avenue for eight performances in October 1901 and then sent on a successful tour with "Baby"
Gladys Smith, soon to be known as Mary Pickford, as Jessie, "the little
mother." Harry made much of his stage debut, so much that some of his

obituaries had him appearing as a "chorus boy" in the play. "Choir boy" would have been more accurate; Harry appeared only in the last scene, which is set in Grace Episcopal Church and requires a boys' choir.

Although Harry never pursued a career in the theater, he spent his adolescence and early adulthood hovering around the New York entertainment scene and at times becoming part of it. To a teenager, New York in the first decade of the twentieth century seemed to offer unlimited opportunities, especially if the teenager lacked any incentive for further education. For Harry, education was not an entrée into the white-collar world; it was an obstacle to stepping onto the Big Street—whether it was 42nd, 52nd, or the Broadway of Harry's adolescence, East 14th Street. It was the street where one could meet the leading practitioners of the twin arts of hustling and performing, both of which Harry learned—the former better than the latter.

Performing has always been among the most egalitarian of professions and one that some of the early movie tycoons attempted. Jesse Lasky did a brother-and-sister act with his sister Blanche (who later married Sam Goldwyn) that toured the country. William Fox and Jack Warner also played in vaudeville. If one could carry a tune, learn lines, play an instrument, or tell jokes, education did not matter.

Harry knew, of course, of his brother's entrance into the flickers but chose not to join him, partly so as not to compete with him but also because, at the time, he found live entertainment more appealing than film. Yet Harry could not ignore the new medium. If he wished to work in the theatre, the chorus was all he could expect. Being neither a humorist nor an instrumentalist, he would never play the Orpheum circuit. What were available to him were musical interludes at the nickelodeon.

Illustrated songs provided an opportunity for the projectionist to rewind and thread up the film for the next showing. A singer, usually spotlighted (unless he or she was an uncommonly poor one), would sing the lyrics of popular songs from slides projected onto the screen. The slides were black-on-white: a fine pen and black ink inscribed the lyrics on plain glass or sometimes transparent fiberless parchment.[6] The singer encouraged the audience to join in. Often the patrons were unruly, but rowdiness would not have fazed Harry. Unfortunately, by the time he began working nickelodeons, this early form of exhibition, which lasted barely a decade (1904-14), was about to end. Harry caught up with the nickelodeon in 1912 when he teamed with Harry Rubinstein (later to be known as Harry Ruby) in an act called Ruby and Edwards, in which "Ruby" would play the piano and "Edwards" would sing from the slides. Rubinstein, who was about four years younger than Harry, would eventually become part of the infinitely better known team of Ruby and (Bert) Kalmar, who wrote such song hits as "Three Little Words," "I

Wanna Be Loved by You," and "Nevertheless." Harry may have gotten the idea for "Edwards" from the name of composer Gus Edwards, whose "In My Merry Oldsmobile" and "By the Light of the Silvery Moon" are among the mainstays of American song. Ruby had worked as a pianist for Gus Edwards around 1908 when the latter had his own music publishing house. And at the time "Ruby and Edwards" were appearing in Bronx nickelodeons, Gus Edwards was in vaudeville with his act, "School Boys and Girls," in which he played "teacher" to a group of "students," some of whom (including George Jessel, Ray Bolger, and Eleanor Powell) graduated to stardom.

Audiences could no more confuse "Edwards" with Edwards than they could nickelodeon sing-alongs with real vaudeville. But that was not the reason for the breakup of Ruby and Edwards. Harry Ruby had higher aspirations, as did Harry Cohn, although in 1912, Harry was not certain what his were, only that they were bound up with popular entertainment. Meanwhile, the age of the nickelodeon was passing. Harry, who by this time had also appeared in an Al Woods production and had hustled pool, was about to embark on another career, not unrelated to his earlier ventures: songplugging.

When Harry entered the world of music publishing, he briefly became part of a business that, like himself, was constantly changing locations. The difference was that Harry moved downtown from the Upper East Side, while music publishing advanced from lower Manhattan to Union Square, then to West 28th Street between Broadway and Sixth Avenue, and had finally reached the West 40s when Harry was about to make his contribution to the field.

When Harry joined Waterson, Berlin and Snyder—"the premier publishing house of popular song hits," as the ad in *Variety* proclaimed (and rightly so, since the Berlin was Irving)—he worked out of their new offices in the Strand Theatre Building on 224 West 47th Street. His brother was right across the street in the Mecca Building at 1600 Broadway, where Universal had its offices. Yet the brothers saw little of each other during this time, not so much by choice as by circumstance. Harry was rarely at Waterson, Berlin and Snyder; he had been hired to do what Berlin and George Gershwin, among others, did at the beginning of their careers, plug songs.

To use a movie analogy, a songplugger had to combine James Cagney's aggressiveness with John Payne's suavity—to huckster with finesse. The songplugger's venue was not just dry goods stores and five-and-dimes but anywhere there was a crowd: pool halls, ratskellers, bike races, parades, and even street corners and elevated train platforms. Pluggers were "known for their piercing voice and stamina."[7] Harry's tenor, while not piercing, was strong enough to sell songs, and he had the stamina to make the circuit of New York from the Bronx to Coney Island, and the ingenuity to get the tunes heard in places other than Woolworth's sheet music counter. Whether Harry had to resort to some of the tricks of the trade—such as whistling from a theater balcony or faking a disturbance in a box to get spotlighted for the song he had conspired with the orchestra to play—is unknown.[8] But one can well imagine his concocting schemes more devious than these.

Jack Cohn, on the other hand, had no need for such gimmickry. While Harry was crooning the latest song hits, Jack was editing films. Jack was barely out of his teens when he discovered film's uniqueness, which, as Siegfried Kracauer pointed out, consists of capturing unstaged or "raw" reality.[9] The Lumière brothers realized it also in 1895 when they brought their camera onto the streets of Paris, photographing men and women leaving work and trains pulling into stations—the latter so realistically that audiences screamed, thinking the train was coming at *them*. Today, of course, the impact of an arriving train is considerably less, if indeed it can even have an impact in a society in which car chases are clichéd and vehicular crackups are commonplace. One wonders if audiences can still appreciate Hitchcock's (then) fresh use of a smoke-belching train in *Shadow of a Doubt* (1943) where the train exudes an air of menace because it is carrying a serial killer.

But in film's infancy, *actualités* like *Workers Leaving the Lumière Factory* or *Arrival of a Train at a Station* had great appeal. What impressed Jack Cohn was not just the films' ability to capture the immediacy of an event but the idea that those who never witnessed the event could have a visual record of it. This is film, or at least one kind of film—the transcribing of objective reality. The transition from filming the actual to filming the possible (potential or probable)—the transition from the nonfiction to the fiction film—would not have been hard for one who began with documentaries and then decided to switch to "movies." Jack Cohn never had much chance to make that transition, but at least he knew he could.

Universal was so impressed by the speed with which Jack was learning the business that in 1912—the year Harry was playing nickelodeons, the year Universal was formed when IMP was amalgamated with four other companies—Jack was entrusted with editing the *Animated Weekly*, a newsreel, not to be confused with the *Universal Weekly*, the studio's trade paper. In fact, both the *Animated* and the *Universal Weekly* came into existence in 1912, no doubt to celebrate the creation of the new studio, whose christening would occur three years later with the opening of Universal City in Los Angeles.

Exhibitors liked the *Animated* so much that they wrote to the *Universal Weekly* asking for information about future newsreels. Their naiveté was understandable; like audiences expecting Previews of Coming Attractions as part of the bill, the exhibitors also wanted "previews" of forth-coming Animateds, forgetting, as often happens in the illusory world of film, that next week's news is yet to be made. While the *Animated* never achieved the status of *Fox Movietone News*, it did provide audiences with the real thing: army maneuvers, fire brigade inspections, socialites on the beach, a Chinese funeral in San Francisco. It also did not shrink from the sensational: one 1912 Animated featured the "Fattest Baby in the World," a 250-pound five-year-old. At the beginning, the *Animated* emphasized national over international news; hence Universal employed twenty-six cameramen in the United States but only fifteen in Europe. With the coming of World War I, the situation did not change much, nor could it, except to include footage of the fighting in France and Belgium.

Perhaps the most exciting moment in Jack's tenure at Universal occurred when he was sent west to film the opening of University City for the *Animated*.[10] For a New Yorker making his first trip to California, it was an unforgettable experience. Had Harry been there, he would have entered the business immediately. On Monday morning, 15 March 1915, Universal opened its gates—literally—at Universal City in the San Fernando Valley as Carl Laemmle, brandishing a key to his own city, marched in with a band to the proud measures of the national anthem. A switch was thrown on the main soundstage, but what was revealed went beyond natural or artificial illumination. The guests who had been issued tickets to "the strangest city in the world" were not disappointed. There was a zoo, an iceplant, horse corrals, a barber shop, a restaurant, and a reservoir, among other attractions. It was indeed a city, but one founded for a single purpose: making movies.

The *Animated* fascinated Jack. Although technically he was not in charge of the newsreel (Aubrey M. Kennedy was), Jack's role was vital: he edited it. From working on the *Animated*, Jack learned that the newsreel, like any documentary, mirrors the beginning-middle-end form of the story film, but with a significant difference: the editor determines the sequence because there is no author. The best newsreels have always evidenced some kind of order, and an editor with a sense of the dramatic can arrange the material so that it has a cumulative effect.

Jack could easily have transferred his documentary skills to the fiction film and enjoyed autonomy of a different sort. While he would be restricted to a narrative, he could at least determine its duration, as he did in 1913 when, by careful editing, he made *Traffic in Souls* Universal's first full-length movie.

The story of *Traffic in Souls* exists in two versions—one not so much apocryphal as embellished, the other more accurate but less imaginative.[11] But since the story bears on Jack Cohn's brief excursion into the fiction film, it deserves a reprise, for it underscores a principle that Jack, and later Harry, would apply at Columbia: economy of length and budget. This Jack had learned even before he edited some 800 feet of film out of *Traffic in Souls*. Once Universal discovered Jack's talent for editing, he was expected to implement the studio's policy of expanding one-reelers into two-reelers by repeating shots or adding stock footage but doing it so unobtrusively that no one would know the difference. Jack even directed some two-reelers himself and played a similar trick on the actors: he saved money in salaries by telling them they were shooting one-reelers which, back in the editing room, he would stretch to two reels. While the names of Jack's films are unknown, they were shot for the most part in upper Manhattan around Broadway and Dyckman Street, where dirt roads could still pass for western trails.

Jack learned how to add to a film in another sense: he inserted the intertitles, which had already been printed on rolls, in the *Animateds* and perhaps even in the one/two-reelers. If one can add, one can subtract; and it was less, not more, that *Traffic in Souls* needed.

George Loane Tucker was never a major Broadway figure. He had appeared in a few plays and also staged some, but he hoped to make his mark in film by directing a movie about a controversial topic: white slavery, which had already been the subject of at least one stage hit, *The Lure* (1913).

Here, the account bifurcates into myth and not-so-much-fact-as-hypothesis. While the true story may never be known, the myth, delightfully told by Terry Ramsaye, is the stuff that Hollywood history is made of. As Ramsaye tells it, the cost of *Traffic in Souls*, $5,000, did not set well with Carl Laemmle. Thus Tucker, Jack Cohn, and three of their friends contributed $1,000 each. Tucker made the movie in ten reels, shooting clandestinely over four weekends at Universal's Fort Lee studio, easily accessible by ferry from 125th Street. Jack reduced the ten reels to six, including intertitles that he wrote himself. When Laemmle finally saw a cut, he was so impressed that, when the board balked at the cost ($700 more than anticipated), Laemmle said he would buy the film for $10,000 and release it as an independent. Few could surpass "Uncle Carl" in one-upmanship. A counterbid came in at $25,000, and the film stayed with Universal, opening at Joe Weber's Theatre on 29th Street and Broadway on 25 November 1913 and eventually grossing $450,000.

Traffic in Souls was a runaway success, and one can certainly see Jack Cohn's hand in it. Newsreel footage of arrivals at Ellis Island is intercut with the main action, which dramatizes the fate of female immigrants who are misled about the land of opportunity and find themselves ensconced in brothels. The speedy denouement, a brothel raid, is also the result of Jack's editing. His intertitles are not filler but integral to the plot; one intertitle even functions as the resolution: a so-called reformer, exposed as a white slaver, commits suicide rather than face trial.

But was *Traffic in Souls* such a conspiracy? I.G. Edmonds and Kevin Brownlow have wondered. While there is no doubt that Jack Cohn recut the movie (he would have been the logical choice), it could not have been shot in four weeks without Laemmle's knowledge, or at odd times in Fort Lee with stars like Ethel Grandin and Jane Gail. And why did it open at Joe Weber's Theatre, owned by the Shuberts, unless it was because the Shuberts helped finance the movie, which cost not $5,000 or even $5,700, but around $25,000? Whatever else may be true, the Shuberts were part of the enterprise from the beginning. Since Universal had no theater chain (except for a brief period in the late 1920s) and *Traffic in Souls* was its first feature, a deal with exhibitors would not have been unlikely.

Harry knew his brother had scored a coup with *Traffic in Souls*; it was common knowledge around Broadway, and the trades made much of it six years later when Jack left Universal. While Harry's relationship with his brother deteriorated from hostility to abuse over the years, in 1913 Harry was only envious. Jack was associated with a box office hit, and Harry, impressed by the grosses (and being at liberty after parting with Harry Ruby), took a job as a traveling exhibitor for the film. Traditionally, the traveling exhibitor was a combination huckster-showman-father confessor who brought entertainment to communities whose only other exposure to urban culture came from road shows and touring companies.[12] By 1913 the position had become less demanding, although it still required specialized skills, particularly the ability to synchronize sound accompaniment with on-screen action.

What cities Harry toured and the length of time he spent on the road are impossible to determine. It may have been just a few weeks; since the exhibitors were now driving to their destinations, Harry may have gone only to Wilkes-Barre, Pennsylvania, where the film had a two-week run at the end of November 1913. At any rate, his stint as a traveling exhibitor was brief and limited to a single film. By 1914 he was promoting songs rather than movies. The difference is significant: bringing the flickers to rural America is not the same as putting over a song in a Broadway venue. Not only was the clientele different but so was the style. Songplugging afforded him a better opportunity to make himself the means of promoting the product. The film is complete at the time it is exhibited; a song comes alive only when it is performed, and the way it is performed has much to do with its success.

The experience was not without its ironic aspect: while Harry may have thought that he had severed his relationship with Universal in 1913, within five years he would be back at the studio in a completely different capacity.

Although Jack Cohn's value to Universal was higher than ever as 1913 ended, even in 1911 he had enough authority to get a job for his old friend from Hampton, Joe Brandt. Since Brandt had a law degree and public relations experience, he did not start at the bottom as Jack did. Brandt became Carl Laemmle's secretary, a term that, in the movie industry, is slightly misleading; administrative assistant would be more accurate. Male secretaries were common in the industry. For one thing, a male's traveling with a studio head would raise fewer eyebrows. The tradition persisted throughout Harry Cohn's regime as well: Harry's best known secretary was William N. Graf. And just as Jack Cohn had graduated from "Doc" Willat's assistant to an esteemed cutter, so Brandt would advance from administrative assistant to more responsible positions.

The business end of the movies held enormous appeal for Brandt, whose marketing strategies and promotional gimmicks were duly noted (and sometimes kidded goodnaturedly) in the trades.[13] Yet within a year of being hired, "homely Joe" became sufficiently important to have a lengthy piece in the *Universal Weekly* (17 August 1912) offering exhibitors suggestions for getting through the summer when the heat kept audiences away from the nickelodeons. Some theater owners had enough property to arrange for outdoor showings during the dog days, but most did not. For the latter, Brandt recommended ice water and fans—but not necessarily their own fans. He stressed the importance of establishing good relations with local businesses which, if made to feel important, would supply the exhibitors with what they needed. And although movie attendance may drop off in the summer, life goes on. Children are still being born, and every mother thinks her baby is prettier than her neighbor's. Therefore, sponsor baby contests: "In your local newspaper start a little ad going that you are going to give a prize to the prettiest baby in the town. Ask the mothers to bring with them . . . a good up-to-date photograph of the baby. . . . Slides would be made and flashed on the screen." It was manipulative, of course, but what gimmick isn't? Even more manipulative was using applause to pick the winning infant.

Another of Brandt's ploys involved firemen. While fires may not be quite as dramatic today as they were in the past (unless they are in a high-rise that produces a "towering inferno"), they were so commonplace at the turn of the century that a movie about a fireman, such as E.S. Porter's *The Life of an American Fireman* (1903), could achieve instant popularity. Even in 1912, firemen (not yet "firefighters") were still important figures in the community. Unfortunately, their profession precluded their being regular moviegoers. So Brandt proposed a fireman's contest, with voting by ballots rather than applause. After all, firemen were not babies.

Brandt had become such a fixture at Universal that, in August 1912, Laemmle sent him to Chicago for the Motion Pictures Exhibitors League

An autographed picture of the young Harry, whose idealistic appearance is at odds with the inscription (an unsubtle reminder to repair an elevator). Museum of Modern Art Film Stills Archive.

Above: Harry with three of his 1930s directors, Frank Capra and Archie Mayo (right), Frank Borzage (left), and an unidentified man. Courtesy of Paul Lazarus. Below: Harry congratulating Capra on his Oscar for *You Can't Take It with You* (23 February 1939), although both knew their association was ending. Museum of Modern Art Film Stills Archive.

Above: Harry in a checked coat upstaged (and partially obscured) by Al Jolson, who was mugging for the camera. Courtesy of Paul Lazarus. Below: Harry with two aspiring actresses, Shirley Patterson (left) and Alma Carroll, at a 1942 premiere. Academy of Motion Picture Arts and Sciences.

Harry in federal court in 1946, when director Charles Vidor tried unsuccessfully to break his Columbia contract because of Harry's offensive language. Security Pacific National Bank Collection, Los Angeles Public Library.

Harry on location at Schofield Barracks during filming of *From Here to Eternity* (1953), conferring with director Fred Zinnemann (left) and producer Buddy Adler. Private collection.

The H. Paulis Studio in 1921 on Sunset Boulevard near Gower, known locally as Poverty Row. With Columbia's arrival, Poverty Row changed from the home of fly-by-night movie companies to that of a major studio. Bruce Torrence Historical Collection.

Columbia's neighbor, Independent Pictures, on Sunset just east of Gower. Bruce Torrence Historical Collection.

Above: The corner of Sunset and Gower in 1930, with the Wolcott Studio at left. Below: The Columbia studio on North Gower, 1938. Both from Security Pacific National Bank Collection, Los Angeles Public Library.

Above: Columbia's official address for almost fifty years (1924-72)—1438 North Gower Street.
Right: An early version of the Columbia logo featuring an Athena-like figure, from a 1925 ad in *Motion Picture News*. Both from Academy of Motion Picture Arts and Sciences.

Convention. Laemmle, realizing that old trademarks die hard, wanted Brandt to bury IMP once and for all and push Universal as the company name. The convention was more of a trade show, an occasion for hawking wares and peddling product. Along with two other executives, Brandt worked the convention beyond anything the exhibitors had ever seen: "No three men ever hit a convention harder or more often. They were simply up and at everything—day and night—From morning to morning it was ever, everywhere 'Demand that Universal Product.'"[14]

Brandt was rapidly becoming one of Universal's most important figures. At Universal's 1914 Christmas party, he was mentioned in the same context as Laemmle and other studio "dignitaries."[15] But Jack Cohn was by no means ignored; at an awards presentation that year, Brandt and Jack were at the head of the grand march.

The symbiosis of their relationship was the result of similar tastes and complementary skills. As filmmakers, Brandt and Jack excelled at shorts; as studio executives, they possessed talents that were different but not antithetical, eliminating the possibility of competitiveness or jealousy. While Jack was a good company spokesperson, he lacked Brandt's gift of salesmanship, which was the proverbial "smile and a shoeshine." Brandt's was a style that had been honed on the road—the result of frequent cross-country trips to exchanges and exhibitors. Universal had a number of film exchanges that in 1918 were placed under Brandt's supervision. When he became assistant treasurer at Universal the following year, he was entrusted with the difficult task of transforming what had been a loose confederation of distribution centers into a multi-outlet conduit for Universal. He was able to achieve greater consistency among the exchanges in terms of prices, policies, and operations by combining business savvy with personal charm. Had he been a performer, he would have spent most of his career touring. "Brandt can do it" and "Brandt will do it" had become catch phrases in the industry, a columnist noted, adding, "and no less familiar is the phrase 'Brandt did it.'"[16]

But Brandt would not be doing it much longer at Universal nor would Jack, despite his being entrusted with the creation of the *Universal Screen Magazine* in 1917. Designed as the film equivalent of the magazine section of the Sunday newspaper, Universal's new short feature was a one-reel magazine-on-film, a weekly that dealt with topics of interest such as travel, diet, and beauty hints. If the titles of the 2 May 1917 *Magazine* are any indication, a typical *Magazine* ran the gamut from ostrich farms and phonograph lamps to new cooking methods and automobile manufacturing.

While neither Brandt nor Jack was ever actively involved in production, each at least had some experience in it. Jack, as noted, did some directing, and Brandt was made head of Universal's serial unit early in

1919 while still assistant treasurer—a mark of his infinitive variety. Exactly what Brandt did in the unit, apart from keeping the scenario, publicity, and stills departments separate, is unknown. "Head" can be a title or a job description; yet it would not come as a surprise to learn that he directed a few episodes of *The Red Glove* and *Midnight Men* (both 1919) and supervised the editing.

Jack might have continued at Universal had it not been for an event in November 1918 that spelled the end of his association with his beloved *Animated*: its sale to William Randolph Hearst, under whom it became the Hearst-International News Weekly (with Universal only as distributor). Jack knew that his role in a Hearst enterprise would be significantly diminished, if not eliminated.

"We Never Thought It Would Happen," *Motion Picture News* exclaimed (12 April 1919) when Jack left Universal. He was departing as the "well-known editor" of the *Animated*. Jack was part of a generation of filmmakers who understood the importance of editing. While they were the first to admit that an editor cannot wring lilies out of acorns, they would also agree that an editor can make an acorn seem less mundane. Harry too would learn to appreciate the importance of editing—of getting the right rhythm, the right pacing, the right sequence, the right mix of tempos; in fact, he understood it so well that Ron Randell, who appeared in a succession of Columbia films from 1947 through 1960, called Harry a "good editor," meaning not that he literally edited Columbia's movies but that when he saw a rough cut or attended a preview he knew automatically how it could be improved, even if it was a B movie.[17]

Jack left Universal to "produce on his own," as the trades said then and continue to say about departing executives. A few months later, Brandt did the same, surprising the Chicago-based *Exhibitors Herald and Motography*, which remarked that Brandt had given no indication when he passed through Chicago in early July that he would be leaving Universal a few weeks later.

The timing was not accidental. Jack's departure in March 1919 and Brandt's in July were part of a decision to go independent—for the time being separately, although neither ruled out the possibility of a partnership. Within a few months of their departure from Universal, Jack and Brandt were neighbors. Jack literally moved across the street, from 1600 Broadway to the Strand Theatre Building. Brandt stayed in the Mecca Building, where several film companies had offices, including the National Film Corporation of America, which he joined immediately after leaving Universal.

The year 1919 turned out to be a critical one for Harry too—it was the year he entered the movie business.

3

From Broadway to Hollywood

There was nothing altruistic about Harry's decision to make movies. It was certainly not to give the world "pieces of time," as Cobb (Brian Keith), the raffish moviemaker of Peter Bogdanovich's *Nickelodeon* (1975), described film's unique gift to humankind. Yet Harry achieved a place in film history through a combination of circumstances that adds one more category to Shakespeare's trio of those born great, those who achieve greatness, and those who have it thrust upon them—namely, those who thrust it upon themselves. Harry understood that while fortune may be incalculable, the incalculable can become the inevitable when a chance occurrence turns into an act of destiny.

For more than a decade, Harry had watched his brother advance in the business. If the flickers got Jack headlines in the trades, they could do the same for Harry; if Jack got a "Good luck to you" sendoff from *Motion Picture News*, Harry could do better. He did, in fact—but not in 1919, when the only Cohn known to the press was Jack.

At some point in 1917, Harry's interest in film revived. It was not film as such: Harry had no intention of returning to the road as a traveling exhib. Rather, he devised a way of uniting his world—popular music— with his brother's and selling movie companies the equivalent of songs-on-slides. Harry rented space in the Strand Theatre Building for his Illustrated Song Service, a one-person operation out of which he produced shorts that offered a visual context for the lyrics. To succeed, he needed the backing of someone high up in the industry. Since the obvious choice was his brother's boss, Carl Laemmle, Harry persuaded Jack to set up an appointment with Laemmle, whom Harry had no difficulty convincing.

In spring 1917, Universal described its Song Hits in Photography as follows: "While the song is being sung, the story the song tells is being acted on the screen."[1] Since these musical shorts involved the cooperation of exhibitors and music publishers, Harry had succeeded in combining two forms of American entertainment, popular music and film. Although Harry was given no credit for this "great combination of all the latest popular song hits and moving pictures to illustrate them," as *Moving Picture World* (19 May 1917) characterized the shorts, he played a major role in producing them.

For the series, Harry was able to draw on his contacts in music publishing. He knew some of the leading music publishers of the day, including Max Winslow, who had discovered Irving Berlin. Winslow became Harry's brother-in-law when Harry married Rose Barker, Winslow's sister-in-law, on 18 September 1923. Since Harry had worked for Waterson, Berlin and Snyder, he knew Ted Snyder well enough to get him for a short centering around Irving Berlin's "The Road That Leads to Love."

This particular short, which delighted audiences at New York's Fifth Avenue Theatre and Harlem Opera House in May 1917, proves that Harry was able to transfer his talent for exploiting songs to film. As a former singer, he knew that one sells a song by integrating voice, face, and gesture into a one-person dramatization; just singing the lyrics is insufficient. The song is a story; the singer, the storyteller. A song also tells its story with great brevity; the telling of that story on the screen must be similarly brief.

The transition from singing songs to dramatizing them on film was not difficult; it was simply a matter of another medium. Harry's idea for "The Road That Leads to Love" short reveals an imaginative sense that one ordinarily does not associate with the precursor of MTV. It also reveals Harry's concept of film narrative: telling a story on the screen skillfully and economically. Before the recording of "The Road That Leads to Love" starts, the title from the actual sheet music is seen, followed by a shot of Ted Snyder driving up Broadway to overtake Blossom Seeley in her car. As he cruises alongside her, he acquaints her with Berlin's new song, which apparently pleases her. Then, the song, sung by Mabel Burke, is heard. But the short does not end here; the song pitch was just the introduction. The purpose of the song short was to dramatize the lyrics, which describe an encounter between a young man, eager for fame, and an older man, who, having known it, tells the youth that "the road that leads to fortune and fame/is paved with gold in your dreams"; and that the only road worth taking is "the road that leads to love."

The song shorts proved a success; Laemmle, who recognized a promoter when he saw one, made Harry an administrative assistant in 1918. When Jack and Brandt left Universal a year later, Harry saw no reason to stay on. But he had not given up on shorts; they illustrated his dual principle of economy: economy of plot and of budget. Harry's next venture would be nonmusical shorts: the Hall Room Boys.

In 1919, Jack Cohn too had an idea for a short: a one-reeler portraying the human side of the business. It would be Hollywood without makeup, "intimate views of movie stars at work and play," to quote the foreword to the many Screen Snapshots, as the series (which lasted until 1958) was called. In a typical Snapshots, one could see Donald Cook backing into a cactus, Ann Sothern crocheting, Fay Wray practicing archery, Ruth Chatterton piloting a plane, and Rosalind Russell trying to count the chairs at a charity ball and never getting the same total twice.

That Screen Snapshots originated with Jack, and the Hall Room Boys with Harry, points up the difference between the brothers. Jack understood the public's need to see its idols, if not with feet of clay, then in flats and loafers. Jack also had the contacts to launch Screen Snapshots in 1919, even though filming did not begin for another year. Harry's connections were in New York, and he capitalized on them.

While Screen Snapshots was a logical series for someone established in the movie business and able to get stars to act like people, the Hall Room Boys was a natural choice for a New Yorker with show business contacts. The Hall Room Boys was a popular comic strip that had appeared for fifteen years in about seventy-five newspapers, including the *World Telegram,* then became an equally popular vaudeville act with the team of (Eddie) Flannagan and (Neely) Edwards. Harry knew vaudeville as Jack never did; he must have seen Flannagan and Edwards as hoboes who deflate the pretensions of the rich.

By July 1919, Harry had wrapped up three Hall Rooms, made in rented studio space in Los Angeles, and brought them to New York for editing and eventual distribution through Joe Brandt's company—or at least that was the original plan. Jack sensed the potential for the series, and since he had not yet done anything about Screen Snapshots, he teamed up with Harry to form Hall Room Boys Photoplays, Inc., renting an office in the Mecca Building where, in addition to Universal, many of the states rights exchanges, which distributed films on a territorial basis, were located, and where the National Film Corporation, the company Joe Brandt represented, was also based. The web of connections seems even more finely spun when one realizes that the National Film Corporation was an independent company that supplied the exchanges in the building with states rights product, which the Hall Rooms would shortly become.

Harry looked upon the series as his, despite the fact that he was only secretary-treasurer of Hall Room Boys Photoplays. It was Harry, now an Angeleno, under whose "personal supervision," to quote the trades, the series was filmed. Jack remained in New York, where he handled distribution. The industry's separation of production (West Coast) and distribution (East Coast) had already polarized the brothers, who only needed distance for their estrangement. Harry's official entry into moviemaking provided that. Henceforth it was strictly business. Production needs distribution; Harry needs Jack. Jack needs product, and Harry delivers it.

Between December 1919 and January 1920, the trades listed the Hall Rooms as "distributed by Jack and Harry Cohn"; then "produced and released every other week by Jack and Harry Cohn"; and finally "produced by the National Film Corporation of America." [2] With the absence of records, one can only assume that "produced" and "distributed by" mean what they customarily do. Harry produced the series in the sense of getting it made; the National Film Corporation could also be said to produce the Hall Rooms (in the same way that a studio can be called a film's producer even though a particular producer is cited in the credits) because they were filmed at its West Coast studio. Harry and Jack distributed the series, which was "released by" their company, Hall Room Boys Photoplays.

Like Laemmle when he founded IMP, the Cohns had become independents. Thus they had to work twice as hard to sell their product. One- and two-reel comedy shorts were commonplace in 1920, and the competition was stiff: Mack Sennett's Keystone comedies, Billy West and Alice Howell in their "comedy effusions," Chaplin, Lloyd, and so on. But the Cohns made it easy for the exchanges to handle the series by furnishing them with elaborate press kits and persuading Flannagan and Edwards to make personal appearances at selected theaters. The Cohns even sponsored a contest with a $100 prize for the best letter about being broke, to be used in a future episode. Since Harry was in that predicament more often than Jack, the contest was probably Harry's inspiration.

Joe Brandt fitted in well with the Cohns. Each was enough of an individual to find his own niche in the business. While Jack and Brandt could claim some credits in production (Jack in the *Animated*, Brandt in Universal's serial unit), production eventually became Harry's province. Distribution was Jack's, with Brandt as the PR man, shaking hands and schmoozing with exhibitors.

The debut of the Hall Rooms coincided with Prohibition. Sensitive to the new morality and a series of scandals that rocked the movie industry, beginning with Fatty Arbuckle's alleged rape of Virginia Rappe in San Francisco during the 1921 Labor Day weekend, the Cohns advertised the Hall Rooms as "the most wholesome comedies on earth." To make the point, two jesters in caps and bells were shown poking at the mask of comedy, as if to say it is all in good *clean* fun.

The press noted the "clean tone," as did exhibitors and audiences. But no series survives on moral inoffensiveness alone. Fortunately, exhibitors held Brandt in such esteem that they booked the Hall Rooms on the strength of his name, which had become familiar to them over the past decade. When Brandt toured the country, Jack remained in New York, leaving only to work the convention circuit and impress on exhibitors the importance of two-reelers despite the growing popularity of features.

As 1919 was about to end, Harry got a notice in the trades: "Cohn Going to Coast"—the Cohn being himself, for a change.[3] His joy must have been short-lived, however, when he read on to learn that while the Hall Rooms were made under his "personal supervision," it was Jack who "planned the picturization of the famous cartoons." The error was never repeated, and while subsequent references attributed the series to Jack *and* Harry , the first names may not have been in alphabetical order but at least the former was not highlighted.

Still, it must have rankled Harry to realize that his baptism in the trades only meant there was another Cohn better known than he. It was Jack who was always quoted, whether he was championing the rights of independents or promoting two-reelers. It was Jack who was singled out for the quote of the day: "Keep the product good and keep the public as your friend."[4] It was Jack who, when Edwards and Flannagan were breaking up, persuaded Edwards to remain in the Hall Rooms with Hugh Fay as his partner. For the time being, Harry suppressed his anger; being in Los Angeles at a time when "Hollywood" was becoming part of the national consciousness partially compensated for what he considered a lack of attention from the press. Ten years later, in 1929, his paranoia would surface, but at least in 1919 he knew that whatever one of the trio did would affect the others—and therefore himself.

In the fall of 1919, the Hall Rooms were booked on the Loew's circuit: "I Told You We'd Pack Them In," a full-page ad in *Motion Picture News* (8 November 1919) proclaimed. Indeed they did, for in addition to Loew's, twelve exchanges had also booked the shorts.

With the Hall Rooms launched, Jack returned to the series that he had been planning for over a year: Screen Snapshots, whose purpose, he told the press, was "to escort patrons of the country's photoplay houses through the mysteries and intricacies of motion picture production in West Coast studios [and] bring the private life of the most famous stars to the patrons of every theatre which books the releases."[5] The rhetoric may have been excessive—Jack not only liked to turn phrases but also to decorate them—but the idea was sound. The series delighted the public as well as the stars, the latter proving unusually cooperative. In fact, there was hardly a major star who did not appear at least once in a Snapshots.

Since Screen Snapshots was Jack's inspiration and did not involve Harry (although Harry later considered himself the producer of everything the company made), Jack persuaded Louis Lewyn to coproduce the series. Lewyn's knowledge of photography proved invaluable when Jack decided to devote an episode to the way underwater sequences were filmed.

Shortly after Screen Snapshots got under way, Joe Brandt, tired of National Film's periodic financial crises, decided to go independent—but not alone. Supposedly he approached Jack, who, despite his penchant for shorts, was also intrigued by the prospect of becoming part of a real film company. While Jack could probably have moved into production after his stint at Universal, the business end of moviemaking began to appeal to him, as did living in New York rather than Los Angeles.

Whether Harry was to have been included at this point is uncertain, although it would have been foolish to exclude him in view of his West Coast experience and knowledge of production. On the other hand, if one can trust the alternate version, a year before Brandt and Jack began discussing a film company, the Cohns had considered the idea themselves. They sounded out Fred Balshofer, who had masterminded the formation of the Quality, Sterling, and New York Motion Picture companies, about joining them in setting up their own and splitting the stock three ways. When Balshofer discovered that the brothers intended to count their shares as one, not two, he bowed out, accusing the Cohns of "trying to pull a fast one."[6]

As is common with conflicting accounts about Hollywood history, one version seems more like a movie than the other. Did the Cohns want Balshofer instead of Brandt in 1919? Did Jack and Brandt want Harry in 1920? Harry's inclusion, much less as production head, struck many in the industry as odd. Eddie Small, who within a quarter of a century would become an independent producer at Columbia, recalls how in 1920 he was having a drink with Jack at Shanley's on 43rd Street when Jack told him Harry would be producing for the company: "You're the creative one, Jack. You're the one with the ideas. Not Harry." "Maybe," Jack answered. "But there's a lot of hambone in Harry. . . . Besides, Joe and I figure we have to watch the business end."[7]

Yet, on reflection, Small had to admit "there was always something in [Harry's] manner that reflected his brash Broadway past."[8] The "something" was the combination of huckersterism and hustle that a movie studio, as opposed to a film company, needed. But the "business end" was equally important, and if Small was quoting verbatim, "watch" was the right word. "Watch" was exactly what Jack and Brandt had to do—and they would be watching both the business end and Harry.

Whether the Cohns teamed up with Balshofer or Brandt, it would still be two C's and a B. Thus it was fitting that the corporate name was the CBC Film Sales Company, a Brandt between two Cohns. In a little more than a decade, it would be just the two Cohns, only one of whom would join the ranks of the movie czars—Harry.

But in the summer of 1920 the industry knew only that a newcomer had joined the independents: "Brandt And Cohn Join Forces," a *Motion Picture News* headline (7 August 1920) read. The Cohn in question was Jack, not Harry, who again had taken a backseat to his brother: "Joe Brandt, former director general of the National Film Corporation, and Jack Cohn, producer of Screen Snapshots and the Hall Room Boys comedies, have become associated in the formation of the CBC Film Sales Company, a distributing medium exclusively for independent productions." As usual, Jack was the spokesperson: "CBC will deal directly with the independent producer [for] the efficient and equitable marketing of his product." As far as the industry was concerned, Harry was CBC's secretary-treasurer; Jack was CBC's vice president, sales.

Thus it was Brandt, CBC's president, with whom the company was identified. The holiday issue of *Motion Picture News* (25 December 1920), which was glutted with paid advertisements from stars, directors, and studios, also contained greetings from Brandt on behalf of the independents. Brandt used the occasion to urge states rights buyers to favor quality over price, dismissing the notion that the independent exchanges were "junk shops for the disposal of cheap pictures." Since CBC's films would cost more than those of many of the independents, Brandt's emphasis on quality was a psychological ploy to make the CBC product less expensive in the long run than "cheap pictures" that would alienate audiences and empty theaters.

CBC began life as an independent like Universal, which started without its own exchanges and under even more discouraging circumstances. In 1912, the year the Universal Film Manufacturing Company (soon to be just Universal) was formed, all but one of the fifty-eight exchanges were owned by the General Film Company, which the Motion Picture Patents Company (MPPC) organized to distribute only the product of those belonging to it. Similarly, Columbia had to depend on states rights exchanges until it could set up its own.

Historically, exchanges began as an alternative to purchasing films outright. In 1902, Herbert J. Miles started renting films to kinetoscope parlor owners at half the purchase price; by the end of 1903 the rental service had been extended to theater managers, especially cost-conscious ones in small towns.[9] Thus began the second phase of filmmaking: distribution. As the industry grew, studios established their own exchanges. But in 1920, independents could not afford that luxury and instead distributed through states rights exchanges, which leased films for a certain period to exhibitors within their territories. There were problems with states rights distribution. First, many exchange members were also exhibitors primarily interested in booking films for their own theaters, which naturally received priority. Since these exchanges handled movies of independents other than CBC, they could not give its films personal attention. Moreover, there were no uniform rental procedures, with some films costing less than their earning power warranted.

It was only a matter of time before CBC created its own exchanges. In the meantime, the company had to guarantee the exhibitors product. Brandt knew that initially CBC could offer few features. In fact, the first CBC film, *The Victim*, was not released until 1921. (CBC was only distributing *The Victim*, which was a Goebel Productions movie.) Realizing that CBC would be proceeding slowly into the feature market, Brandt toured the country, sympathizing with theater owners who complained of having to book for an entire year because they were afraid of being without product. While Brandt could do nothing to help them, he listened to their tales of woe, which included such acts of desperation as booking two films for the same day. Since he knew he would be quoted in the trades, Brandt deplored block booking, arguing for at least twelve open weeks so exhibitors could have some leeway. He inveighed against the inferiority of the current movie crop, arguing for "fewer but better pictures." If his philosophy prevailed, the exhibitors would start turning to the independents and book whatever they wanted. That happened thirty years later, although even after the so-called end of block booking and blind bidding, there were—and still are—abuses.

In 1920, there were about eighty independents, and a newcomer could last only under the right management. Fortunately, CBC was headed by Brandt, who now had enough friends in the various exchanges to ensure that CBC's movies would find their way to the theaters.

Early in 1921, CBC, which had yet to release a feature, suddenly became respectable. On 22 January 1921, the bill at New York's Strand Theatre featured, as the main attraction, George Arliss in *The Devil*, preceded by a stage show that included the overture to Boito's *Mefistofele*, a rendition of Rossini's "Una voce poco fa," and an organ arrangement of the Pilgrims' Chorus from *Tannhäuser*. While one would think a short would lower the tone of such rarefied entertainment, the Strand management did not: it even added "A Dog-gone Mix-up," a Hall Room Boys short. The bill broke previous house records, although one suspects audiences came more for Arliss than for the Hall Room Boys. But the Hall Rooms were now legitimized, and the engagement also brought delayed recognition to Harry, who claimed he had perfected the series to such a degree that it had a discernible structure, with each episode "made to follow a definite thread wherein all the action is logical and has a real meaning."[10] Harry never knew it, but he was expressing the principle of linear narrative: a unified action that moves progressively toward its resolution and is not "jumbled up with a lot of extraneous . . . matter."

Beginning–middle–end construction also became his credo when he assumed control of Columbia ten years later.

The Hall Rooms may have been flourishing, but CBC needed features, which had to be bought since the company had no production facilities of its own. Since Jack was busy with Screen Snapshots, which were being booked in major New York theaters such as the Rivoli, State, and Criterion, it fell to Brandt to acquire features. Finding a story that he liked, "Heart of the North, or the Twins of Destiny," Brandt purchased it and arranged for its filming; he then went into partnership with George H. Davis to form Quality Film Productions solely to make *Heart of the North* for CBC.[11]

Although CBC's first releases were not major fare, Brandt believed they could be made attractive to exhibitors. Thus he handled the advertising himself. Unfazed by travel, he embarked on another tour of the states rights circuit. Curtailment of production in 1921 resulted in the exhibitors' demand for lower rentals; hence film, for a time, became a seller's market. When the exhibitors discovered they had open dates that could be filled with the independent product, Brandt used the occasion to release CBC's first features.

Like Jack Cohn, Brandt considered himself a New Yorker, yet both must have realized the days of filming in upper Manhattan and on the Hudson Palisades in Fort Lee were ending. Harry, who severed ties with New York when he began producing the Hall Rooms, knew the future lay in southern California. As far as Harry was concerned, New York was where the Hall Rooms were shipped for editing, titling, and distributing; Los Angeles was where they were filmed.

Harry may have had foresight, but Brandt got the lion's share of the publicity even after CBC entered the feature market. In May 1922, Brandt was elected executive director of the Federated Film Exchanges of America. *Motion Picture News* (3 June 1922) congratulated him, noting that "he's happiest when busy and when busy he's a dynamo." A dynamo was what Brandt had become. Throughout 1922 he was on the road promoting *More to be Pitied than Scorned*, CBC's first feature (the others being films CBC distributed). Even when national distributors begun wooing CBC, Brandt was determined to release on the open market, if for no other reason than to gain time until CBC could establish its own exchanges. The more popular CBC features became, the easier it was to distribute them through CBC's exchanges, which began operating in 1924.

CBC wanted exhibitors to know it had more than one feature. Thus, the company announced four others for 1922 that, together with *Pitied*, would constitute the Big Six—a paltry figure compared with Paramount's

Super Thirty-Nine. Even so, CBC promoted each film individually, while at the same time announcing future releases.

More to be Pitied opened in New York at the B.S. Moss Broadway on 18 September 1922; in Chicago, it played the Randolph, the first independent movie to open at that theater. Soon it was being booked into other first-run houses, and as its popularity increased, so did Harry's reputation. Ads made it clear that *Pitied* and the rest of the Big Six were directed by Edward Le Saint and produced by Harry Cohn.

Pitied's success emboldened CBC, which advertised its second release, *Only a Shop Girl*, before the film was even finished. Brandt, who knew every marketing trick, went on a two-and-a-half-month tour, touting the movie with exhibitors, exchanges, and chambers of commerce; he even worked out tie-ins with department and novelty stores to spotlight their own "shop girls." Brandt was riding high on the success of *Pitied*, which was being shown as the sole attraction in theaters that ordinarily ran double features.

If *Pitied* was a hit, *Shop Girl* had to be a bigger one. CBC had taken a chance, promoting the film before it was available. Completed in November 1922, it had still not been released at the start of 1923. Yet the exploitation had begun in earnest, with announcements of shop girl contests (in which the finalists would be judged by a committee comprising the film's stars, Estelle Taylor and Mae Busch, Joe Brandt, Harry, and Edward Le Saint, with the winner getting a chance to appear in CBC's third movie, *Temptation*). Anticipating charges of gimmickry, Jack Cohn insisted the contest was a sincere attempt to help girls who "have the yearning for better things," although "circumstances" have placed them behind counters.[12]

Using one film to advertise another was not uncommon, nor were promotional stratagems. The industry, in fact, has always relied on advertising gimmicks, the difference being that in the early 1920s there was a greater attempt to involve the community. In their Sunday editions, newspapers often featured fictionalizations of movies; stores showcased replicas of clothes and jewelry from current films. While press kits offered ideas for exploitation, exhibitors also came up with their own, resulting in some ingenious lobby displays: an entrance way in the shape of a white mask for *White Masks* (1923); a peep hole revealing a fog-enshrouded face for *The Face of the Fog*; barns for *The Village Blacksmith*; a bar (serving only soft drinks) for *Ten Nights in a Barroom*.

Joe Brandt was a master of exploitation. For *Temptation* (1923), he encouraged exhibitors to use their imaginations; if theirs had grown dull, his had not. Brandt offered, among other suggestions, fake diamond rings inscribed with the movie's title; message pads with "We've got your number—watch out for 'Temptation'"; and miniature roulette wheels (gambling being the cause of the temptation).

Musical tie-ins were probably Harry's inspiration, reflecting his days as a songplugger. For *The Barefoot Boy*, a Mission Film Corporation feature that CBC was only distributing, Harry got Percy Wenrich and Gus Kahn to write the title song, making the deal with Forster Music Publishing of Chicago. He worked out a similar arrangement with John Franklin Music Publishing in New York for the title song of *Forgive and Forget* (1923). For the most part, though, Harry had little to do with exploitation. Feeling that he had come into his own as production chief with *Shop Girl*, edited and titled in Los Angeles and not New York, Harry ordered leatherbound albums and lavishly illustrated pressbooks for the exchanges. Jack, who frowned on extravagance, limited the ads to a single page to save impatient buyers the trouble of poring over pressbooks. Eventually Harry's prodigality and Jack's conservatism would result in a polarization so total that only one of them could head the studio that would be known as Columbia.

Regardless of how the Cohns and Brandt felt about each other, they put CBC before all else. Their specialities reflected the division of labor on which the studio system would be based. Harry settled into production; while he had some ideas for exploitation (he had, after all, mastered the art of the hustle), he lacked Brandt's flair for hype. Brandt, on the other hand, could never be a production head; he was too gregarious and genuinely enjoyed working conventions and visiting exchanges. Jack might have been an executive producer or a New York–based studio president; he never lost his ability to edit and was widely respected in the business. Yet he lacked both Brandt's charisma and Harry's street smarts. He was, as Eddie Small said, "a sweeter-tempered man than Harry."[13] Torn between two personalities more powerful than his own, Jack decided to stay in distribution until he could no longer tolerate Harry's excesses.

But in 1924 the triumvirate was functioning smoothly, or at least not acrimoniously. Since CBC's 1922 and 1923 releases had been well received, it seemed the right time for the company to shed its "shorts stuff" image. The Hall Room Boys, the series that had brought the company into prominence, was about to end, and while shorts would continue to be important, the emphasis would have to be on features if CBC was to be taken seriously. But features alone would not do the trick; CBC also needed its own exchanges, which might rid it of its inferiority complex. The company could not help but feel like an outsider with its one-room office at 1600 Broadway, where Universal occupied the entire third floor with views of both Broadway and Seventh Avenue and "fixtures and office furniture . . . of massive mahogany and plate glass."[14] Worse, Universal now had its own exchanges.

The states rights circuit initially suited CBC's purposes when it was just a movie company. In 1923, as it was about to evolve into a studio, Brandt and the Cohns came up with a name for a "big first run caliber series" consisting of four films: *Yesterday's Wife, The Marriage Market, Discontented Husbands,* and *Traffic in Hearts.* This "special" would be called the Columbia series, and in August 1923 CBC completed arrangements with De Luxe Film Corporation to distribute the Columbias throughout eastern Pennsylvania and south Jersey, and with Federated Film Exchanges and the Southern States Film Company to book the series in their territories.

Although CBC was planning to abandon its states rights image as it evolved into Columbia Pictures Corporation, it had no intention of altering its reputation as a company catering to mass audiences, or of making movies whose budgets were so high that exhibitors would have to raise ticket prices during their engagement. What bothered Brandt—and he was not loath to say it—was the rash of million-dollar features that required a $2.00 top. He criticized producers for their indifference to an "industry [that] was originally based on entertainment for the masses"— a principle that would be articulated in the Production Code preamble.[15] Brandt, in fact, predicted fewer big pictures in 1924 and a policy of retrenchment, which was exactly what happened.

January 1924 marked Columbia's emergence from the cocoon of CBC. The metamorphosis was not immediate but gradual, occurring in two stages: CBC's establishment of its own exchanges and the adoption of the first exchange's name for the new studio. Early in 1924, Brandt announced that CBC would be opening its own exchanges, the first of which would be in Omaha and called Columbia Pictures Corporation— "corporation" being a common designation for an exchange (as in Merit Film Corp., Southwestern Film Corp., Consolidated Film Corp.)[16] CBC had a reason for selecting "Columbia": it was also the name of a special kind of CBC film. Hence, the name of the first exchange inspired Brandt and the Cohns to divest themselves of the "corned beef and cabbage" image that "CBC" had inspired. Columbia was certainly as distinctive as Universal, the studio the trio wanted to rival.

"Columbia" was not an arbitrarily chosen name, unlike "Universal," which became the studio's name when a Universal Piping Company truck passed under Carl Laemmle's window. A decade earlier, there had been another Columbia Pictures Corporation, one of Metro's producing companies that was absorbed into Metro in 1917.

"Columbia" had other associations, richer than Peerless and Mascot and more American than Eclair: the patriotic song "Columbia, the Gem of the Ocean" (1843). A studio called Columbia, the personification of America as a woman whose most famous representation is the Statue of Liberty, would be unique if its logo could evoke that image. Paramount's mountain and Universal's globe would pale in comparison.

The first logos did not entirely succeed. What became the famous lady-with-the-torch began first as a medallion depicting an Athena figure, her head garlanded in the Grecian style. Then the lady brandished a torch, sometimes holding it at an angle as if lighting the way for exhibitors still skeptical of the Columbia product. By about 1930, the lady held a sparkler. Finally, in 1936, a torch-bearing lady draped in a flag and standing on a pedestal replaced the inanimate fourth-of-July queen. The Columbia logo underwent a great deal of experimentation during the 1920s. Sometimes the Athena medallion appeared at the end of the film rather than the beginning. In such cases, the film might open, as *Ladies of Leisure* (1926) does, with the credits appearing against the full Athena figure, a considerably more feminine image than the one on the medallion.

How Athena evolved into Miss Liberty is another matter. Joan Perry, Harry's second wife, whom he married on 31 July 1941, claimed she was the inspiration. Perry had come to Columbia as a contract player in 1935, the year the logo was about to change to the one identified with the studio ever since. Indeed, there is a publicity still showing Perry in a pose not much different from the Athena that opened *Ladies of Leisure*. It almost seems as if someone was trying to make the lady more lifelike by using a live model. Yet the Perry pose is too studied, tending to be more vampy than statuesque. The story told by former Columbia bit player Amelia Batchler is more credible. Batchler's specialty was the hands close-up— hers being so exquisite that they were used whenever such a shot was necessary. Apparently hands were not her only asset. Harry was so struck by her bearing that he told her to report to wardrobe, where she was appropriately costumed for the portrait of the torch-bearing woman that became the permanent Columbia logo.[17] Even the change to laser beams in 1971 did not substantially alter her look.

The change of logo coincided with Columbia's own change of image: seven Academy Awards on Oscar night, 27 February 1935—five for *It Happened One Night*, two for *One Night of Love*. With Columbia's entry into the majors, it was impossible to continue with Miss Firecracker.

In 1924, however, a change of name took precedence over a logo. Although "CBC" lent itself to parody, it was a familiar name among independents and, at least until the summer of 1927, functioned as the distribution name of Columbia Pictures Corporation. If it seems odd that CBC coexisted with Columbia for three years, the trades thought so, too, often putting "CBC" in parentheses after a Columbia movie to prevent confusion. Yet the situation was not very different with Universal, which began life as IMP in 1909 and, through a merger with other companies, became the Universal Film Manufacturing Company in 1912. Until the studio officially became Universal in 1915, "Universal" and "IMP" were used interchangeably.

Columbia—first the name of a series, then an exchange, and finally the studio that made the series along with others distributed by CBC—did not sever the cord with the parent company until the end of 1927, when all the exchanges were in place. Then there was no need for a distributing arm with a name that was different from the studio's.

It was one thing for a movie company to reconstitute itself as a studio. A company can distribute the films of others, but a studio must also create its own. And if the Cohns and Brandt really wanted to rival Universal, where they had begun their careers, they would have to emulate its distribution methods and offer exhibitors groups of films, each with its own designation. Universal's films fell into four categories in increasing order of cost: low-budget Red Feather programmers, Bluebirds, Jewels, and Super Jewels. Similarly, Paramount had its Personality Pictures, Commander Specials, Leader Specials, and New Show World Specials—the last (such as *Glorifying the American Girl*) commanding $1.50 and $2.00 a ticket because of production values. Columbia, not having enough films to warrant four categories, after only a year as a studio announced eighteen movies: three series (Columbia, Perfection, and Waldorf), each consisting of six films. Eighteen may have seemed low compared to Fox's forty-nine and Universal's fifty-four, but it was still impressive for a newcomer.

While Paramount and Universal distinguished between their low budget and big-budget movies (a Bluebird is not a Jewel and a Leader is not a Commander), there did not seem to be much difference between the Columbias, Perfections, and Waldorfs. With Columbia as the name of the studio, a Columbia could not be inferior to a Perfection, although the latter name might lead one to think so. *S.O.S. Perils of the Sea* was a Perfection; *Ladies of Leisure*, a Columbia. Both starred Elaine Hammerstein. Initially, the distinction was geographical, with the Columbias restricted to Omaha, Eastern Missouri, and Southern Illinois; that would no longer be the case as other exchanges came into existence. But *Ladies of Leisure* is the better of the two films.

Ladies of Leisure is typical of the CBC and early Columbia films that were, for the most part, melodramas about women misunderstood, blackmailed, or deserted, and men wrongly accused of murder or wrongly accusing their wives of infidelity. Yet, visually *Ladies of Leisure* is not Poverty Row; it may lack the MGM aura, but it is definitely high gloss. The credits appear against a logo of the Athena figure in her billowing gown. Then a woman opens a compact as the camera captures her reflection, setting the tone for a study in doubles (the wealthy Marian and her paid companion, Mamie) and contrasts (Marian's pursuit of Eric as opposed to Mamie's feigned indifference to Jack, Marian's brother).

Despite the elegant production, *Ladies of Leisure* suffered from stodgy direction, a problem that affected many early sound movies and one that Columbia tried to remedy by hiring directors who understood that while film can be theatrical, it is not the same as theater. Director Thomas Buckingham seemed oblivious to D.W. Griffith's innovations in *The Birth of a Nation* and *Intolerance* (not to mention *The Lonely Villa* [1909]), staging the script rather than filming it and allowing entire scenes to be played out instead of intercutting them.

At least Albert Lewin's script makes the plot easy to follow despite the paucity of intertitles which, when they appear, are decoratively printed, providing their own touch of class. The denouement is also ingenious: After saving Mamie from suicide, Eric brings her to his apartment. To work Jack and Marian into the resolution, Lewin has Mamie hiding in the bedroom when Jack arrives at the apartment. When Jack insists on knowing who is behind the bedroom door, out comes Marian, who uses the occasion to get Eric to marry her: Marian merely tells her petulant brother that she is in Eric's apartment because they have just married, leaving Eric no choice but to agree with his "bride."

The next five years saw Harry getting increasingly more attention from the trades, since it was he who was producing the films and signing the stars and directors. *Forgive and Forget* and *The Marriage Market* (1924) were advertised as "Harry Cohn Productions." A *Motion Picture News* headline (29 March 1924) attests to Harry's ascendancy: "Brandt on West Coast to confer with Harry Cohn about CBC's production expansion." A few years earlier, Harry would have been conferring with Brandt. By 1925 Harry was quotable: "New ideas, fresh viewpoints, and clever angles to movie materials are the most vital needs of the films today."[18] Columbia's pictures were his pictures: "I am personally proud of the pictures I have made for Columbia," he told the press in the fall of 1925.[19]

Harry started thinking of the company as his when he began making the Hall Rooms. Once he settled in Los Angeles, he turned into a producer. He needed studio space, which he leased from Wilnat Films at 6070 Sunset Boulevard in the heart of Poverty Row, a stretch on Sunset and Beachwood Drive where the studios that turned out one- and two-reelers (such as Gold Medal, Quality, Loftus, and Chadwick) were located. Since many of them went out of existence as quickly as they came into it, the area was dubbed "Poverty Row."[20]

In the 1922 Los Angeles Directory Harry's address was given as Wilnat Films. In the 1923 Directory he had a title and a residence: Production Manager, Wilnat Films, with a far more fashionable address than 6070 Sunset. The production manager resided on the west side of Los Angeles at 3089 West Seventh Street in the same apartment building where Mabel Normand lived, and where a duplex like hers cost $250 a month. "Production manager" was a bit of an overstatement, since Harry was really using Wilnat to obtain product for CBC. On the other hand, Wilnat was known in Los Angeles, while CBC was New York-based.

In 1925, the year after CBC became Columbia, the Directory reflected the transformation: Columbia's address was given as 6070 Sunset, which was understandable, since the studio had not yet found a home of its own. The rest of the listing would not have raised an Angeleno's eyebrow's but an Easterner who followed the trades would have been stunned to read that Harry was president and Al (sic) Brandt was secretary-treasurer. While "Al" may have been a legitimate mistake, "Harry Cohn, President" was not. More telling is the absence of any reference to Jack, who finally made it into the 1928 Directory. But even there he failed to get his due: Jack was identified as secretary-treasurer, although he was really vice president, sales.

Harry wanted to convey the impression of wielding more authority than he had. He was working on Poverty Row, off Gower Gulch—the northwest corner of Sunset and Gower, which in the first decade of the century was lined with corrals where the makers of westerns kept their horses. By Harry's time it had become a hangout for cowboy actors looking for work.

Poverty Row would be impressed by anyone claiming to run a studio, and Harry considered himself a studio head. He also felt his was the most important job in the company. Certainly his salary indicated that: Harry made more than either Jack or Joe, each of whom was averaging $1,000 a week in 1928, compared to Harry's $1,500. In 1929, the year Columbia issued the first stock offering, Harry's and Jack's salaries, including bonuses, were $127,000 and $91,000, respectively. Federal Trade Commission figures for 1930 reveal that Brandt and Jack made the same amount that year: $103,916; Harry made $189,333. In 1933, the year after Harry became Columbia's president, Jack earned $82,200; Harry, $145,600—the decrease in both salaries reflecting Columbia's modest net profit for fiscal 1932, which was only $14,000 more than the previous year's.[21]

If Harry regarded Columbia as his studio, it was because he literally bought it. A permanent home was necessary for both the studio and its soon-to-be head, especially as the industry faced the challenge of sound. In July 1926, when the Los Angeles Directory still listed Harry as Columbia's president, he and his first wife, Rose Barker Cohn, took out a $118,500 mortgage for property on Gower Street that had originally been the home of California Studios, adjacent to which was another movie company, Bischoff, Inc. Within two years, Columbia had a real home, as 1432-38 North Gower became 1438 North Gower. That same year, 1928, Sam Bischoff, who owned Bischoff, Inc., joined Columbia as production supervisor, leaving in 1931 for Universal and then Warners; he returned in 1941 for five more years before going independent.

The year after Harry and Rose found Columbia a home, they moved into their own home at 135 Fremont Place in the (still) exclusive Hancock Park section on mid-Wilshire. By October 1929, Harry, encouraged by Columbia's net profit of $250,000 for 1928 and knowing the studio needed even more space, bought the last tract of the old Gower Ranch on 1400 North Gower. Since Columbia had a similar piece of property on the Beachwood side, the studio now owned a complete square lot: 114 feet on Gower and 114 feet on Beachwood, with a depth of 270 feet.

Even with its new and relatively modest addition, Columbia still had to rent space and would continue to do so into the 1930s. To enter the sound era, even if just to add sound effects to movies shot silent, Columbia had to rent facilities and equipment. Renting was not cheap. The service charge alone for making five movies at Metropolitan Sound Studios on North Las Palmas was $15,000 for each of the first two films, $14,500 for the third, and $14,000 for each of the last two. There was also a daily charge for the facilities—$1,800 a day for the first two days, $1,700 for the third, and $1,600 for the last two. Columbia could afford only two films at Metropolitan, preferring (until about 1935) to negotiate with less expensive outfits such as Alexandria.

Until spring 1929, Harry's star was in the ascendant. But as the summer wore on, he began feeling less secure, wondering whether a reorganization at the studio would reduce or undermine his authority. Although he had been pressured to imitate other studios and find producers to whom he could delegate authority, he hesitated to do so. Thus Harry was disturbed to read the contract issued to Edward Small, later one of Columbia's major independent producers. Although Small's real association with Columbia did not begin until the mid-1940s, he received a contract in October 1928 to produce three films for Columbia "under the general supervision of Harry Cohn or any such executive of Columbia Pictures . . . which latter shall be known as General Supervisor."[22] But there was no General Supervisor in 1928—only Harry.

On 5 April 1929, Nathan Burkan, Columbia's New York attorney, wired the West Coast attorney Loyd Wright, claiming that Harry was "confused"—a word Burkan used twice. Harry was confused because he suspected Brandt would use Columbia's going public to replace him, or at least to saddle him with an assistant production head or an executive producer. Harry's point was, simply, that Jack and Brandt enjoyed the privilege of a New York address, far removed from America's movie capital, while Harry was at its center, getting New York the product it could distribute. His status, reflected in his salary, merited greater respect. From Harry's point of view he was right: he was involved in the creative end of moviemaking—production. Until 1928 he had to make movies without a studio of his own, renting space and working deals. To Harry, Brandt and Jack were in the catbird seat.

Thus Harry felt he should have complete control of production. Brandt, however, did not agree. On 5 June 1929 he wrote Harry personally, refusing to give him the autonomy he craved and limiting his role in the company. "As long as you and Jack and myself have control of this company you will be the 'representative' of the company and with sufficient control to carry on production along lines that are for the best interests of the company."[23] Brandt did not buckle under; there was no need, since he had been a vital force in the business when Harry was plugging songs in five-and-dimes.

Brandt treated Harry as one would a child having a tantrum. Eventually, Harry had to loosen the reins and bring in some executive producers, who, as the history of Columbia shows, were few. But in 1929 Harry was experiencing a form of paranoia common to autocrats. Sharing authority frightened him; reporting to a "general manager" or a "general supervisor" infuriated him.

Brandt refused to indulge Harry. He made light of his complaint that his name was absent from a Screen Snapshots; he dismissed Harry's fear of being replaced in case of sickness as "something . . . I must accept in a humorous vein." He also reminded Harry that he had never approved of Harry's including "Produced by Harry Cohn" or "A Harry Cohn Production" in the main title, yet had done nothing about it. Harry would have answered that the films were his productions. His name, appearing with the title (even though below it), meant much to him. It would not have mattered to Louis Mayer, who agreed to join Metro-Goldwyn in 1924 if his name was added to the company's. If one's name is part of the studio's, it becomes better known with each movie.

Harry wanted a signature and continued to use his name on the main title, first as producer, then as president. No doubt he was influenced by the way the Universal movies opened: with "Carl Laemmle, President" at the bottom of the main title. In the late 1930s Harry felt secure enough to drop "Harry Cohn, President" from the main title—which is more than Jack L. Warner did. Even though Warner was one of the Warner Brothers (and the brother identified with the studio), he made his name part of the Warners logo, adding "Jack L. Warner, Executive Producer" at the bottom of the sky-borne WB shield. Including one's name in the main title is one thing; incorporating it into the logo is another. Harry, at least, kept his name off the Lady's pedestal.

Anyone other than Harry would have been chastened by Brandt's letter. Unfortunately, Brandt tried to be rational; attempting to allay Harry's fear of being replaced as production head, he posed a rhetorical question: "Since Jack, you and myself control the stock, who is going to do the appointing?" Harry may not have known what a rhetorical question was, but he had his answer: It would make no difference what producers had in their contracts; Harry Cohn was head of production.

But even in that capacity, Harry could not supervise every film. Brandt knew that (and so did Harry, although he would not admit it). Thus in 1928 Brandt brought Eddie Small to the studio. Brandt and the Cohns knew Small from the New York days when Small was an agent. Although he was given a three-picture deal at $5,000 a picture, only *The Song of Love* was made—a vehicle for Belle Baker, one of Small's clients, who received $7,500 for her efforts. There would be no more Edward Small productions at Columbia for two decades.

Brandt was still determined to neutralize Harry's power. In October 1931 Columbia announced that associate producers would be coming to the studio "to confer with [Harry] on story selection, adaptation, choice of director, cost, budget, etc." [24] While Columbia eventually established its own (comparatively small) cadre of producers and played host to a number of independents, it was not until the mid-1930s that a producer's name was acknowledged in the credits. Until Harry became president, "Harry Cohn, Producer" was often part of the title. It may not have been in the most conspicuous position, but even at the bottom of the frame it could not be missed.

Since Harry never relinquished the title of production head when he became president, Columbia had few producers with any real authority. The exceptions were Sidney Buchman, Virginia Van Upp, and probably S. Sylvan Simon, whom Harry was grooming for executive producer. Simon's sudden death in 1951 makes it impossible to know what responsibilities he would have been given, particularly since he had joined the studio only in 1948. Unless a film was an outside production, one involving Buchman or Van Upp, or one made by a director important enough to have his name before the title (John Ford's *The Whole Town's Talking* [1935]; George Stevens's three Columbia films, *Penny Serenade* [1941], *The Talk of the Town* [1942], and *The More the Merrier* [1943]), one can assume that the producer's chief responsibility was to bring the movie in on budget—the function of a line, not an executive, producer.

Producers may have solved the problem for Brandt, but not for Jack, who was convinced that Columbia had taken a turn for the worse under

Harry. Jack, whose filmmaking had consisted almost entirely of one- and two-reelers, decided his brother had become a liability: Either Harry's extravagancies had to be curbed or Harry had to go—at least as production head. Jack did not understand that product does not come cheap, nor do stars and writers. Mentally, Jack was back at CBC—before CBC moved forward and became Columbia. Jack also knew that if he was to do anything about Harry, he had to find an ally other than Brandt, who, in fall 1931, had become little more than a figurehead.

Two years earlier, Brandt had been firm with Harry—or so he thought. In 1931, he must have realized that Harry's moviemaking talent outstripped his. Harry was another breed: he was in the creative end of the business, while Brandt and Jack were in the promotional. To use the familiar distinction, Harry was Los Angeles; Brandt and Jack, New York.

The dawn of the new decade saw the end of Joe Brandt's presence at Columbia; Brandt, in fact, would be dead before the 1930s were over. But even as they started, he was losing the drive that had made him famous. Although not yet fifty, he had begun showing signs of strain. One of the last times he behaved like a studio president was when he saw a print of *Murder on the Roof*, a forgettable and forgotten 1930 movie running fifty-five minutes, meaning it was 5,500 feet, 500 feet under the 6,000 feet requirement for British features.[25]

Harry had forgotten the requirement; *Murder on the Roof* was not a major movie (it was shot in two weeks), and there were twenty others, including two by Frank Capra, that took precedence. Besides, while fifty-five-minute films were rare, Columbia continued to make them well into the 1950s, primarily low-budget westerns.

Harry's and Brandt's reactions to the *Murder on the Roof* incident show how different they were. Harry, always the con artist, would have lied; he would have told the British they had received the wrong print. In the meantime, he would have gotten the additional 500 feet somewhere—from outtakes or stock footage. But it was too late; the movie had already been previewed in Britain, and exhibitors wouldn't book it because it was under an hour.

The lost bookings did not bother Brandt, who hoped the experience would teach Harry a lesson. But what Harry learned was not that he should never release a movie that ran under an hour (Charles Starrett's westerns averaged fifty-five minutes) but that he should never release one that exceeded two hours. Only in rare cases (such as *Lost Horizon* [1937], *Mr. Smith Goes to Washington* [1939], and *The Jolson Story* [1946]) did Harry make an exception. Despite his love for *From Here to Eternity* (1953), he would not let it go beyond 118 minutes—the same running time as *The Talk of the Town*.

Far more important than Britain's losing the opportunity to see

Murder on the Roof was the matter of pressure groups, who were becoming increasingly vocal about film content. Since movies from before 1934 (the year the Production Code was enforced and the Legion of Decency formed) were more open about infidelity, prostitution, and illegitimacy, Columbia could get by with Capra's *Ladies of Leisure* ([1930], not to be confused with the 1926 film of the same title), in which the main character was, if not a streetwalker, then a tart, to use a term of the time. The title was self-explanatory, and the movie itself was totally unapologetic about the ladies' morals. Like *Pretty Woman* sixty years later, the heroine eventually finds the dream husband, whose love—and wealth—keep her at home.

Capra's *The Miracle Woman* (1931) posed a different problem; in a way it too is a "fallen woman" movie except that the woman is not a tart but an evangelist, and her fall is not from morality but from grace. From the outset, Brandt was nervous about the film, whose main character, Florence Fallon (Barbara Stanwyck), was modeled after evangelist Aimee Semple McPherson. Yet the film should never have been a problem—not in 1931 or even in 1934, when Joe Breen assumed the directorship of the Production Code Administration (PCA) and judged scripts from a Catholic viewpoint. The characters in *The Miracle Woman* are not Catholic; Florence is a minister's daughter seeking revenge on the religious hypocrites she blames for her father's death. A con artist plays on her bitterness and makes her into a famous evangelist with her own radio station. Eventually she sees the light and repents by joining the Salvation Army.

The script was shown to various Protestant clergymen, but the changes they requested would, if made, emasculate the film. Unable to deal with their objections, Brandt passed the criticisms on to Harry, who accepted a few of them.[26] He agreed to delete "bring the fish," which the clergy had interpreted as a snide reference to the miracle of the loaves and fishes. When a minister demanded that "Jesus Christ" not be uttered, he settled for "Christ," which Stanwyck said so reverently that no one could object to it, or to the line "down with sin with good old gin," delivered at a party at which the drunken guests mock Florence's evangelism. But Harry would not budge on the more controversial "Religion's like everything else; it's no good if you give it away." This was the con artist's philosophy and therefore part of his character. Harry also refused to heed the clergy's suggestions about the first sequence, in which Florence berates the parishioners from her father's pulpit. The clergy hoped her invective could be photographed in such a way that it would not be a wholesale indictment of the congregation; perhaps the guilty could leave in a huff and the innocent remain in their pews. The sequence remained intact.

Harry could hardly have taken their objection to the use of the "Holy

Land" seriously. The con artist blackmails Florence into going to Europe with him, planning to tell the press she is traveling to the Holy Land. But the most ludicrous request was the deletion of his line "Buck up, I know how you feel. I'd have the blues myself if it wasn't for the good times I'm expecting to have on the Riviera. That'll shake the blues out of you. The only blue down there is the Mediterranean, and, sister, you know how blue that is." Either the clergy thought the Holy Land was being trivialized by being compared to the Riviera (or the Jordan to the Mediterranean), or they took "blue" in the sense of suggestive or risqué.

What is distressing about the teletypes between Harry and Brandt is the latter's passivity, as if he were beset by a lethargy more psychological than physical. He would simply enumerate one series of objections after another, including those of the New York censors, who were upset by references to traveling salesmen and "farmer's daughter jokes." Either Brandt or the censors were confused; there were references to the farmer's daughter but no jokes.

Harry, who would later challenge any attempt to change his films, was of the same mind in 1931 when he used an argument on Brandt that he would use on Joe Breen: "Cuts ordered will vitally affect quality [of] picture." In the same context, when he reminded Brandt that New York was less rigid than most states, Brandt replied feebly, "Impossible to do anything about New York censorship."

While *The Miracle Woman* was not a great success (and Capra's memories of it are not entirely accurate[27]), it is still a powerful movie that makes no attempt to reconcile a belief in God with a desire for satisfaction but only suggests that, once that desire has been fulfilled or has played itself out, the individual may be restored to an even higher state of grace, as Florence discovers in the Salvation Army.

While Brandt was loosening the reins of authority, Jack was tightening them. Brandt must have shared his 1929 reprimand to Harry with Jack, who was already disturbed by his brother's growing power and free hand in production. Bringing associate producers to the studio to "assist" Harry was not the answer. Harry would never be content until he moved Columbia into the front ranks, a goal that only someone who thought in the grandest of terms could achieve.

What Jack foresaw for Columbia was different; lacking his brother's vision, Jack thought of the studio as a provider of product, superior to Tiffany and Mascot but never the rival of MGM. He also might have thought Columbia would go the way of other Poverty Row studios. Brandt may have felt similarly; he had been associated with short-lived companies, and after leaving Columbia in 1932 worked for a few more. Both Jack and Brandt were accustomed to seeing studios thrive for a while and then wither away. No doubt if either had been told that Columbia would outlast RKO and that before the end of the century Columbia would move to the old MGM lot in Culver City, he would have laughed.

Although Jack resented the cost, he must have been impressed at the way his brother obtained product for the studio. There is also a strong possibility that Jack envied his brother's abilities as a producer and, in fact, wanted to produce features himself. It is certainly not coincidental that in the crucial years 1929 and 1931—the latter being the year he conspired to remove Harry as head of production—Jack acquired producing credits.

Since Jack's expertise lay in shorts and newsreels, the only explanation for his sudden interest in features is his desire to rival his brother, perhaps with the idea of replacing him. The extent to which Jack was involved in either *The Younger Generation* (1929) or *The Last Parade* (1931) will probably never be known. Capra directed the former, which will always bear his signature. One can understand Jack's attraction to the subject matter—a Jew who repudiates his origins, thereby causing his father's death and dooming himself to a life of guilt. Neither brother could be characterized as religious, although Jack was more observant than Harry and perhaps thought each of them could profit spiritually from the film. Jack apparently did; he developed a reputation as a humanitarian, while his brother was dubbed "White Fang."

The Last Parade may have been a personal film too, but in a different way. The success of Capra's *Submarine* (1928) and *Flight* (1929), with their successful pairings of Ralph Graves and Jack Holt, inspired Jack Cohn to duplicate the formula with Holt and Tom Moore as two buddies in love with the same woman. The male bonding theme, however, is limited: either one of them wins the woman while the other grieves for a while and then resigns himself to being a guest at Sunday dinner, or the woman proves to be faithless and the men are reunited. In *The Last Parade*, written by Dorothy Howell and Jo Swerling from a story by Casey Robinson, one friend (Moore) goes into law enforcement while the other (Holt) goes into the rackets and then to the electric chair.

Obviously, Jack did not envision a similar fate for Harry: removal, yes, but not electrocution. Yet it is odd that Jack was so attracted to a screenplay that he gave it his imprimatur. There is nothing overtly autobiographical about the plot: neither Jack nor Harry served in World War I, as the main characters do, nor did they court the same woman. While it is tempting to think that Jack imagined Harry walking the last mile (metaphorically, out of Gower Street), it is more likely that Jack wanted a hit that would bear his name. Since his brother was nominally the producer of *Submarine* and *Flight*, Jack saw no reason why he could not be the producer of another buddy movie that would differ from its predecessors by being a crime melodrama as well. Little did Jack know that he was anticipating a cycle of films portraying friends on opposite sides of the law that would become increasingly popular during the decade (for example, *Dead End* [1937], *Angels with Dirty Faces* [1938], and *The Roaring Twenties* [1939]).

While *The Last Parade* was well received, it had to compete with *Dirigible*, the third of the Graves-Holt movies, which was released a few months earlier and proved considerably more successful.

Producing features was not Jack's forte. He was vice president, sales—a position that made him acutely aware of figures. He saw how Harry, in his eagerness to win respectability for Columbia, committed the studio to expensive projects which, in turn, meant higher salaries for everyone involved. *Submarine* cost $100,000, but at least it was a hit. *The Miracle Woman* was not, even though, by 1931, Capra was getting $3,000 a *week*—a far cry from his starting salary of $1,000 a picture in 1927; *The Miracle Woman* took four weeks to shoot.

What Jack regarded as extravagance, Harry considered necessity. Jack, who was never a big spender, was appalled by Harry's high living; Harry's home on Fremont Place, with its spiral staircase and projection room, was a prime example. But the heart of the matter was Harry's growing fame; by 1930 it was obvious that Harry had eclipsed Jack, although from Harry's point of view he was only making up for all the years he had been overshadowed by his brother.

Now it is time to amend, or at least offer an alternate version of, the Abortive Attempt to Unseat Harry—an example of Hollywood's notion of received opinion, which is usually gossip fortified by random facts, some of which may be correct but when combined indiscriminately only make the gossip more enticing.

Supposedly, late in 1931, Brandt and Jack decided that Harry should step down or, preferably, leave Columbia. Apart from the fact that at the time Harry was too well known to be dismissed summarily, the story does not mesh with Brandt's diminishing role at the studio. If there had been an attempt to remove Harry, and apparently there had, it would not have come from Brandt, who was contemplating his own departure, but from Jack and someone who thought as he did—Abe Schneider, then assistant treasurer and, like Jack, fiscally conservative. Yet neither could have dislodged Harry by himself.

The average moviegoer might not have known about Hollywood's dependence on bankers, but in 1931 it was common knowledge in Los Angeles that the Bank of America and the East River National Bank in New York had been making loans to producers in a variety of ranges.[28] One Hollywood story that is at least credible concerns the $100,000 loan Brandt and the Cohns received from A.H. "Doc" Giannini to create CBC. The Gianninis—Amadeo Peter Giannini, founder of the Bank of Italy (later the Bank of America), and his younger brother, Attilio Henry Giannini, president of the East River National Bank—had by the end of the 1930s "financed more than one hundred films, extending more than $55 million in credits to the industry."[29]

Like the Cohns, the Gianninis were bipolar opposites in every respect: tempermanent, lifestyle, even base of operations. A.P. was the flashy dresser, the West Coast extrovert. After A.H. moved to New York in 1919 to manage the East River National Bank, he assumed the demeanor of an eastern banker—sedate and reserved. The tension between the brothers was not entirely due to their opposite natures. A.P., whose education ceased after the eighth grade, resented his younger brother (whom he dubbed the Prima Donna), a University of California graduate who had completed medical school in two years. It was not enough that when a Giannini was mentioned it was usually A.P. While A.P. garnered the lion's share of publicity, A.H., whom he put in charge of film financing, was the Giannini with whom moviemakers preferred to deal because he was more sympathetic to their needs.

A.H.'s criteria for loans were simple: the three C's—character, capacity, and capital.[30] When he came to the aid of Brandt and the Cohns, he felt they had all three. As a banker, A.H. was aware of CBC's metamorphosis into Columbia; he also knew that, at a time when, of the Big Five, only MGM was showing a profit, Columbia was in the black. Its first feature, *More to be Pitied Than Scorned*, made $110,000; for fiscal 1931 the studio reported a net profit of $560,292, down from the previous year— but so was MGM ($12 million in 1931 as opposed to $15 million in 1930). Nevertheless, Columbia was making money; the same could not be said of Warners, which registered a net loss of $7,918,604 for 1931 (in contrast to a net profit of $7,074,621 the previous year), or RKO, whose 1931 net loss was $5,660,770.

Although A.H. was temperamentally more like Jack than Harry, he also knew who was responsible for Columbia's features and would have attributed their success to Harry; and, like any banker, he expected an investment to pay off. If it came down to Harry or Jack, the choice was easy. Anyone reading the trades between 1928 and 1930 would have known that the Cohn associated with Columbia was no longer Jack but Harry. It was Harry who was credited with getting first runs for Columbia's pictures at the prestigious Pantages Theater on Hill and Seventh; Harry who was interviewed about the movie scene in Europe when he returned from abroad in fall 1928; Harry whom Louella Parsons not only called "head of Columbia Pictures" in the *Los Angeles Examiner* (1 June 1930) but also described as "young," "interesting," and "dynamic."

At the end of 1931, Robert Riskin's script for a film about a liberal banker who believes that character is a valid form of collateral was taking shape. The film, originally entitled *Faith*, became *American Madness* (1932), which Capra ended up directing. Although it did not go before the cameras until early spring, Harry would not have missed the opportunity to tell A.H. he would be canonized on the screen in the character of Thomas Dickson (Walter Huston). Politically, it would have been foolish for Giannini to sanction Harry's dismissal or even a diminution of his authority; financially, it would have been senseless.

In 1950, when Paul Lazarus, who eventually became vice president, publicity, at Columbia, arrived at 729 Seventh Avenue (where Columbia then had its New York office), he learned the facts of the attempted coup plus one additional detail: "Harry took over the company when Jack Cohn and Abe Schneider went to Dr. Giannini . . . to complain about Harry's gambling and profligate ways. The story I'm told is that when they had finished their list of complaints and had left the office, Giannini picked up the phone, called Harry and said, 'You'll never guess who just left my office.' It's always been my assumption that Giannini then helped Harry on the buyout . . . or obtaining control."[31] A.H. knew who ran Columbia; he also knew that without Harry there would be no Columbia.

Never content to let a Machiavellian matter rest, writers have darkened the story, giving it the look of a low-budget gangster movie. According to one account, the $500,000 Harry needed to buy out Brandt came from his "betting advisor."[32] Another version is a scenario unto itself: "Harry in the Underworld," in which "Harry consulted his bookie, who put him in touch with a well-heeled gentleman . . . known . . . as 'Longie.'"[33] The gentleman was the gangster "Longie" Zwillman. The extent to which one finds the Longie Zwillman story credible depends on one's tolerance level for error and inconsistency. The same source claims that "Jack [Cohn] studied law," obviously confusing Jack with Joe Brandt, and that gangster Johnny Roselli was the one who made the arrangements with Zwillman for the $500,000.[34]

Neither account, it should be added, is documented; and if Bob Thomas is correct, Harry met Roselli (called "Charlie Lombard" in *King Cohn*) in the mid-1930s *after* he became president of Columbia. Although the bookie/Roselli/Zwillman versions seem to be known only to a select and unnamed few (Paul Lazarus, who had been part of the old regime, never heard about them), they fit in well with Hollywood mythology. While moviegoers want to believe the worst about the industry, that has never stopped them from supporting it. An underworld connection elicits an "I told you so," yet anyone who knew Harry will admit that while he numbered Frank Costello among his acquaintances and patronized the hotel casinos of Las Vegas, he never let his reputation be tainted by mob connections.

With "Doc" Giannini on his side, Harry had no need to look elsewhere for the $500,000. Since A.H. believed that Hollywood was a better investment than bonds, he could easily have arranged for one of his typical loans, making it possible for Harry to get the money from a reputable source. Although 1931 was not a banner year for banks (and the Bank of Italy and the Bank of America of California merged in 1930 to become the Bank of America National Trust and Savings Association), the Gianninis were still loaning money to filmmakers. If A.P. could loan $1 million to Sam Goldwyn to make the Eddie Cantor movie, *The Kid from Spain* (1932), A.H. could certainly loan half that amount to Harry. A.H. was in charge of the East River National Bank in New York, and it was in New York that the abortive putsch occurred. The loan was also an investment in Columbia's future, of which A.H. became part when he was made a voting trustee early in 1934.

When A.H. formally became part of Columbia Pictures, it was more as a late arrival than a surprise—a presence once felt and now acknowledged. By 1934 A.H. was affiliated with a studio that was no stranger to fraternal rivalry, a studio whose head had found a director capable of visualizing a world of diversity and tension but also of resolving what appear to be extremes. Capra was the link between Harry and A.H.; like the "Doc," Capra put people first. The "Doc," in fact, resembles a Capra hero—endangering his health to treat typhus and smallpox victims, advocating lower trolley fares, arguing for free physical examinations in schools, lobbying Congress for aid to San Francisco after the 1906 earthquake.

The "Doc" also understood what it was like to be in an older brother's shadow; thus he had no difficulty empathizing with Harry. Columbia was the ideal place for all three.

This was Harry's finest hour, but the press did not know it. "No Truth in Columbia's Rumors," the *Motion Picture Herald* (16 January 1932) insisted—the rumors being Harry's plan to buy out Brandt as well as his brother! *MPH* also mistakenly referred to Jack as "Joe," perhaps out of confusion with Joe Brandt; the error must have delighted Harry, whose Hall Rooms had occasionally been attributed to his brother.

Brandt naturally denied the rumors, informing *MPH* that "the Company remains as it is and so do the partners." He explained Harry's presence in New York as "an annual visit to secure new story materials and for home office conferences with regard to the new production schedule" (16 January 1932).

Three weeks later, *MPH* (6 February 1932) told a different story: "This week's realignments in Columbia Pictures Corporation, by which Mr. Harry Cohn becomes president, with Mr. Joe Brandt retiring to a post on the board of trustees and Mr. Jack Cohn vice president in charge of distribution bring sharply to attention one of the most significant and interesting developments of recent years. The rise . . . of Columbia might well be taken by students as a markedly perfect type . . . of corporate development . . . from a states' rights concern to a substantial production and distribution concern."

Columbia's rise, however, was attributed not to Harry but to Jack, who "all the film world knows . . . conspired [to make] that first great Universal feature drama, 'Traffic in Souls.' It was a beginning which got somewhere, and is still going."

In one way *MPH* was correct: it was a beginning, and Jack was partly responsible for it. But a beginning was all it was. Out of loyalty to Jack, the trades sentimentalized the event, showing him bidding a sad fare-well to his two "lieutenants," Walter Wanger (whom Harry was obliged to take on as vice president, production in 1931) and director Harlan Thompson, as they left for Los Angeles. Harry, on the other hand, was jubilant: "I am going to do what I always wanted to do," he told *MPH* (20 February 1932).

Henceforth, the Cohn associated with Columbia was Harry. Jack was relegated to the background, suffering the fate New York-based film executives often face: semi-oblivion. While Jack had always been happier in New York than in Los Angeles, he took his defeat as a form of retirement from the creative end of the business, which was incompatible with his temperament and abilities. His eclipse, however, did not make him bitter. Jack worked tirelessly for the Motion Picture Pioneers, an organization devoted to helping needy members of the movies' eastern establishment who had spent twenty-five years in the industry and were often overlooked in favor of their West Coast colleagues.

Those who knew Jack before the reorganization have remarked that he was never the same afterward. But that change must be attributed in part to Jack's realization that movies were no longer the same. Sound had irrevocably altered the way films would be made and seen. And while Jack understood editing and sales, these were skills he had acquired when both he and the movies were young. Jack and Brandt lacked the vision to see Columbia into an era that marked the beginning of Holly-wood's Golden Age. Brandt, whose health began failing in 1931, may have decided that, in light of the new Columbia, he would be better off out of the picture. In that case the story reported in the press (that when he balked at the market price of Columbia's stock at $6 a share, the Cohns bought out his 20,000 shares at $50 a share) was a way of saving face for everybody.[35] Since the cost was reported as $1 million (not $500,000), there was no hint of unofficial loans or failed takeovers. With Jack included in the buyout, a reputation was untarnished, at least until the death of the Cohns, after which variant readings arose to challenge the established text.

Between 1932 and 1935 Joe Brandt held several positions, all related to film: first, as president of World Wide Pictures, which he left to become vice president of Educational Films, then as president of Associated Publications, a film trade paper group, and finally as founder of Nuovo Mondo, which distributed Italian films. In 1935 ill health forced him to retire to Los Angeles, where he died on 22 February 1939 at the age of fifty-six.

Variety noted Brandt's passing in a simple obituary; two decades later, *Variety* treated Harry's death as a news item, complete with head-line: "Death Strikes 'Last of Studio Czars.'" Brandt may have been a studio president, but Harry was a studio czar.

4

The Patriarch

Columbia conformed to the studio model of a pyramid with a strong base of actors, directors, and writers; executives as the triangular faces; and, at the vertex, the studio head. There is no other way to describe Mayer, Zanuck, and Harry: they were heads of studios but, except for Harry, never presidents. They were like the great newspaper publishers or directors of symphony orchestras who set the tone for the group and were therefore responsible for its success or failure. Just as the members of an organization think of themselves as a family, so too do studio workers. The moguls encouraged that mentality; it was not only good for morale but also allowed studio heads to play father (never mother, since the line of succession was male) to their children-stars, rewarding the docile with choice roles and punishing the disobedient with suspension.

The Columbia family was like the Warner family—partly natural, partly synthetic. There were, of course, Harry and Jack, at opposite ends of the country and the business. And like Albert and Sam Warner, Max and Nathaniel Cohn, the oldest and youngest Cohn brothers respectively, also worked for the studio. Yet when Warners is mentioned, the name that first comes to mind is Jack L. Warner; then, perhaps, Harry. Similarly with Columbia: Harry Cohn first, Jack, second. Like his colleagues, Harry did not hesitate to find positions at Columbia for family members in need of work; he was able to place his brother Nathaniel in sales and Max in the short subjects unit.

While children of movie executives often find their niche in the industry, it was different with the children of the moguls. Even actors' offspring have an easier time carrying on the family tradition. The patriarchal nature of the studio system discouraged the moguls' sons from following in their fathers' footsteps, at least while their fathers were alive. Power, once acquired, was relinquished only through death, retirement, or removal; and the thought of being displaced, much less by one's own child, was anathema. Samuel Goldwyn, Jr., only surfaced as a producer after his father's death; Carl Laemmle, Jr., suffered in comparison with Carl, Sr. Only Richard Zanuck managed to win a lasting reputation in his father's business. Richard may have had no choice; in 1970 when Richard was president and head of production at Fox and Darryl was chairman of the board, the chairman had to fire the president because Fox had released a series of disasters, one of which was Darryl's brainchild *Tora! Tora! Tora!* (1970). Darryl Zanuck became the first mogul to fire his son. Harry would have loved to be in that position in regard to his brother.

While Jack Cohn's children could at least claim some connection with the business—and in the case of his son Ralph, with television as well—Harry's sons avoided moviemaking almost as a matter of principle. The late Harrison Perry Cohn, who legally changed his name to Harry Cohn, Jr., in 1956, became a rancher. John Cohn lives in Santa Barbara with his mother, as devout a Roman Catholic as she. On the other hand, all three of Jack's sons could claim to have been "in the movies."

Ralph Cohn, born in 1914, grew up hearing about his father's days at Universal when he edited the *Animated Weekly*.[1] Jack brought up his sons differently from the way he had been raised. Yorkville held too many unpleasant memories for Jack, who preferred to live on the Upper West Side, first on West 101st Street. But like many New Yorkers, he discovered Westchester County and moved to Katonah, keeping a pied-à-terre in New York, generally on the West Side and eventually at the San Remo on Central Park West.

By the time Ralph was fourteen, CBC had become Columbia and his father was vice president of a studio. In 1928 Ralph was old enough to be initiated into the mysteries of moviemaking. Each summer Ralph made the five-day train trip to Los Angeles to work in Columbia's film library, where he discovered, as his father had, the importance of editing. And having made that discovery, Ralph advanced from clerk to assistant cutter.

Jack was determined his sons would have the education he never did. Ralph went to Cornell; since there was no film major at the time, he studied speech and theater, as did his brother Robert at the University of Michigan. After graduating from Cornell, Ralph used his family's connections to get into Irving Briskin's B-unit at Columbia as an assistant producer—a position that, in view of Harry's twin title of president and production head, carried little responsibility. Ralph won his first screen credit for *Panic on the Air* (1936), and by 1941 he had acquired thirty-nine more.

World War II brought a temporary halt to Ralph's film career. When he returned to civilian life, he sensed the industry was changing; when he saw television for the first time, he knew the change was irreversible. His plan—and it was quite revolutionary in 1948—was to get Columbia to create a television subsidiary. Accordingly, he drafted a fifty-page rationale, hoping to persuade Harry to move into the television vanguard.

While Ralph was not Harry's favorite nephew (if indeed any of Jack's sons was), Harry agreed, and Screen Gems was born.

Screen Gems began small, with commercials.[2] When DuPont decided in 1952 to continue the radio program *Cavalcade of America* on television, Screen Gems was the logical choice to film the series. *Cavalcade of America* led to other dramatic programs such as *Ford Theatre* (1952-57) and *Alcoa/Goodyear Theatre* (1958-60), as well as such sitcoms as *Father Knows Best* (1954-58), *Dennis the Menace* (1959-63), *The Donna Reed Show* (1958-66), and *Hazel* (1961-66). Beginning in 1966, Screen Gems took on another function: leasing Columbia films to television. Thus when Columbia's movies of the 1930s, 1940s, and 1950s are telecast, "Distributed by Screen Gems" appears over the logo at the end of the movie.

Ralph was the third Cohn to die within three years. Jack died in 1956, Harry in 1958. Ralph Cohn died of a heart attack on 2 August 1959. The brothers were sixty-seven; Ralph was forty-five.

Ralph's brother Robert also began his career at Columbia. A speech and theater major at the University of Michigan as well as a star football player, Robert decided to spend the 1941 winter recess in Los Angeles with a college friend, the All-American Tom Harmon. While Robert was giving Tom a tour of Columbia they encountered Irving Briskin, who hit upon the idea of having Tom play himself in a football movie costarring Anita Louise. Since Anita Louise would be playing Tom's wife in the movie, Briskin worked out a promotional scheme for her to travel to Ann Arbor as Tom's date for the senior prom. When Tom graduated in June, *Harmon of Michigan* (1941) was ready to be filmed; its release coincided with the start of the football season.[3]

In 1941 Robert Cohn seemed headed for a career in movies; he had just finished serving as assistant director of *Bedtime Story* (1941) when the war intervened. When it ended, he returned to Columbia in a different capacity—as a producer. Like his brother Ralph, Robert discovered there was little prestige in Columbia's B-unit. Even the location was different: Robert was not working on the main lot but at Columbia's Sunset Studios, near Vermont and Sunset. B-unit producers were line men whose primary responsibility was bringing the picture in on time and on budget. Since they were working primarily with contract players and directors, they were not consulted about casting and scripts.

The prospects for B-unit directors were equally bleak. Except for a few, notably Joseph H. Lewis and Budd (then Oscar) Boetticher, the directors of Columbia's series and programmers rarely achieved recognition even though they did respectable work, despite being given a week's notice to prepare a script for shooting.

Columbia's B producers, like most of its B directors, rarely moved into the upper echelons, either at Gower Street or elsewhere. Yet what inspired them to do quality work regardless of the material was the desire to leave the limbo of the lost. Robert Cohn also aspired to do something higher than producing *The Killer That Stalked New York* (1950) and *The Barefoot Mailman* (1951). He eventually went into independent production but, except for *The Interns* (1962), without much success.

Like his brother Ralph, Joseph Cohn died prematurely. Joseph, who changed his last name to Curtis at his wife's request, was even younger than Ralph when death came: thirty-six. Joseph too found a job at Columbia, although not one that carried much responsibility: he placed the movie ads. Yet, like his brothers, Joseph harbored a desire to produce. He bought the rights to Malcolm Johnson's Pulitzer Prize–winning account of waterfront crime that had appeared in the *New York Sun* and hired Budd Schulberg to write the screenplay. Harry would not produce it, and when Joseph's option expired, Sam Spiegel took it up. The film became *On the Waterfront* (1954).[4] Joseph believed he had been robbed of his one chance to succeed in the business in which his father, uncle, and brothers had achieved varying degrees of success. Joseph Curtis died within a week of the 1955 Academy Awards when *On the Waterfront* received eight Oscars, one of which was for best picture.

In Hollywood "my film" is a recurrent phrase, used by everyone from writers to art directors. When a critic referred to William Wyler's *Wuthering Heights*, Goldwyn corrected him: "I made *Withering Heights* [sic]. Wyler only directed it."[5] If Joseph Curtis had been lucky enough to produce *On the Waterfront*, it is doubtful he could have made the kind of film that the team of Elia Kazan-Budd Schulberg-Sam Spiegel did. For one thing, he lacked Spiegel's contacts and financial methods, which may have been byzantine but resulted in a film for which even Harry could not take credit. *On the Waterfront* was produced by Spiegel's own company, Horizon.

The Cohns constituted one Columbia family, but there was another—less diverse but more stable—that complemented it. But stability is unexciting copy, and, compared to the Cohns, the Briskin-Schneider-Jaffe axis seems almost faceless; to a great extent it was. Columbia's other family was a mirror image of the Cohns; it was a microcosm of brothers and brothers-in-law whose relations with each other were less extreme than those between Jack and Harry but still far from fraternal.

From the beginning, the movie industry relied on accountants. Harry knew that, but it did not stop him from calling them "bookkeepers." Yet two of Columbia's bookkeepers, Abe Schneider and Leo Jaffe, succeeded him as president.

Harry's first "bookkeeper" was Samuel J. Briskin. Fresh out of City College with a degree in accounting, Briskin joined the company in 1920 when it was still CBC. By 1935 he had become vice president and general manager. Although Briskin had a long association with Columbia, it was never his permanent home, as it was Schneider's and Jaffe's. Briskin left Columbia at different times—once, to join Frank Capra, William Wyler, and George Stevens to form Liberty Films, known mainly for *It's a Wonderful Life* (1946). But he returned periodically, and when Harry died in 1958 Briskin, who was then at Paramount, came back to Columbia as a vice president.

It is impossible for brothers to enter a business as competitive as film without becoming rivals, even if they gravitate to different areas of moviemaking. What was true of the brothers Cohn was also true of the brothers Briskin. Sam and Irving Briskin were never models of brotherly love to begin with. The situation worsened when Irving joined Columbia and became part of the studio's B-unit, where he met Ralph Cohn. Realizing that Sam had carved out his niche at Columbia, Irving joined Ralph at Screen Gems.

The Briskins' sister, Ida, married Abraham Schneider, another "bookkeeper" with a degree from New York University. Schneider also went back to the days of CBC. Like Sam Briskin, Schneider moved up the ranks: assistant treasurer (1930), treasurer (1935), treasurer and vice president (1942), first vice president and treasurer (1957). At the time Harry died, Schneider, whom the press always called A. Schneider, had acquired the reputation of being one of the top financial experts in the industry. Inevitably, he was Harry's successor.

Leo Jaffe knew Schneider at New York University, where he too studied accounting. A summer job at Columbia led to a permanent position in 1930, and almost every time Schneider was promoted, so was Jaffe. Similarly, Jaffe succeeded Schneider as president of Columbia in 1967. Like Schneider, with whom he was linked, Jaffe was considered a financial wizard and thus fitted in well in the New York office, which was largely the domain of accountants, publicists, and lawyers.

Neither Schneider nor Jaffe had much use for Hollywood. Schneider used to boast of never having read a script; there was no reason to, since he was not in production. Schneider and Jaffe were businessmen, and movies happened to be the business they were in. Columbia was the company at which they started and from which they retired. Star-gazing meant no more to Schneider and Jaffe than it did to Jack Cohn; thus a bond arose between the three of them that Harry could not break.

Another Jack Cohn ally was Abe Montague. Once Harry became Columbia's president and Jack executive vice president, someone had to take over sales, which had been Jack's province. Montague, who started in exhibition in New Hampshire and then entered distribution, obtaining a Columbia franchise in New England in 1929, was the ideal choice for general sales manager, a position he held from 1933, when he joined the studio, until 1943, when he became a vice president. In 1958 Montague inherited the title Jack had at the time of his death; executive vice president.

Ben Kahane was also a longtime Columbian. Since Kahane was a West Coast lawyer as opposed to an East Coast accountant, he was on better terms with Harry than the New York bookkeepers. Kahane had a background in the business that the others lacked: in 1932 he went from secretary-treasurer of RKO to president. When RKO developed a reputation as Hollywood's "most mismanaged studio," [6] Kahane found himself demoted to vice president, production. In 1936 Kahane left RKO for Columbia, where he quickly became Harry's budget adviser. Kahane's RKO replacement was another Columbian, Sam Briskin.[7]

Despite occasional defections, there was little executive turnover at Columbia during Harry's presidency. If there was to be a major change, Harry would demand, as an act of loyalty, that the one departing find a worthy successor, as Nate Spingold did. Although Harry had no great love for anyone in the New York office, he felt differently about Spingold. While Harry and Spingold were not cut from the same cloth, they were doubles in the classic sense: men from totally dissimilar backgrounds but with common interests (women, good food, and especially an obsession with success).

Spingold started out as a journalist. Between trains in Chicago, a representative from the William Morris Agency, confusing him with Jack Lait, interviewed him and was so impressed that he offered Spingold a job at what was then the premier talent agency. As an agent, Spingold numbered among his clients Harry Lauder and Sophie Tucker. Because Spingold managed his money wisely, as did his wife Frances, he was able to retire in his mid-forties to the Waldorf Towers. Frances, knowing her husband had a roving eye and, more important, would be wasting his talent with early retirement, paid Harry a visit. Harry was not unaware of her existence: Frances Spingold was Columbia's second largest shareholder and thus had no trouble getting what she wanted: a job for her husband. Although Spingold came on board in the nebulous capacity of "general executive," his real ability lay in advertising; in 1943 he became vice president in charge of publicity and advertising.

At the start of the 1950s, Spingold began losing interest in his job. Perhaps he sensed the days were dwindling down to a precious few (he died in 1958). At any rate, he preferred to divide his time between Manhattan and Palm Beach and arrange for a permanent home for his art collection, deciding on Brandeis University, whose theater arts center he also endowed. Harry extracted a promise from Spingold that he would not leave before he found a replacement. Spingold did more: he found a successor, Paul N. Lazarus, Jr., whose father had been the first director of publicity for United Artists when it was formed in 1919. But Paul, Sr., who believed a college education would offer his son more options than writing studio copy, sent Paul, Jr., to Cornell, Ralph Cohn's alma mater. And just as Ralph went from Cornell to Columbia, so did his fraternity brother, Paul N. Lazarus, Jr.

To ensure that Lazarus would be treated as a successor and not a replacement, Spingold insisted that Lazarus's name appear on the office door in the same size letters as his own.[8] Such magnanimity is rare in any business, even more so in film.

While Harry's executives were a relatively stable lot, his assistant production heads were another matter. Once the shareholders decided they did not want one person holding the reins of production, Harry was obliged to take on assistant production heads. But none of them wanted to stay. Walter Wanger served briefly as vice president, production, lasting little more than a year—from 1931 to the end of 1932. By January 1933 Wanger was off to MGM, where he remained for an even shorter time before returning to Paramount (which he had left earlier because of a salary dispute). Then Wanger set up his own production company, releasing through United Artists (1938-41) before finding a niche at Universal. For a time, Everett Riskin, the brother of Capra's most famous collaborator, Robert Riskin, functioned as executive producer of such films as *One Night of Love* (1934), *Theodora Goes Wild* (1936), and *The Awful Truth* (1937), continuing the kind of romantic comedy spiked with a dash of screwball that his brother had pioneered in *It Happened One Night* (1934).

Significantly, Harry's next assistant was the writer of Capra's *Mr. Smith Goes to Washington* (1939), Sidney Buchman. After graduating from Columbia, Buchman set out for London, where he found a job as assistant director at the Old Vic. Determined to be a playwright, he returned to New York where his play *This One Man* was produced in 1930; although it starred Paul Muni, the play was a failure. As the 1930s dawned, Hollywood was wooing playwrights, successful and otherwise. Although Buchman was one of the latter, Paramount offered him a job. It was at Paramount that Buchman acquired his first screen credits for such films as *The Sign of the Cross* and *If I Had a Million* (both 1932).

In 1934 Buchman changed studios; it was a move that many would have questioned. Although Paramount and Columbia were within walking distance of each other, Paramount had won five Oscars at the first Academy Awards presentation in 1928; Columbia had yet to win one. Yet Buchman's timing was perfect: on Oscar night 1935, Columbia won seven; Paramount, one. Buchman did some of his best writing at Columbia, working on scripts for some of the studio's most important films, four of which (*Mr. Smith, Here Comes Mr. Jordan, The Talk of the Town*, and *Jolson Sings Again*) were Oscar nominees.

Just as a special bond developed between Harry and Nate Spingold, so, too, did one between Harry and Buchman, this one more complex. Like Spingold, Buchman was Harry's opposite in background and education; yet he became a son figure to Harry, even though there was a difference of only ten years between them. Although Harry would have been reluctant to admit it, he was looking for, if not a successor, then someone able to share the burdens of production without undermining his authority. Thus Harry made Buchman vice president, production, in 1942 when Everett Riskin left for MGM. Throughout the war years Buchman proved so useful to Harry that in June 1945 he accompanied Harry and other studio heads (including Zanuck and Paramount's Barney Balaban) on a government-sponsored three-week tour of Europe. Although the tour was ostensibly to acquaint members of the movie industry with conditions there, the government, assuming postwar Europe would be as familiar a movie theme as wartime Europe, was hoping Hollywood would continue to rely on the expertise of military advisers and consultants.

It was also around 1945 that Buchman began losing interest in being an assistant production head. His goal was to have his own production company, releasing through Columbia—an ambition he realized with *Over 21* (1945). While Sidney Buchman Productions gave Columbia *To the Ends of the Earth* (1948), *Jolson Sings Again* (1949), and *Saturday's Hero* (1951), among others Buchman was also responsible for a movie that does not bear his name, *The Jolson Story* (1946).

Columbia was an odd choice of studio for a movie about Al Jolson; logically, it should have been Warners, which released the George Gershwin and Cole Porter biopics, *Rhapsody in Blue* (1945) and *Night and Day* (1946), respectively. Columnist Sidney Skolsky brought the project to Warners, which showed no interest; Jolson was neither a Gershwin nor a Porter, although his ego was bigger than either's. Skolsky convinced Jolson that Columbia would give him the kind of treatment he would not get at a larger studio. Jolson was in no position to argue; his career was in limbo. The project then moved to Columbia under Buchman's supervision.[9]

Although one would not know it from the credits, which cite Skolsky as producer and Stephen Longstreet as screenwriter, the concept was Buchman's. It was Buchman who decided that the key to Jolson's character was his overriding need for an audience, which made it impossible for him to sustain a relationship with anyone, including his wife. In a movie filled with memorable scenes, the most dramatic occurs at the end when Jolson's wife, Julie (Evelyn Keyes), modeled after Ruby Keeler, walks out of a club where her husband is mesmerizing his fans because she realizes he prefers mass adulation to one person's love.

While neither Buchman nor John Howard Lawson, who developed a preliminary script among Buchman's suggestions, received screen credit, the industry was aware of their contributions. Everyone associated with *The Jolson Story* knew Buchman was the creative force behind it. Evelyn Keyes recalled that the only direction she received from Alfred E. Green, who had been in the business since 1912 and did little after *The Jolson Story*, was "Color it up, Evelyn."[10] She and Larry Parks, who played Jolson, lip-synching his songs to perfection, spent their evenings working with Buchman on the blocking and getting pointers for the next day's shooting.

Harry was determined that *The Jolson Story* be not just a hit but a blockbuster. Just as he was obsessed with seeing how *Born Yesterday* played before an invited audience before it was filmed, he insisted not merely on previews for *The Jolson Story* but also on hiring Audience Research, Inc., to ascertain the reaction.[11] Each viewer was given a reaction recorder that fitted into the palm of the hand, allowing the viewer to register responses from "very dull," "dull," and "neutral" to "like" and "like very much." When audiences reacted negatively to a song sung in Yiddish, it was dropped.

The year after *The Jolson Story* was released, the witch hunt began. Although Harry knew Buchman had been a Communist party member between 1938 and 1945, he was relieved when the House Committee on un-American Activities (HUAC) did not call Buchman to testify in 1947 along with the Hollywood Nineteen, one of whom was Larry Parks. By 1951 the situation had changed. As Lillian Hellman would do a year later, Buchman told HUAC, when he was subpoenaed in the fall of 1951, that he was willing to answer questions about himself but not about others. Buchman's ordeal, however, was just beginning. In January 1952 he received another subpoena, which he ignored, claiming he had said all he cared to say the previous fall.

When a contempt citation (and a jail sentence) seemed inevitable, Buchman branded the second subpoena harassment. Since HUAC was notoriously inconsistent, Buchman received a $150 fine and a one-year suspended sentence. Similarly, Lillian Hellman never went to jail, probably because her famous "I cannot and will not cut my conscience to fit this year's fashions" letter was read into the minutes, so she could hardly be called contemptuous of a congressional committee that was itself beneath contempt.

In Buchman's case, there was an irregularity in the September 1951 hearing. For some reason, HUAC member Donald R. Jackson left the chamber, whereupon Buchman's attorney immediately called for a quorum, the lack of which brought the testimony to an end. Buchman should never have been subpoenaed a second time, especially since he was being cooperative—on his own terms, of course—by consenting to answer HUAC's questions about himself (but not to name names). Many in Hollywood interpreted the second hearing as Jackson's revenge for the embarrassment incurred by his "mysterious walk." Buchman was right in charging HUAC with harassment, and the committee knew it.

Even in 1950 Harry knew Buchman would not be at Columbia or any studio much longer. In a revealing 3 August 1950 teletype, Harry, learning that Buchman had called Abe Montague, wanted an explanation. Buchman had a "hell of a good story," Montague replied; but rather than encourage Buchman, Montague told him (as if Buchman did not know) that screen properties were Harry's province. Although there is no way of determining tone of voice from a teletype, Harry's response seemed tinged with sadness: "Well, didn't know he called. May let him go." Within a year Buchman left.

When Buchman decided to form his own production company in 1945, Harry had to find another assistant production head. His selection resulted in an appointment that, in 1946, was without precedent: Harry designated a woman as executive producer, giving her the same title that Jack Warner had. The industry was stunned. Women were editors like Maggie Booth or costume designers like Edith Head. Some were writers (Mary McCall, Dorothy Howell, and the most famous of all, Dorothy Parker and Lillian Hellman); hardly any were directors. The chief exception was Dorothy Arzner, who made two films for Columbia: *Craig's Wife* (1936) and *First Comes Courage* (1943). But there had been no women producers at Columbia; men had a difficult enough time with Harry.

While sex mattered to Harry, gender did not. Virginia Van Upp had been a reader, casting director, and screenwriter before coming to Columbia in 1944. To Harry, she was doubly talented: first, she could write a script; second, unlike the typical screenwriter who thought a script should be free of studio interference, Van Upp appreciated the myriad details involved in getting a movie made, among which was the need to subject a script to a diversity of opinion.

Virginia Van Upp was what Harry wanted: a writer like Buchman who could make the transition to writer-producer. Van Upp wrote Rita Hayworth's best musical, *Cover Girl* (1944), and produced her signature film, *Gilda* (1946). In between were *Together Again* (1944), a charming romance with Irene Dunne and Charles Boyer; and Jean Arthur's last Columbia film, *The Impatient Years* (1944).

If any film affirms Harry's faith in Van Upp, it is *Gilda*. Although Marion Parsonnet is credited with the screenplay, Van Upp monitored it. Van Upp sent a first draft of *Gilda* to Humphrey Bogart, who rejected it, rightly sensing it would be a woman's film. Although Parsonnet and Van Upp had not been thinking in those terms, Bogart's refusal to play Johnny Farrell (a role that went to Glenn Ford) inspired them to make not just a woman's film but a special kind—a woman's film unlike any other: a film noir with musical numbers, homoerotic overtones, an underworld more colorful than criminal, a faked death, and a climactic real one. Yet the main character is still a woman—not a fallen woman (although Gilda is defiantly postlapsarian) or even a victimized one. Gilda is woman wronged; woman misunderstood. Even so, self-pity is alien to her. Her opening line says as much: when asked if she is "decent" (i.e., dressed), her reply is the self-deprecating, "Who? Me?"

While Gilda is not above enumerating her grievances, she does it in song—twice to be exact, and always with the same lyrics. Everyone who has seen *Gilda* can recall Hayworth's rendition of "Put the Blame on Mame." Yet few remember that Gilda sings it twice: once, plaintively, while strumming a guitar; then publicly, as she begins a striptease that, although it consists only of peeling off arm-length gloves, is really a baring of the soul.

Gilda, whose zest for living is mistaken for promiscuity, is like Mame, who was blamed for everything from the Chicago fire to the San Francisco earthquake. Grammarians might argue that "put" is the imperative (and that Gilda is asking us to consider Mame, and woman in general, as the eternal scapegoat). But Gilda is subverting the imperative, mocking the command it implies. She is suggesting that the myth of woman as bringer of destruction is so ingrained in human consciousness that it has become a social mandate. Being an ironist, she can mock the mythology that holds her prisoner.

Gilda is also the dark intruder who threatens male friendship. When Johnny Farrell discovers that his friend and patron, Ballin Mundson (George Macready), has married Gilda, he uses every opportunity to degrade her and remind her of past transgressions. It takes Farrell almost the entire picture to realize that Gilda is more sinned against than sinning. His discovery of her worth results in a dual transformation: Farrell becomes more sympathetic; Gilda, less sensual. After a kindly washroom attendant kills Mundson (who was presumed to be dead), Farrell and Gilda are free to begin a new life. But Mrs. Johnny Farrell is no longer a femme fatale in black satin; dressed in a traveling suit, she is merely *femme*. Gilda's humanizing of Farrell has robbed her of her allure, making her less provocative (and ultimately less interesting).

"The age demanded" a conventional resolution: love goddess sheds divinity and marries mortal. This was the same problem Van Upp faced with *Cover Girl*, in which Hayworth played a former nightclub performer who graduates to Broadway stardom, much to the displeasure of the club's owner (Gene Kelly), and then returns to her tacky roots (much to the delight of those who believe a woman's place is in a dump). The denouement is a concession to 1940s chauvinism, although what preceded it was uncommonly intelligent.

After *Gilda*, Van Upp, who seemed the perfect Hayworth scenarist, could no longer take the pressures of production; she left Columbia in 1947, returning five years later for a single film, the *Gilda* clone *Affair in Trinidad* (1952), which reunited Hayworth and Ford.

Since Harry never knew how long an executive producer would last, he began grooming S. Sylvan Simon for the position in 1948. While Simon was not a writer, he had credentials Harry respected: a Michigan M.A. Simon was at the studio barely a year when he delighted Harry with his direction of the Red Skelton comedy *The Fuller Brush Man* (1948). Harry then made him producer of *Born Yesterday* (1950). While Simon was flattered, he did not realize the extent of Harry's determination to replicate the Broadway original and the pressure it would entail. Within a few months of the film's opening, Simon died at forty-one of a heart attack.

Except for Jerry Wald, whose tenure was slightly longer than Van Upp's, there would be no more assistant production heads until Harry accepted his own mortality. There would only be independent producers.

It was also important for Harry to have what are known in the corporate world as executive assistants. That term is almost as nebulous as administrative assistant, as Harry knew, having been Carl Laemmle's. But just as Harry needed producers to get a movie on the screen, he also required assistance in other areas. While "casting director" is a standard term in both theatre and film, during the studio years casting was such a complex matter, involving suggestions from everyone from readers to directors, that a casting credit would have been impossible (although today it is commonplace). Nominally, Max Arnow handled casting at Columbia in the 1940s, as he had at Warners a decade earlier. But even at Warners his title was not casting director but executive assistant—the same title he was given when he joined Columbia in 1941.

For a year, 1939-40, Columbia had one of the best story editors in the industry, Sam Marx, who held a similar position at MGM. Each studio had a story editor and a stable of readers (or story analysts, as they are now called), who, depending on the studio, were housed in a couple of offices, a separate building (such as Paramount's writers' building), or a "firetrap," to use Dore Schary's description of the MGM facility, although the "firetrap" offered a librarylike setting where the readers found novels in galley, articles, books, and plays ready for synopsis and commentary.

Marx's stay at Columbia was brief; Marx loathed Sam Briskin, and although he found Harry difficult, he respected Harry's often pedantic method of annotating scripts by writing marginalia in black pencil and circling what was unclear.[12]

The story editor most associated with Columbia was Eve Ettinger, who worked behind the scenes, always looking for properties for the studio to buy. She was instrumental in persuading Harry to purchase the rights to *From Here to Eternity* and hire Daniel Taradash to write the screenplay; the film won Oscars for Taradash, Frank Sinatra, Donna Reed, director Fred Zinnemann, cinematographer Burnett Guffey, sound director John P. Livadary, and editor William Lyon. Indirectly, it won an Oscar for Harry: *From Here to Eternity* was voted best picture of 1953.

Such was the Columbia family. If the patriarch had had his way, he would have created emanations of himself to perform all the duties that a business like film demands. Given an imperfect universe, Harry did not do badly.

5

The Boss

"He had to be boss."[1] That is how Evelyn Keyes characterized Harry in 1990, forty years after his accusations of promiscuity became so frequent that she could no longer bear to be at the studio to which she came in 1940.[2] She left Columbia in 1951 even though she had to pay the studio 20 percent of her earnings for the duration of her contract. As she recalled the 1949-51 period, when Harry accused her of having sex with every man she dated, she realized those tantrums were his pathetic way of expressing love: "What he was really doing was proposing." Not understanding Harry's unorthodox manner of courtship, she spurned him.

But the obscenities that upset Evelyn Keyes in 1950 were by 1990, "only words." Since she was living in Spain when Harry died, she could not attend his funeral; had she been in the States, she would have. Even by 1958 she was thinking differently about Harry; and three decades later, after embarking on a new career as a writer, she genuinely lamented his absence: "I wish there were a Harry Cohn, now that I've become a screenwriter. I could go to him with my script, and I know he'd make it into a movie. The reason so many showed up at his funeral was that they owed their fame to him. He made them look good; he protected them. He had to play the tyrant, which gave him the image he has now: a vulgar, foul-mouthed mogul. But he had to do that because it was the only way he could get the best out of us—and the only way he knew how to be boss."

He had to be boss. In a sense the other moguls felt the same. But while they perceived their studios as households (MGM) or factories (Warners), Harry, if he knew the word, would have reluctantly called Columbia a diarchy. He would have preferred an absolute monarchy, of course, but he never became such a megalomaniac as to discount the importance of New York.

If Harry could not be a monarch, he could at least have the trappings of monarchy. In 1933, Columbia released a documentary, *Mussolini Speaks*, which Jack edited, using the skills he had honed during his Universal days. Mussolini was delighted with the result; he was already thinking of film as a medium of propaganda. In 1935 he authorized the construction of Cinema City, Cinecittà, on the outskirts of Rome. Like Universal, it was to have been a city in microcosm and eventually became Europe's largest studio.

Fascism held no appeal for Harry, although others, including "Doc" Giannini and Walter Wanger, were looking for joint ventures between Rome and Hollywood.[3] Nor was Harry part of the welcoming committee for Mussolini's son, Vittorio, who came to Hollywood in 1937 to study moviemaking, American style. By then, Italy had invaded Ethiopia, the Spanish Civil War was raging, and Fascism meant much more than getting trains to run on time. Except for Hal Roach, the Hollywood community ignored Vittorio, who thereupon returned to Rome.

In 1933, however, Harry did accept an invitation from Mussolini to visit Italy. On the same trip he met Pope Pius XI, but Il Duce left a greater impression—or rather his sixty-foot office in the Palazzo Venezia did. Harry was determined to duplicate it, but without mosaics and reliefs. If he could not be Il Duce, he could still be Boss, which meant an office so overwhelming that anyone entering it would feel simultaneously awestruck and insignificant.

Harry's office was on the second floor of 1438 North Gower, next door to the three-story rabbit-warren of a building that housed the writers and producers. The office was completely in white—white chairs, a white piano, a white couch. Entering was an ordeal in itself: Harry's version of the grail quest. After sitting in an outer waiting room for what would seem an hour, the visitor was finally admitted to the secretary's office. Since the door between the secretary's and Harry's office had no knob, it had to be opened by a press of the buzzer under Harry's desk. When Harry was ready to receive the visitor, he buzzed, expecting whoever was waiting to push the door at the same moment. If the push did not coincide with the buzz, he would express his annoyance over the intercom.

Once admitted, the visitor made his or her way along a white shag rug to the thronelike desk. Since this was a movie czar's office, the effect would best be captured by subjective camera: the recording of sheer movement, with the camera standing in for the visitor as it takes in all the details, more slowly than in real life.

Approaching the desk, the visitor would notice something odd about the placement: the desk was elevated—on an eight-inch riser, to be exact—so that the visitor would be looking *up* at Harry, who would be looking *down* at the visitor. There was an aura about the room that came partly from the royal ambience, partly from the spectacle behind the desk: Columbia's Oscars, dramatically spotlighted. On shelves behind the gold statuettes was merchandise—nylon stockings and perfume. Each represented recognition: the Oscars, recognition for the studio; the merchandise, recognition for Harry from obliging young women who, in return for their favors, could choose what they wished from the shelves of plenty. Studio insiders referred to the practice as "bartering with the natives," with the white couch as the ratification of the trade agreement.[4]

While Harry could affect an imperial air when granting an audience, lunch was an entirely different matter. Unlike MGM, which was known for its commissary, and Fox, which had the Cafe de Paris, Columbia had no comparable dining facility unless one was a producer or a guest; everyone else lunched in the neighborhood, usually at the nearby drugstore. Harry set up a private dining room where he insisted the producers join him for lunch. It was not that he enjoyed their company (he preferred writers); Harry simply wanted to hire his own cook, and as inexpensively as possible. Thus the producers, who did not dine free, paid for both the cook and the upkeep.[5]

Harry never entered until everyone was seated around the one enormous table. Then he strode in, taking his place at the head. The luncheons served a dual purpose: they enabled Harry to conduct business and at the same time to criticize each producer individually, even if nothing had been done to merit it. The exceptions were Virginia Van Upp, who, when Harry made her an executive producer, found flowers in her office to mark the occasion, and Sidney Buchman, who liked to use words in front of Harry that he knew Harry did not understand. Unlike Goldwyn, who, lacking an education, respected those who had one, Harry took pride in never having attended high school. While he was awed by writers (never showing it, of course), he felt differently about producers, whose presence he basically resented except for the few who were handpicked. In view of his limited education, Harry felt he had the right to belittle those (chiefly producers) who had not only high school diplomas but also college and postgraduate degrees.

When he chose, Harry could compose a well-written letter or a tersely worded memo; but since part of his persona was the scrapper from Yorkville who had in his employ graduates of some of America's finest colleges, he behaved accordingly. Harry took great delight in asking producer Collier Young, a Dartmouth graduate and at the time Ida Lupino's husband, to pronounce words Harry claimed he did not understand. Harry would then say, "Gentleman, the only reason I have Collier Young here is to piss on him. Isn't that right, Collier?" "Yes, sir," Collier would reply. He treated University of Pennsylvania alumnus Buddy Adler similarly. Adler, who left Columbia in 1954 and moved to Fox, died in 1960. Yet shortly before his death, Adler called Harry "the toughest man I ever worked for but a great showman."[6]

Harry had the knack of finding a person's vulnerable spot. If he sensed weakness (which he despised), he would not relent until he destroyed every vestige of the person's self-worth. If one retaliated or showed some mettle, Harry often backed down. Still, dealing with him was an ordeal. Perhaps S. Sylvan Simon and Jerry Wald were destined to die young, but one suspects their deaths at forty-one and fifty, respectively, were not unrelated to having worked for Harry. Nor did Robert Rossen develop bleeding ulcers from a careless diet.

Harry's ultimate torture was reserved for Jack. When Harry phoned him in New York, some of the operators, out of loyalty to Jack, would alert him to the call with two staccato rings that would send him rushing into the bathroom. But that did not stop Harry, who would then call someone else, usually Abe Schneider, with instructions that he would be phoning Jack again at a certain time and expected his brother to be in his office. When Jack finally had to take the call, he would keep transferring the phone from one hand to the other as if it were burning his fingers.

While Columbia was not bugged, Harry was nonetheless privy to most of what was happening at the studio. Although each executive had his or her private phone, Harry thought nothing of having the operator interrupt a call to learn the caller's identity. If Harry called on a private line and received no answer, he would call the security guard to inquire if the executive had left the studio. Harry would then confront the executive with proof of absence; a trip to the bathroom was no excuse. Although some might argue otherwise, Harry was not being malicious as much as perverse. It was, as Evelyn Keyes would say, his way of being Boss.

The teletype outside Harry's office was another form of technology with an even greater potential for intimidation than the telephone. A phone conversation at least allows one to detect tone and nuance, to interrupt or outshout the person at the other end. But to frame responses to questions flashing across the page in lightning-swift print, to express oneself standing behind a teletype operator, dictating questions or answers to a party one can neither see nor hear—these are skills that give those who have mastered them power over those who are capable only of face-to-face confrontations. Harry's mastery of communication by teletype enabled him to wear down the opposition, to pick up on certain words and score points as secondary school debaters do when they turn an infelicitous or ambiguous phrase against the user.

When Abe Schneider criticized Harry for allowing *Born Yesterday* to go over budget (7 August 1950 teletype), Harry accused him of sarcasm. Since his authority had been questioned, Harry turned the tables on his critic. Focusing on "budget," Harry began repeating the word in various contexts, questioning New York's insistence on two copies of each film's budget when financial statements would have been sufficient. "You know very little," Harry added, arguing—rightly—that budgets can fluctuate during production. "I don't think that's fair," Schneider replied; "I think we should have those reports for our records." Not only did Harry disagree; he also announced he would no longer send budgets. Then he waxed formal, using the clichés of business correspondence: if a "particular situation" arises, a budget will be sent "on request." Of course Harry could not withhold budget sheets, but he could get the last word.

Neither New York nor Los Angeles could act unilaterally; theirs was a relationship of checks and balances, complicated by a form of one-upmanship common to families whose members seem to be at odds but who rally in a crisis and present a united front. It was therefore not a question of who tipped the scales or to whose advantage a deal turned out. While New York and Los Angeles might appear to be in competition, they were not competing against each other. Each was testing the other to achieve the one goal in which both believed: Columbia Pictures Corporation.

Although each coast had its hobbyhorse, each knew not to ride it to death. New York had its concerns, which Los Angeles might not appreciate but eventually learned to understand. Los Angeles had to deal with types (actors, agents, directors, producers, writers) that New York would not ordinarily encounter; and when New York did, it considered them assembly line workers manufacturing the dream that New York had to sell to the world. So who are the real moviemakers: the ones who get the films into cans or the ones who get the cans into the theaters? It is rather like asking if there is sound when a tree falls in a frozen waste where no one is within hearing distance. The traditional answer is "Yes" in the sense that a sound occurs; "No" in the sense that the sound is not heard. Without Los Angeles, there would be no movies; without New York, there would be no outlet for them. Without either there would be no Columbia.

Understanding the way Los Angeles and New York served Columbia's interests requires an appreciation of paradox, specifically, the way one self-interested party can rise above its own concerns, joining with another self-interested party for the good of the whole. While each liked to think of itself as autonomous and often acted as if it were, each knew it could not exist without the other. But that did not stop both of them from behaving autocratically.

What New York did not know about movies, Los Angeles did not know about money, except that it was to be spent making movies that New York promoted and distributed so the studio could make money to make more movies. Such a relationship can either lead to a schism—in which case the studio will fold—or to creative tension, resulting in ulcers and angina but also in good films and healthy profits. Tension took more of a toll at Columbia than elsewhere because the usual East-West friction was intensified by a parallel friction between Harry and Jack.

Likewise, the obsession with budgets, typical of any New York office, was greater at Columbia because of Jack's monetary conservatism. Even when Jack was not replying personally on the teletype, there was the same concern with budgets and the same disbelief when inordinately high amounts were paid for properties that would be hard to sell to exhibitors. Jack never lost the "Short Subjects Kings" mentality, nor did he appreciate the way immediate need for product drove the studio to pay more for a property that, in a calmer moment, might have been acquired for less.

Since the New York office was run by accountants and marketing experts who had their own notions about how cash should be spent (less is more), it was often shocked by what it considered excess. A case in point was Harry's lifestyle, which appalled Jack yet had nothing to do with the way Harry ran the studio. Harry could be as penny-pinching as Jack. In 1955, Fox and MGM each gave $12,500 to the Community Chest, which asked Columbia to increase its contribution from $4,000 to $7,500. Harry refused.

Harry also berated New York for using the teletype for irrelevant questions: "This teletype is not a plaything and it isn't necessary to put a lot of junk on it that can be postponed for the next wire. . . . Use this the same as you would a telephone—it costs plenty of money and use Western Union when it's only about wires" (6 January 1944).

New York was Columbia's conscience. Los Angeles knew—but rarely let on—that New York had the studio's interests at heart even when it questioned budgets. Secretly, Los Angeles was hoping New York would provide a financial solution (which it often did) to a problem that seemed irresolvable. For example, Los Angeles knew $200,000 was too high for the rights to *Snafu*, a mediocre 1944 play that closed after 158 performances. New York's objection was not to Columbia's making the movie version but to paying so much for a comedy of adolescence that would only invite comparison with *Kiss and Tell*, which Columbia had purchased earlier and planned to release in 1945. Since the rights were so expensive, New York hoped some money could be saved on the script by offering the writers $15,000 instead of the $30,000 they were asking, thereby reducing Columbia's investment in *Snafu* (1945), which would be an outside production. The writers would not come down, claiming, rightly or wrongly, that Mary Pickford, who was about to enter independent production (and shortly did), would meet their terms. Thus Columbia had no choice but to pay them $30,000.

While New York would often defer to Harry, addressing him as "chief" ("Would I kid you, chief?"), it naturally favored its own, perhaps thinking, as Jack did, that New York worked harder than its laid-back double in the palms. Thus Harry was both angry and hurt when New York advertised *A Song to Remember* as "A Sidney Buchman Production" but failed to credit Virginia Van Upp as the associate producer of *The Impatient Years*. It was more out of ignorance than sexism that Van Upp's name was omitted: New York had known Buchman during the period when he was assistant production head, while Van Upp was a newcomer. Since Harry respected Van Upp, he was embarrassed by the omission: "There must be some way in which the studio will have to check these ads. . . . It isn't the first time that it has happened and you are always ready with some excuse. . . . Well, I can't get away with it any longer because the minute they leave my office, they go upstairs and check and find out that it has happened to other people . . . and I cannot make an apology to them" (31 August 1944 teletype). Van Upp merited an apology, and the incident led to a new policy: ads were airmailed to Harry.

There were actually moments of harmony between Los Angeles and New York. Los Angeles knew that New York, in addition to handling exploitation, supplied copy to the fan magazines, which had their offices in Manhattan. With magazines like *Movie Story* and *Screen Romances*, which fictionalized films, scripts or script synopses were as important as publicity material. Realizing that New York, which had the ear of magazine editors as well as exhibitors, was a good barometer of audience preference, Los Angeles would offer suggestions—Lizabeth Scott or Veronica Lake for *The Dark Past* (1949), for instance. When New York dismissed Lake as "poison" and Los Angeles admitted that Scott was a "very bad actress," the role went to Nina Foch.

Sometimes the teletypes were almost civilized, showing that New York and Los Angeles understood each other. In June 1948, Los Angeles, about to cast *Mr. Soft Touch* (1949), checked first with New York, suggesting two of its contract players for the leads; or one contract player, Glenn Ford, and Ida Lupino, who would cost $85,000. "Would you prefer Ford-Lupino at the additional cost or Ford and one of our girls?" Los Angeles queried (18 June 1948).

The exchange began without belligerence or defensiveness. When New York asked for a budget for *Mr. Soft Touch*, Los Angeles admitted it had not worked one out except in terms of a rough estimate—$800,000-$850,000, more with Lupino. New York was either being generous or realistic; probably the latter, since initially it did not balk at the figure or the possibility of Lupino's increasing it. But when Los Angeles said Ford and Evelyn Keyes would save the studio $75,000, New York wasted no time on deliberations: "Would rather go with Keyes and hope you can cut down cost still further" (22 June 1948). Los Angeles was delighted: "Will do our best." *Mr. Soft Touch* costarred Ford and Keyes.

Titles were another source of friction between the two coasts. With so many studios competing for titles in the 1930s and 1940s, there had to be a central office where they could be registered. Since the industry made the Motion Picture Producers and Distributors of America (MPPDA) its arbiter of morality when it chose internal censorship in 1922, it authorized the same organization to act as a clearinghouse for titles. When a studio registered a title with the MPPDA, the Association, as the MPPDA was known in Hollywood, prepared a Title Registration Report (TRR) that determined priority of use, depending on whether the studio was the first to request the title or whether the same or a similar title had already been approved. Columbia's New York office would receive the TRR and notify Los Angeles if there were any similarities to former or forthcoming releases. If New York failed to inform Los Angeles, or if Harry discovered another studio using a title reminiscent of one of Columbia's, New York would hear about it.

When Harry learned that MGM was about to release a movie called *The Bride Goes Wild* (1948), he rushed into arbitration, alleging that Columbia was planning to remake *Theodora Goes Wild* and had already spent a considerable amount of money on it. The Association ruled there was no conflict, pointing out that when MGM had protested Columbia's use of "Honolulu Lil" because of its similarity to MGM's own *Honolulu* (1939), the arbitration had gone in favor of Columbia. Harry was unimpressed: "That Honolulu statement is a lot of junk. How can you claim priority on a country?" (14 January 1948 teletype). "It has to do with similar words," Nate Spingold explained to the combative Harry. MGM wouldn't call its film "Alicia Goes Wild" because then there would be "harmful similarity." Harry understood, but his was the logic of the embittered and the hurt—a logic that changes to illogic as reason turns to unreason. Harry therefore decreed that if MGM could release a movie called *The Bride Goes Wild*, there would be no *Theodora Goes Wild* remake.

Harry reacted the same way when he heard that Warners had made *The Daughter of Rosie O'Grady* (1950). Columbia owned the rights to the song "Sweet Rosie O'Grady," which it allowed Fox to use in the 1943 musical of that name. New York reminded Harry that Warners had registered "The Daughter of Rosie O'Grady" and had used it for a 1942 short. Columbia could do nothing, New York maintained; after all, Warners had never stopped Columbia from making *Fortunes of Captain Blood* (1950), although its own *Captain Blood* (1935) had become a classic. Harry knew it was futile but still demanded a fuller explanation, which New York provided so elementarily that most studio heads would have been embarrassed: Columbia had the rights to *a* song; Warners had a property with the name of another song. Harry would not yield: "Doesn't this come down to the fact that our New York office forgot to protest?" That there was nothing to protest did not seem to matter.

A real problem occurred in the mid-1950s when Goldwyn and Warners both registered "Seventh Cavalry," the same title Columbia planned for a Randolph Scott western. Since Goldwyn had been given priority over Warners, Columbia would get the title only if neither used it. When Goldwyn's movie failed to materialize, priority went to Warners, which decided against making a cavalry film and waived its rights in favor of Columbia. Thus one of Columbia's 1956 releases was *Seventh Cavalry*.

Film titles were a joint decision. Harry knew New York had to give the sales staff titles that could be presold to exhibitors. Despite his bias against New York, Harry could not dismiss its marketing expertise. Similarly, New York knew Harry's days as a songplugger made him sensitive to a title's commercial value. Harry also had to deal with stars and directors, whose suggestions, if unheeded, could leave Columbia without big names. When Cary Grant was cast in *The Talk of the Town*, his preferences had to be taken into consideration. Since Grant suspected that Ronald Colman, who had the better role, would steal the picture, he strenuously objected to the proposed title, "Mr. Twilight," because it implied that the movie revolved about a single male character. To get the title everyone agreed was right, Columbia had to relinquish "Sin Town" to Universal in return for "The Talk of the Town." Columbia got the better title in addition to making the better film.

Stars were not the only ones who balked at unsuitable titles. Jerome Kern had written the score for a 1942 Fred Astaire and Rita Hayworth musical that included, among other songs, "You Were Never Lovelier." New York wanted to call the picture "The Gay Senorita," but Kern would have no part of it, nor would he sanction "The Girl from Argentina," "Rita from Argentina," or "The Senorita from Argentina." The musical became *You Were Never Lovelier*. But New York had not given up on "The Gay Senorita," which three years later was used for a Jinx Falkenburg movie.

While it may seem unlikely that a weak title can lessen a film's stature, one wonders if *The Talk of the Town* would be the classic it is if it had been called "Mr. Twilight," or if *Casablanca* would be a film for all seasons if it had the name of the play on which it was based, *Everybody Comes to Rick's*.

One of Frank Capra's best films is *Mr. Deeds Goes to Town*, whose title Harry championed despite New York's preference for "One in a Million" ("too many million pictures," Harry complained) or "Cinderella Man" ("a nance title," as both Harry and Capra agreed). When New York came up with "Gary Goes to Town," Harry exploded: "How can you possibly suggest 'Gary Goes to Town' when the character in the story is named

Longfellow Deeds?" (30 January 1936 teletype). *Mr. Deeds* and *Mr. Smith* are thought of as a pair (the latter's title clearly determined by the former), but that might not have been the case if Harry had not prevailed.

It was not an easy battle. At one point Harry grew tired of defending "Mr. Deeds Goes to Town," but he could not stomach "Spendthrift," "Opera Hat," or "A Wise Fool." "Town" was going to be in the title, one way or another. When Harry proposed "A Gentleman Goes to Town," New York, exhausted, conceded. But when Columbia tried to register the title, it discovered that it conflicted with a similar one MGM was planning to use. Nicholas Schenck, president of Loew's (MGM's parent), wired Jack Cohn, whom he held in high regard, to inform him that MGM had paid $50,000 for a *Cosmopolitan* story called "The Lady Comes to Town." Schenck's argument was that if "A Gentleman Goes to Town" comes out first, "when people see our picture advertised they will confuse it in their minds with your title. . . . The very purpose of regulation of titles is to avoid such situations" (25 February 1936 teletype). Schenck also reminded Jack that when Columbia had wanted to change the name of "Night Bus" to "It Happened One Night," MGM, which had registered "It Happened One Day," deferred to Columbia. New York, feeling chastened, agreed to "Mr. Deeds Goes to Town."

While MGM was gracious about "It Happened One Night" in 1934, Columbia was not when MGM wanted to call a 1942 film "A Yank on the Burma Road." Columbia had registered "Along the Burma Road" and would not relinquish the title. Since Columbia had gone no further than the title and MGM had almost completed its movie, Columbia waived its priority right, knowing that arbitration would favor MGM.

Titles mattered to Harry, whose primary considerations were the title's appeal, its relevance to the film (as encapsulating theme or identifying genre), and its suitability to the star. Thus Harry objected to "The Lady Is Willing" for a Marlene Dietrich vehicle about an actress who wants to adopt a baby but must first find a husband. When the alternatives proved unavailable, Harry had no choice. Moviegoers agreed with Harry and stayed away from *The Lady Is Willing* (1942).

While Joan Bennett was not an icon like Dietrich, she was still too glamorous to appear in an anti-Nazi movie called "Heil-ly Irregular." The film became *The Wife Takes a Flyer* (1942). But should it be "flyer" or "flier"? "wife" or "lady"? Should "Counter-Attack" be hyphenated? (It was, although the hyphen never caught on with orthographers.) Should the studio's first Technicolor release be called "The Last Desperado" or the more dramatic "Desperadoes"? (The latter won.)

Although these matters may seem trivial, executives on both coasts spent much time searching for the right word. Querying back and forth at least prevented Columbia from releasing too many movies with similar titles. This was particularly a problem with the series film. If Columbia was releasing "The Secret of the Lone Wolf," "The Secret of Boston Blackie" would have to be changed to something else, New York observed, "as we don't want [to] use identical phraseology" (4 August 1941 teletype). When Los Angeles replied that it preferred "Secrets of the Lone Wolf," New York concurred: the plural has greater power of suggestion than the singular. The Boston Blackie movie was also put in the plural, and in 1941 *Secrets of the Lone Wolf* and *Confessions of Boston Blackie* went into the theaters.

Obtaining permission to use the name of an actual company in a title was not a simple matter. Before Columbia started filming *The Fuller Brush Man* (1948), it was forced to give the Fuller Brush Company script approval—something Harry was always loath to do, although with Red Skelton in the lead, Fuller Brush would hardly go under. It was different when the studio was about to make *The Good Humor Man* (1951). Harry refused to indulge the makers of Eskimo Pie; as a result, the title cost Columbia $50,000.

Studios even had to clear titles so much a part of the vernacular that it was inconceivable that anyone would have a prior claim on them. Although "Sing for Your Supper" was a song from the Rodgers and Hart musical *The Boys from Syracuse*, it also harked back to the "Little Tommy Tucker" nursery rhyme. Thus Columbia released *Sing for Your Supper* (1941) without incident; there was also no problem with *She Wouldn't Say Yes* (1945), which even Jerome Kern agreed was not a copyright infringement on his song "She Didn't Say Yes."

On the other hand, two colloquialisms, "three's a crowd" and "the more the merrier," were, as Columbia found out, not in the public domain. When Columbia wanted to use the former, it discovered that Howard Dietz, who had conceived the famous musical revue *Three's a Crowd* (1930), would not waive the title rights for less than $5,000. Deciding that the title was not worth the amount, Columbia called the film *The Gentleman Misbehaves* (1948). *The More the Merrier* had been the title of a 1941 play, whose authors were litigious enough to force Columbia to pay them $4,500 for the rights, even though all the studio wanted was the title—not the film rights to a show that had run for only sixteen performances. But Columbia wanted that particular title because it fit the movie, which concerned the housing shortage in Washington during World War II. "The More the Merrier" was preferable to the proposed "Washington Story" and "Washington Merry-Go-Round"; in view of the film's continuous appeal, the $4,500 was well spent.

Once World War II began, titlemania intensified. Four days after Pearl Harbor, Columbia registered "Remember Pearl Harbor." Since it had no immediate plans for such a film, Republic, which did, got the title;

Republic's *Remember Pearl Harbor* was in the theaters by spring 1942. Nevertheless, Columbia did not want to miss out on a battle or a locale that was a potential title; and so it registered "The Spirit of Wake Island" and "Siege of Corregidor," although it made neither. *Wake Island* (1942) became a Paramount film; *Corregidor* (1943), a PRC release.

Finally, Columbia registered a World War II title that figured in one of its films. In 1940, "commando," a term coined by Britain's Lieutenant Colonel Dudley Clarke after the Afrikaans word for military unit, entered the vocabulary of war. A 1941 commando raid on occupied Norway caught the attention of Columbia, which registered "Commandos Story," thinking the title was general enough to spawn one, and maybe two, movies. "Commandos Story" became *Commandos Strike at Dawn* (1942). The following year, when Columbia was about to release its second film about the Norwegian resistance, with Merle Oberon and Brian Aherne, Harry wondered why "Commandos" couldn't be the title; after all, it had been registered. Here Harry was off base. When New York pointed out the possibility that *Commandos Strike at Dawn* could be playing across the street from *Commandos*, thereby confusing the public, Harry scoffed: "The public isn't that stupid." Intelligence was not the issue; the issue was Merle Oberon's image, which would be poorly served by a title suggesting a combat film. Since Oberon was playing a woman who joins the resistance, *First Comes Courage* (1943) may not have been the most evocative of titles but it was at least accurate.

Providing New York with a final title was Harry's idea of a coup. When Columbia was about to release one of its most expensive films, the $2.2 million story of Frederic Chopin and George Sand, the title was all-important. When the Hays Office vetoed "The Affair of George Sand" because "affair" was unacceptable, Harry fumed: "The sooner we get Hays out of here, the better we will be" (13 April 1944 teletype). Harry knew full well there were "affair" films—*The Affairs of Annabel* (1938) and *Love Affair* (1939), to name just two. It took the prudishness of the Hays Office to inspire a better title, one less redolent of a woman's film and more in keeping with a biopic about Chopin, whose music would be heard throughout.

Harry concluded that no matter what the film was called, critics and audiences would refer to it as "the Chopin movie." Then why not call it "Music by Chopin"? New York, which could be firm but was rarely caustic, responded: "Everyone fainted. It is a credit or a title?" Harry was not amused. He defended his suggestion by showing its superiority to "The Eternal Flame," "Duel in Hearts," and "We Dream at Night." But New York insisted, perhaps rightly, that any title with "Chopin" would doom the picture at the box office. Harry, who gave the public more credit than New York did (perhaps because he gave moviegoers their dream while New York only packaged it), reacted with a candor that explains why minimally educated studio heads like Harry and Goldwyn were attracted to films that would elevate the public's taste. A Chopin movie need not be completely accurate; even historical fiction is not. But a filmmaker should not shrink from using names that audiences may not have heard before; once they hear the names, they may remember them and even want to learn more about them. "You know," Harry said, "I give a lot of credit to a man named Goldwyn. One of the biggest grosses was 'Wuthering Heights' and I still can't pronounce 'Wuthering.' And I give credit to Warners for 'The Life of Emile Zola.' . . . Do you think the public knew who Zola was?"

Harry's point—that those who didn't know who Chopin was would after the movie—was wasted on New York. He must have been hurt when, desperate for a title that New York would not mock, he offered "The Professor and Madame Sand," only to be told, "This is a title that is so obviously bad." "Go ahead," Harry sneered. "Try anything." When New York countered with "The Song That Lived Forever," it was Harry's turn to laugh: " 'The Song That Lived Forever' doesn't even fit the picture. There is not a song in the picture that lived forever." New York, which had apparently lost its sense of humor, took Harry literally: " 'Song' is used in the proposed title symbolically." As if Harry didn't know.

At the 19 June 1944 preview, the audience was polled: 158 preferred "The Song That Lived Forever" to "The Eternal Flame," which garnered only 103 votes. While it seemed that New York had won, Harry made one last attempt to have his way. "Frankly I liked 'A Song to Remember,' but I didn't try it out." Finally New York was impressed: "Between you and I [sic], I like it better than 'The Song That Lived Forever.' " To most people, christening a film would hardly represent a victory; to Harry it was cause for rejoicing. The film is entitled *A Song to Remember*.

It was one thing for Harry to hear someone from the New York office other than his brother challenge a title or measure Columbia's films against another studio's; it was something else to hear it from Jack. On 11 August 1944 Harry received a letter from Jack wondering why Universal had more forthcoming releases than Columbia. Unable to get back at his brother, Harry went after Montague, Schneider, and Jaffe, all of whom apparently agreed with Jack. Harry excoriated them for daring to compare quality with junk: "You do not compare Woolworth's with Altman's." He dismissed Universal's so-called star attraction, Deanna Durbin: "If I gave you a pic as bad as 'Christmas Holiday' you'd have a fit." Harry had a point there; known primarily for the bizarre pairing of Gene Kelly and Durbin (the latter in a dramatic role) and perhaps for Durbin's rendition of Frank Loesser's "Spring Will Be a Little Late This

Year," *Christmas Holiday* may not have been "junk" but it was hardly the film by which either of its stars would wish to be remembered.

What bothered Harry was not so much the comparison as the one who made it. Yet, as New York tried to show, the comparison was valid: neither studio had a theater circuit, and both courted the same clientele, unlike Woolworth's and Altman's. Harry would not accept the explanation: "Who has Universal got that compares with Cary Grant, Irene Dunne, Charles Boyer, Rita Hayworth, Rosalind Russell?"

Nothing could mitigate Harry's rage, which briefly subsided into self-pity before swelling into vituperation. Harry, who had castigated others for abusing the teletype, was doing the same, making it the medium for his tirade against his betrayers, who included Jack and his New York accomplices. The anger unleashed in the 11 August teletypes with their childish repetition, illogic, and circularity explains why Jack would shake and Robert Rossen's ulcers would bleed after a confrontation with Harry.

This was not a rational outburst, a release of displeasure after which the conversation is resumed. Harry kept returning to Jack's comparison of Columbia and Universal: "I just can't stand for this continuous comparison with Universal." It was not the comparison that was continuous; it was the invective. If New York wanted to make Universal's "crap," Harry would take vacations twice a year because he would not "have to waste . . . time reading scripts or worrying about production." Furthermore, New York was an ingrate: "No matter what is given to you, you are never satisfied." Worn down by Harry's hostility, New York tried to make amends: "Please understand that there hasn't been one line here for the purpose of complaining." Harry, who never understood the difference between query and complaint, would not accept what was tantamount to an apology: "I don't know how you can say your teletype has not contained one line of complaint. In any event Jack's letter was nothing else." And Jack, as Harry knew, had been highly regarded at Universal.

Harry demanded a meeting in Los Angeles, at which he could preside: "I can't let this thing wait. . . . This doesn't start with this teletype. It starts with a letter written by Jack Cohn." Suddenly, Harry realized he could score by making a point that had nothing to do with a West Coast meeting but with a matter discussed earlier: theater chains. "I notice you don't make any comparison of Columbia with United Artists. They haven't got a circuit of theaters." Bringing up United Artists (which was more of a distribution company than a studio) at this stage was a non sequitur, but so was most of Harry's monologue. But New York, which was trying to answer unreason with reason, explained that Columbia and United Artists are not competitive in the way Columbia and Universal were. There was a sudden pause; then Ben Kahane came on and said, "Harry exhausted and disgusted and left machine."

Harry would never have gone on at such length, and with such immaturity, if his brother had been at the other end; he would have been too ashamed. When Harry and Jack communicated, it was the studio head addressing the executive vice president in a tone a superior uses to someone lower on the organizational chart. Harry could drop his guard with the others, but not with Jack; like all paranoids, Harry knew the limits of paranoia.

On another occasion, learning from an outside source that *A Song to Remember* would be opening in London, Harry, who had not known about it, demanded an explanation from Jack, whose reply was pathetically direct: "Things slip my mind occasionally" (20 November 1944 teletype). Forgetfulness was no excuse. Harry adopted a formal tone, quiet different from the stridency he had exhibited three months earlier; it may have been imperious, but at least it was not infantile: "The utter disregard for the president of the company is very appalling. The utter disrespect for people who make pictures in the studio is worse. . . . It looks like we have to go back to putting someone in the New York office who will keep the studio informed." Whether this was a threat or a reprimand is uncertain. Harry, who never forgot that Jack had once tried to unseat him, looked for every opportunity to remind him that being the president's brother was no guarantee of continuous employment.

Whenever Harry could find something to criticize about Jack, he did so. Harry wanted the authority, which New York would not grant, to decide whether a movie should be previewed in theaters to get the audience's reaction, or in a projection room if it was just another run-of-the-mill picture. Harry was shocked that a mediocrity like *Meet Me on Broadway* (1945) was previewed in a theater. Complaining that New York "has no faith in my judgement," Harry described what he would have done: "If I were in New York and a bad pic were sent in, instead of previewing it, I would look at it in a projection room and decide which is the best way to handle it" (13 December 1945 teletype). New York was at fault, but specifically *who*? "I am blaming it on you." It was obvious the "you" was Jack.

Harry, who despised MPPDA President Will Hays ("the thin long Presbyterian," as Harry called him), was curious about an Association meeting that resulted in Hays's getting a $500,000 pension, which would come from dues and a contingency fund. Harry was curious about the way Jack had voted, suspecting (as was the case) that it was "yea." Realizing he could do nothing about the pension, Harry tried to make Jack feel guilty about his vote: "I wouldn't care what the rest . . . did, but . . . if you were a party to this yourself there is nothing I can do about it" (27 July 1945 teletype). Jack stood firm, knowing that Harry was powerless; it must have delighted Jack to tell Harry that "no one feels that anything less than $500,000 would be fair." This was one of the few opportunities Jack had to reduce his brother to silence.

While Harry could never forgive Jack for his complicity in the 1931 putsch, he might have been on better terms with him if Jack had been more sensitive to the magic of movies. Harry loved the creative end of film: working his way through a script, quizzing the writers, dictating notes on rough cuts, analyzing preview cards. When Harry and Abe Montague were arguing as to whether *Kiss and Tell* should be previewed in New York or in Chicago, Montague's preference for Chicago threw Harry into a rage. Montague tried to appease him: "Please be assured, Harry, I am not trying to be arbitrary, but I want to protect this job" (18 April 1945 teletype). Harry's reply summed up himself, his studio, and his view of his brother: "Please, this is not a job or as Jack Cohn would say, a piece of merchandise. Remember you're talking to an artist."

That was the difference: Jack was the salesman; Harry, the artist. Harry never understood that whatever zest Jack had for film had ended in 1932. Jack, who was in the industry long before his brother, had gone from thinking of pictures as the stuff dreams are made *on* to the stuff they are made *of*. What was once a dream became a commodity that Jack had to distribute—not make, but merely funnel.

With the sapping of his creative energy, Jack took to merchandising what he could not produce. When his suggestions were naive, Harry did not hesitate to criticize them, even in his brother's absence. Jack thought "Curly" would be a good title for a Cary Grant comedy about a dancing caterpillar, especially since Curly was the caterpillar's name. Harry became hysterical: "That is a cute idea from the executive vice president. I personally don't care if you call the pic 'Cheese,'" Harry told New York (22 December 1943 teletype). Embarrassed, New York offered a feeble apologia: "The trouble is poor Jack never meets people who believe in fairy stories."

The very mention of Jack's name drew venom from Harry, but this time not in profusion. Although the topic was now whether *Counter-Attack* should be made with Paul Muni or someone less expensive, it still involved Jack, who thought Muni's name meant nothing at the box office. "Stop with those silly questions," Harry snapped. "Let's wait until we get the script." Meanwhile, Harry proposed to keep Jack in Palm Springs, where he was attending a sales meeting, "so I won't have to worry about whether Muni is a draw or not or whether we will have to change any more titles."

During the next decade, the gulf between the brothers widened into a chasm, then an abyss. As they settled into their sixties, sensing length of days would not be theirs, the gap increased and the outbursts became fewer. One of the last times they differed was over the title of the musical version of *My Sister Eileen*. The exchange was comparatively civil; although Harry had his way, he showed that he was at least capable of carrying on a dialogue.

Encouraged by the success of *Wonderful Town* (1952), Rosalind Russell's Broadway triumph, Harry thought it would be a natural property for Columbia. *Wonderful Town* was the musical version of Columbia's 1942 hit, *My Sister Eileen*, which also starred Russell. *Wonderful Town*, however, was *My Sister Eileen* with a score by Leonard Bernstein and lyrics by Betty Comden and Adolph Green. Columbia would not be remaking *My Sister Eileen* but making the movie version of *Wonderful Town*, which, even if the rights were available, would be costly. The alternative, as everyone agreed, was to remake *Eileen* with an original score. But with what title? The old one or a different one?

In September 1954, Jack informed his brother that the musical *Eileen* needed a new title to avoid confusion with the original and to give the remake a "big lift." Harry was unusually calm, but he would not let Jack get away with misinformation, reminding him that *Show Boat*, *A Star Is Born*, and *Magnificent Obsession* were all remade with the same title.

The matter was still unresolved in August 1955. Harry was holding out for any title with "Eileen" in it; he would have been happy with just "Eileen" except that it was the title of a Victor Herbert operetta. Because he had seen the latest Rodgers and Hammerstein musical, *Me and Juliet* (1953), Harry toyed with "Me and Eileen." When Jack countered with "Here Comes Eileen," Harry took the opportunity to display his knowledge of film, rattling off fifteen "Here Come(s)" movies and noting that a "Here Comes" title cheapens any film.

Tired of haggling over the title, Jack asked to "finalize 'My Sister Eileen' and discuss other problems" (10 August 1955). Now Harry became furious; the film was scheduled for a fall release, and it was still untitled. "That's a hell of a way to give me the answer," Harry retorted. Admitting he didn't have an answer, Jack was on the verge of capitulating: "Don't think we're getting anywhere by spelling this out on TT." Harry agreed: "Call me immediately, number to number on regular phone." Whatever was discussed on the phone, Harry got what he wanted, which was what he had wanted a year and a half earlier: that the remake bear the same title as the original.

My Sister Eileen was released in October 1955. During the next year there appears to have been little communication between Harry and Jack. "Read in paper that Jack Cohn had surgery. What was this?" Harry asked New York on 7 December 1956. The next day Jack died. More than a thousand people, including Harry, attended his funeral on 11 December. The turnout was impressive, especially in view of the obscurity to which he had been relegated for a quarter of a century. Naturally, Harry would have a grander service, but Jack did not do badly. The eulogy was spoken by former State Supreme Court Justice Ferdinand Pecora.

Those who had witnessed the way Jack shook after one of Harry's phone calls were surprised at Harry's grief over his brother's death. While Harry and Capra had their share of shouting matches, Harry never heaped the abuse on Capra that he did on Jack; Capra would not have tolerated it. Harry did to Jack what one brother could do to another but not to an outsider. Because they were brothers, Harry felt free to criticize, berate, and, on rare occasions, commend; because they were brothers in the same business, in positions that each perceived as antithetical (but really complementary), Harry thought of Jack not as his older brother but as the executive vice president, whom he was forced to consult on properties, budgets, and titles. If Jack had shown greater interest in the magic of movies, Harry might have been better disposed toward him. But Jack was neither a showman nor a moviemaker; Harry was both. What Harry loved in Jack—but could never admit—was Jack's ability to endure his wrath without retaliation. That Jack took it is a tribute to his endurance.

A man rarely kills the thing he loves; more often he tortures it for reasons ranging from ego gratification to perfectionism. In *Citizen Kane*, Charles Foster Kane loves Susan Alexander, transforming her into an opera singer despite her limited vocal range and forcing her to perform before indifferent audiences until she attempts suicide to convince him she has no talent. Yet when a reporter, interviewing her after Kane's death, admits to feeling sorry for him, Susan replies, "Don't you think I do?" If Harry had died first, Jack would have expressed the kind of sorrow Susan felt for Kane. What Harry felt for Jack was not sorrow lessened by pity but sorrow intensified as much by guilt as by love.

6

CapraCohn

If the 1930s were the American film's golden age, much of the splendor could be credited to writers, who, while they may have scoffed at "Hollywood," nevertheless succeeded in making movies literate. Because he lacked an education, Sam Goldwyn held writers in high esteem—higher certainly than Louis Mayer did. Goldwyn, in fact, committed the Goldwyn Corporation to a "scripts first" policy in 1919 with the formation of Eminent Authors, a group of writers (including Rupert Hughes, Mary Roberts Rinehart, and Rex Beach) who gave Goldwyn the movie rights to anything they wrote under contract. While the "eminent authors" were not eminent screenwriters (one might even question their authorial eminence), the concept reflected the industry's need for good scripts.

Harry Cohn favored writers also, yet that did not stop him from pressuring them into producing the kind of scripts he wanted. Thus some supremely gifted screenwriters passed through Columbia, some staying for long periods (Jo Swerling, Sidney Buchman, Robert Riskin), others just long enough to give the studio a single classic (Charles MacArthur and Ben Hecht with *Twentieth Century*, Donald Ogden Stewart with *Holiday*). But scripts alone were insufficient; Columbia's best pictures of the 1930s were the result of directors who, if they were not writers themselves, were able to work with writers to bring the film to life. It would be more accurate, then, to speak of Columbia's writer/director teams who, aided by studio technicians (the same director of photography and editor for all of their films or, when that was not possible, the kind of crew to which the director was accustomed), helped forge the Columbia signature.

When Frank Capra arrived at Columbia in October 1927, there was no such policy; the studio was still in its infancy. Capra described his Columbia years in his 1971 autobiography, which, while endearingly told, is not always reliable (for example, Harry knew who he was when he came to Columbia). Some two decades after Capra reinvented himself, Joseph McBride revised the reinvention in his exhaustive biography of the director, setting the record straight by crediting those whom Capra had slighted or ignored.[1]

Since the "real" Capra lies outside the purview of this book, one can only say that McBride's biography is to Capra's body of work what William Wright's and Carl Rollyson's biographies of Lillian Hellman are to hers: a standard by which to measure the artist but not the art. Capra pursued ambivalence long before it was sanctified by the Academy. One can cheer Longfellow Deeds and Jefferson Smith and at the same time feel uncomfortable about the personality cult each inspired, recalling how easily popular leaders turn into dictators. If Capra worked both extremes of the political spectrum, creating leftists who could pass for right-wingers, Republicans who sounded like New Dealers, and capitalists who acted like populists, it was because he mirrored the confusion of the times. Americans wanted an end to the Great Depression, and to many it made no difference whether the means were democratic or totalitarian. But Capra mirrored more than the 1930s: if he seemed to be a New Deal Democrat (but was really a Republican) and an antifascist on the surface (but within an admirer of Mussolini), he reflected all the unresolved tensions of humankind. Like Robert Frost, whose private and public selves were equally contradictory (and whose poetry revealed someone more than casually acquainted with the night), Frank Capra could no more be mistaken for William Saroyan than Robert Frost could for James Whitcomb Riley.

Regardless of how future generations regard Capra, the fact remains that he achieved an unusual degree of autonomy in an industry based on the principle of division and specialization of labor. Although he may not have had the right of final cut, he became a rarity among American directors: Capra was able to tap into the American consciousness and express the public's aspirations as well as its fears.[2] For all his "Capra-corn," he understood that 1930s audiences—the ones for whom he made his best movies—were dreamers who thought their dreams could come true. But the realization of the dream required a miracle.

If they could come to life, Jefferson Smith (*Mr. Smith Goes to Washington*) would admit that he never thought Senator Payne would confess to his complicity in the shady land deal; "Apple Annie" (*Lady for a Day*), that she could never fool her daughter into thinking she was a lady; Conway (*Lost Horizon*), that there is no Shangri-La.

Capra may have thought so, too. While he was never completely able to conceal his dark side (such as the persecution of "John Doe," the what-might-have-been sequence in *It's a Wonderful Life*), Capra's view of humanity was basically compassionate, at times even tolerant. It depended, of course, on the characters. The self-righteous (*The Miracle Woman*) and snobs (*Platinum Blonde*) come in for their share of ridicule. But for the persecuted, Capra was all tears; for idealists, he was all enthusiasm. They get the miracles.

Whether Capra could have made his special kind of movie at any other studio than Columbia is doubtful.To embellish his obscurity-to-fame saga, Capra would have us believe that his coming to Columbia was accidental: his name headed Harry's list of unemployed directors, and Harry, believing God had made Abraham the founder of Judaism because his name began with an "A", had hired him.[3]

Any insider would have been suspicious of Capra's account, which makes Harry seem as pixillated as Longfellow Deeds. As McBride has shown, it would have been impossible for Harry not to know who Capra was.[4] Apart from having been involved in the making of *Life's Greatest Question* (1921), a Quality film that CBC distributed, Capra was also a Mack Sennett gag writer. More important, he was the director of two Harry Langdon features; the second, *Long Pants* (1927), proved such a failure that the rupture in the relationship between Capra and Langdon was common knowledge. But the first, *The Strong Man* (1926), combined sex, comedy, drama, and social consciousness into a whole that soon acquired its own epithet: Capraesque. Fired by Langdon, Capra was looking for a job, and Harry knew it. Harry also knew that Capra could make the kind of film he envisioned for Columbia.

Harry, who had the most diverse background of any of the moguls (pool hall hustler, trolley car conductor, nickelodeon performer, song-plugger, musical shorts producer, traveling exhibitor, administrative assistant to Carl Laemmle), wanted movies that, like himself, were not easily categorized. Rather than repeat the successes of other studios, Harry sought to surpass them by adding to the hit formula. To paraphrase a song from Irving Berlin's *Annie Get Your Gun* (1946), anything the competition can do, Columbia can do, if not better, then differently; it would make movies that were neither single-plot nor single-genre but a mix—and not just a narrative mix but often an ideological one.

Since Harry had no patience with the theoretical, he would never have discussed his philosophy of film with Capra, who shared Harry's disdain for the speculative. Each was a moviemaker in his own way; each took the road to Hollywood, but it was a road that bifurcated (production for Harry, direction for Capra), then converged in the fall of 1927.

As a Sicilian-American, Capra believed in a heterogenous society (or at least wanted the world to think he did). His films are not easy to classify. Even when he directed *Arsenic and Old Lace* (1944) at Warners, he did not treat it as the black comedy it was on the stage; he made it a screwball comedy for an autumn night—Halloween. Thus the Brewster sisters appear more quaint than barmy, and their poisoning of elderly gentlemen with elderberry wine seems more an act of charity than homicide. Capra's *Prelude to War* (1942), the first in the *Why We Fight Series* that was originally intended for the armed services, was more a feature film than a documentary; it is a Capra film, complete with the director's tolling bells trademark and Christmas hymns on the soundtrack. In fact, when *Prelude to War* was released to theaters in 1943, it was advertised as a "movie," not a nonfiction film.

Capra was well compensated for his kind of film, although he considered his initial salary, $1,000 a picture, beneath him; on the other hand, he had no other offers. But that salary, which Harry offered him in October 1927, was doubled within two months. Capra makes no mention of this rather substantial raise, nor does McBride—understandably, because Columbia has Capra's December 1927 contract.[5]

If any further proof is needed that Harry believed Capra could give Columbia an identity, it is Capra's salary history. Capra began filming *That Certain Thing*, his first Columbia movie, on 21 November 1927, completing it on 7 December. Harry was so impressed by the film (rich boy marries poor girl and together they become successful entrepreneurs) that, even before Capra began his second film, *So This Is Love* (which also took him about two weeks—21 December-6 January), Harry offered him a new contract, on 13 December 1927, guaranteeing him $2,000 a picture.

Capra's salary rose over the next two years: in 1928 he was receiving $3,000 a picture for a minimum of six pictures, each to be called "A Frank Capra Production." There was also the option to extend the contract for another year at $4,000 a picture. Columbia picked up the option, and in 1929 Capra was getting that amount. His 15 August 1932 two-year contract stipulated a weekly salary of $3,000. By 6 June 1935 he was making $100,000 a picture and 25 percent of the profits.[6]

When Capra claimed Harry gave him artistic freedom, he meant he was allowed to dramatize his vision of America as a melting pot, an image that has become synonymous with the immigrant experience. With writers like Jo Swerling and Robert Riskin, who shared that vision, Capra was able to translate the blending of cultures and races into a blending of narratives and motifs. "Pure Capra," then, is different from "pure Ford." The purity of style in Ford's classic westerns (*Stagecoach* [1939], *My Darling Clementine* [1946], *She Wore a Yellow Ribbon* [1949], *The Searchers* [1956]), comes from the subordination of narrative to myth and iconography. A mythmaker in his own way, Capra did not have Ford's singleness of vision. Ford could poeticize life in a Dublin slum or on the frontier. Capra may have glorified or idealized, but he never poeticized. One can wax poetic about the frontier, but there is no Monument Valley in Capraville. There is class, though, and Capra never made a movie without reference to class. Nor did he ignore change and innovation. He was always on the lookout for the topical: motor courts (*It Happened One Night*), bank runs (*American Madness*), evangelism (*The Miracle Woman*), farmers in revolt (*Mr. Deeds Goes to Town*), turmoil in southeast Asia (*The Bitter Tea of General Yen, Lost Horizon*). Capra stretched his talent to accommodate whatever fate ordained, history decreed, or the competition produced.

As a commercial filmmaker, Capra did not share the naiveté of some of his characters. He may have understood Longfellow Deeds and Jefferson Smith, but he was neither. While Capra made class a moral as well as a social matter, so that audiences knew with whom to identify, he never resorted to an upper class-evil/working class = good dichotomy. Harry and Capra both knew that moviegoers of the 1930s were a mixed lot, comprising the affluent and the needy, Republicans (who were perceived as advocating self-help) and Democrats (who were assumed to be New Dealers).[7] Since Harry was a Republican (as was Capra, although audiences presumed he was a liberal Democrat), Columbia would never launch a frontal attack on the rich. On the other hand, there was nothing wrong with exposing their foibles as long as they were given some measure of humanity. The millionaire father in *It Happened One Night* is a better human being than some of the other characters on the lower rungs of the social ladder (such as the jovial suitcase thief, the puritanical motel owner). Capra worked through comedy to class and from class to humankind; thus his movies are examples not merely of social consciousness but of class consciousness as well.

The Capra dialectic consists of focusing, first, on one class, then on another, and finally on people. What matters, ultimately, is not class but species; in Capra, there is only one species that counts: homo Capranensis, a breed that includes the audience, too. A Capra person, after seeing *Prelude to War*, which visualized democracy and totalitarianism as two globes (one bright, the other dark), would know which to choose without waiting for Walter Huston's off-camera voice asking for a decision.

In the 1930s, however, Capra was not so obvious about allegiance, even though he was asking the same question: Do you side with the People or the opposite, the latter including the crooked lawyers of *Mr. Deeds Goes to Town*, the religious hypocrites of *The Miracle Woman*, and the fascist publisher in *Mr. Smith Goes to Washington*. In between are the other-than-good-but-not-necessarily villains: the teller of *American Madness*, who masterminds the robbery of his own bank to pay off his gambling debts; the spoiled heiress of *Platinum Blonde*, who tries to turn her middle-class husband into one of the idle rich; the senior senator of *Mr. Smith Goes to Washington*, who becomes a party to a real estate scam. If one can judge from Capra's mail, which was addressed to him personally, Americans understood the principle behind the auteur theory before the

French articulated it. They knew a Frank Capra film was different from any other.

Capra helped establish a policy that Columbia implemented during the 1930s; it was a policy that combined ingredients that had worked individually and might work even better in combination. If topical movies succeeded at Warners and marital romps at Paramount, Columbia would make romantic comedies with a social dimension. In Capra, blending is all, as he showed in his second film for Harry, *So This Is Love* (1928), his first truly Capraesque work. It begins with a trio of characters, each belonging to a different world: Jerry McGuire (William Collier, Jr.), a dress designer who prefers to paint; Hilda (Shirley Mason), a delicatessen clerk; and Spike Mullins (Johnnie Walker), a macho boxer. Capra then polarizes the trio, situating Hilda between two extremes of masculinity. Although at first she is drawn to Spike, she gradually begins to favor Jerry, who, to win her, learns how to box. When Jerry must fight his rival, Hilda betrays Spike by plying him with so much food that he overeats and loses the match.

Jerry's transformation from esthete to boxing champion is one of many such Capra metamorphoses (hayseed into philanthropist, derelict into lady, vagrant into celebrity, cynic into idealist). While such transformations were not new in 1928, Capra gave them the semblance of novelty by evoking current events or similar films, thereby ensuring recognition. *So This Is Love* opens with an iris; but unlike an iris that is an optical effect, Capra's is a natural one: Hilda is washing the window of the delicatessen, moving her arm in such a way that a circle appears through which she sees a poster advertising a fight. A boxer's face appears in iris—this time one created optically. The artful transition from natural to artificial extends to the film itself, which neatly resolves what would otherwise have been two extremes.

The opening also suggests Chaplin, who often began a movie with an iris, as he did in *The Gold Rush* (1925), for example.[8] *So This Is Love* is Capra's *Gold Rush*. Just as Chaplin's Lone Prospector progresses from adventurer to millionaire, Jerry McGuire advances from loser to winner. The women in both films also change. Chaplin's Georgia renounces golddigging; Hilda, her standard of measuring masculinity in physical terms. The endings of both films are wish-fulfillment, although Capra's is more realistic than Chaplin's. Chaplin offers the charm of fantasy: the triumph of an empathetic figure who had been subjected to humiliation and abuse and thus was especially appealing to immigrants who had been similarly treated. Capra made the fantasy a reality by incorporating it into a narrative in which the characters are both types and individuals, not nameless figures like the Lone Prospector, another form of the Little

Tramp, who resemble allegorical abstractions that make up in universality what they lack in credibility.

While Capra, like Chaplin, understood the traditional distinction between tragedy and comedy, he also knew, as did Chaplin, that there are tragic elements—or at least serious ones—in comedy. And by comedy, Capra meant the same thing the medieval rhetoricians did: a work with a happy outcome, no matter how stark or tearful are the events preceding it. Within such a work styles can mingle as long as the successful resolution is achieved. Thematic blending, however, works only with narratives that are antithetical or complementary. Thus, the hallucinatory sequence in *It's a Wonderful Life* does not alter the film's texture so much as deepen it by showing the infernal city Bedford Falls would have become if George Bailey had never been born. Capra was fortunate in having such writers as Jo Swerling, Robert Riskin, and Sidney Buchman, who were able to create diverse or bipolar classes. With the right collaborator, Capra could expand the film's social dimensions beyond the parameters set by the script—but only if class was the narrative matrix. And when it was, the result was pure Capra: a movie in which romance, social differences, political conversion, and the triumph of goodness coalesced into a myth of America as not just a melting pot but a crucible in which everything becomes gold.

Capra was not always successful in his blendings, however, as a comparison of *The Younger Generation* (1929) with the less satisfying *Rain or Shine* (1930) reveals. The latter is Capra's most chaotic picture, although it has some historical value. Those who imagine vaudeville as a prehistoric form of popular entertainment at least have the opportunity to see what it was like in the verbal duels between the comedians Joe Cook and Dave Chasen in which non sequiturs, double entendres, and puns multiply at a dizzying rate. But the vaudeville routines are more like set pieces than integral parts of the film—a tale of circus life as well as an upper-class boy/middle-class girl love story. One's reaction to the scene in which a couple of stooges wreak havoc at a dinner party depends on one's ability to overlook Capra's pacing, for which "slow" is an understatement. It is as if Capra was savoring every bit of mayhem. Dorothy Howell and Jo Swerling, who usually gave Capra tighter scripts, wrote one with two climaxes—or rather with a climax and an anticlimax. The circus is saved from falling into the wrong hands, but a fire breaks out, causing a stampede (a similar disaster occurs in a later film, *The Miracle Woman*) and destroying the big tent. In another film, this would have meant the end of the circus, but not in Capra: the wagons roll on, rain or shine.

Rain or Shine reveals Capra's fascination with water imagery and its various associations: loneliness (eyes filled with tears as rain trickles down a window in *It Happened One Night*; an ex-hero making his way past a jeering crowd as the driving rain intensifies his humiliation in *Meet John Doe*); passion (a kiss behind glass sprayed by the rising waters of a fountain in *Platinum Blonde*); and the erotic (the waterfall beneath which Sondra bathes in *Lost Horizon*).

Rain dominates the opening sequences of *Rain or Shine*; the circus wagons make their way through a stormy night, their wheels sinking into the mud as Mary (Joan Peers), whose last name is appropriately Rainey, looks out of the rain-streaked window of her trailer. The addition of rain to a face wet with tears or of cascading water to a lovers' tryst spiritualizes, or at least mythicizes, passion. Certainly the imagery purges passion of its more physical aspects. Capra did for sex what he did for America: just as he scoured the melting pot, he sacramentalized lovemaking by juxtaposing it with a universal symbol of cleansing.

The Younger Generation (1929), made the previous year, is part talkie; there are three sound sequences that unfortunately slacken the generally taut narrative line, slowing down the pace as spoken dialogue can do in a largely silent movie, especially when it is delivered in the stage tradition of projecting up to the second balcony. The exception is Jean Hersholt, who gave the ethnic role of Julius Goldfish a shading of ethnicity rarely achieved in movies of that period.

The Younger Generation was an attempt to capitalize on the success of Warners' *The Jazz Singer* (1927) while going one step further. While *The Jazz Singer* chronicled Jacob Rabinowitz's journey from the ghetto to Broadway (where he changed his name to Jack Robin), *The Younger Generation* used the same idea (minus Broadway stardom) but added a new twist: the youth's repudiation of both his religion and his family. In *The Jazz Singer*, Jack does not disown his father; Morris Goldfish (Ricardo Cortez) in *The Younger Generation* does. In the company of his friends, Morris happens to encounter his parents; he is so ashamed of them that he gives his companions the impression they are only servants. The rejection sends his father back to the Lower East Side and eventually results in his death.

The Younger Generation may not have been successful in its integration of sound with action that was shot silent, but it was in its interweaving of upward mobility and domestic tragedy. Related to the escape-from-the-ghetto theme was the rejection of the ghetto and those who still had its mentality. The film succeeds because there is a sociological connection between these themes as well as wrenching drama in a son's disowning his parents.

Rain or Shine and *The Younger Generation* brought out different sides of Capra: the former, his love of physical comedy and vaudeville shtick; the latter, his empathy with immigrants. *The Younger Generation* was a sentimental journey for Capra, an immigrant himself who left Sicily when he was five. Thus he depicts life on the Lower East Side with a reverential awe, giving it purity along with a lack of squalor. Still, love is all to Capra, even love among school children. A girl holds out a loaf of bread to a boy in an adjacent tenement as they extend their arms through an air shaft. Later, Capra repeats the composition when the children, now grown up and married to each other, are separated again—this time by the bars of a prison in which the husband is serving a sentence for a crime he did not commit.

Capra allows nothing to deflect from the heart of the narrative, even using dissolves to get the Goldfish family from Delancey Street to Fifth Avenue. While this is the kind of script a more political director might have turned into an indictment of materialism (in addition to shortening his surname to Fish, the son also changes his first name from Morris to Maurice to seem less Jewish), Capra does not forsake social drama for social criticism. Nor does he make Morris a villain. Although Morris prevents his sister's letters from reaching their father, whose death he indirectly causes when he passes his parents off as servants, he remains an object of pity rather than scorn. When his mother moves in with her daughter and son-in-law, Morris is left alone in his mansion; shadows cast by slats from the venetian blinds form bars against the fireplace where he sits wearing his father's prayer shawl. That double image of isolation and imprisonment crystallizes, in an extreme long shot with neither dialogue nor titles, the fate of those who renounce their roots. Given the theme, *The Younger Generation* is unusually subtle; while Capra's sense of subtlety disappeared a decade later (the classic example is the filibuster in *Mr. Smith*), it was intact when he shot Julius Goldfish's death scene: Julius raises his eyes to heaven as his face goes out of focus.

As the 1930s approached, Capra's pace did not slacken. Driven by a desire for recognition that coincided with Harry's plans for Columbia, Capra continued making movies that emulated other studios' successes, going so far as to challenge the preeminence of Paramount's *Wings* (1927) with a trio of films (not planned as such originally) that proved Columbia was capable of making high-tech pictures. But while *Wings* was at least classifiable, Capra's trio was characterized by the same eclecticism that distinguished his earlier features. The films, each of which celebrated a particular kind of technology (*Submarine* [1928], sea power; *Flight* [1929], marine aviation; and *Dirigible* [1931], aircraft), grafted the male bonding of *What Price Glory* (1925) and *Wings* onto the combat film, resulting in an anomaly (unless one prefers "peacetime combat film") that portrays the peacetime military in action—a Latin American skirmish in *Flight*, rescue operations under water in *Submarine* and at the North Pole in *Dirigible*.

Thus audiences, getting adjusted to talkies, would get their money's worth just from the sound of gunfire or the whir of an airplane propeller.

Friendship between males is central to all three movies, each of which offers a variation on the bonding theme. In *Submarine*, a woman temporarily comes between two men who discover her duplicity in time to keep their friendship intact. In *Flight*, the men vie for the love of the same woman. While one of the friends in *Dirigible* is married, his rescue by his unmarried buddy is more an act of love than of heroism.

Of the three, *Submarine* offers the most direct affirmation of the superiority of male friendship to physical desire. Bessie (Dorothy Revier) entices Jack Dorgan (Jack Holt) into marriage and then seduces his best friend Bob (Ralph Graves) when her husband is on maneuveurs. Eventually she is unmasked, but not until Jack rescues Bob from a submarine that sank when it collided with a destroyer. Until then, her allure is real, as an underwater scene with Bob confirms. All Bessie can offer is sex, not love—the word she and Bob inscribe on the sand, only to see a wave wash over it. Bessie lives up to her nickname, "Snuggles," as she presses herself against Bob while they swim. But she cannot extricate him from a deadlier form of underwater entrapment when the submarine sinks. A male can, and *Submarine* is a man's, or, as some might say, "masculinist" film. Men console each other in the submarine on the ocean floor; men ponder suicide as an alternative to death by suffocation; when one of the sailors dies, Bob holds his body in a *pietà*.

Flight presents the other side of the anima: the virgin rather than the whore. Again, Capra and his screenwriter, Howard J. Green, are responding to *Wings*: if *Wings* could feature Clara Bow, the "It" girl, as a nurse, *Flight* would offer the public a nurse (played by Lila Lee) who at least looked like someone Florence Nightingale might recognize. A former football player (Ralph Graves), disheartened after losing a crucial game, joins the Marines. When his commanding officer (Jack Holt) becomes his rival in love, the plot branches out into romance (the officer asks the private to court the nurse for him, *à la Cyrano de Bergerac*) and melodrama (a jungle rescue). During a bombing raid on Nicaraguan rebel bases, the private's plane crashes and the officer rescues him for the woman they both love but whom only one of them—the private—can marry.

Dirigible is the least effective of the three Jack Holt–Ralph Graves movies; it also suggests that the male bonding theme had run its course. Since Frisky (Graves) is married, he and his friend Bradon (Holt) do not clash over a woman but over aircraft: the merits of the plane versus the dirigible, with Frisky championing the former and Bradon the latter. From the title alone, one knows which will prove superior and who will emerge as hero. Just as Holt rescued Graves in *Submarine* and *Flight*, he does the same in *Dirigible* when Frisky's plane crashes at the Pole.

Periodically, Capra would make a summary film, bringing together past themes and anticipating future ones. *Dirgible* looks back to *Flight*, where suicide was a possibility; here it is a reality. The amputation of a gangrenous leg in *Flight* recurs in *Lost Horizon*, along with a crash landing in the snow.

While there are fewer references to *Submarine*, *Flight*, and *Dirigible* in film histories than to *Wings*, Capra's films merit more than a footnote. There is nothing in *Wings* comparable to the scene in *Flight* when Lefty (Graves) provides a makeshift cremation for a dead pilot by setting fire to his plane and standing at attention as Taps is heard on the soundtrack. Capra does not stop there; Lefty's hand, rigid in salute, loosens and moves down his face, his fingers separating but not enough to mask his grief.

Capra's ability to infuse sentiment into the unlikeliest narratives gave Columbia's 1930s films an interest and distinctiveness they would not otherwise have had. While film historians attribute Columbia's rise in that decade to Capra's presence, it might be more accurate to say Capra's influence. While fallen woman films became a subgenre of the era, most of them either went soft or stayed tough as nails. Capra sensed that such movies demanded a certain toughness of attitude on the part of the fallen, who were still women and therefore more than hookers or good girls gone bad. What makes *Ladies of Leisure* (1930) different from, say, MGM's *Susan Lenox, Her Rise and Fall* (1931) is the recognizable humanity of the main character, played by Barbara Stanwyck, who always insisted she learned more about film acting from Frank Capra than from any other director; it was Capra who brought out a tenderness in Stanwyck that few directors could.

In *Ladies of Leisure*, Capra's favorite theme, the disparity between the classes—usually rendered as rich/poor—was treated seriously, stopping short of a tragic ending. Realizing moviegoers wanted boy and girl to remain together (even though the boy is an artist from a wealthy family and the girl is a "lady of leisure"), screenwriter Jo Swerling makes the audience wait until the fade-out and endure the suspense of a suicide attempt that, under ordinary circumstances, would have meant death. Although Kay (Stanwyck) jumps from an ocean liner into the Atlantic, she survives.

Capra was always circumspect about sexuality, which is not to be confused with sex. Sex is the act; sexuality is the metaphor for the act, the trappings that cloak it in mystery. Sexuality is the silhouette of a man bending over a woman in a position that would come to represent intercourse. Capra used this composition first with Ralph Graves and Stanwyck in *Ladies of Leisure*, repeating it in the haystacks scene in *It Happened One Night* when Clark Gable hovers over Claudette Colbert. Although both men are interested in doing more than casting their shadows over women, Capra separated the position from the act, which never takes place.

Eventually, Capra would explore what he considered the highest form of love: the sacred. But first he had to confront the profane, which was easier to do at Columbia, where there was no high gloss, no elaborate *mise-en-scène*, no sumptuous decor, as there was at MGM, where Camille was the paradigm of the fallen woman. In *Camille* (1937), everyone looked as if he or she belonged to the same class—the world of the salon. *Camille* also followed the parental opposition plot in which the fallen woman either yields to a father's plea (as Camille does) or weakens under a mother's tyranny (various versions of *Madame X*).

The fallen-woman cycle at Columbia was primarily the work of two writers, Jo Swerling and Robert Riskin, both of whom were Capra collaborators and could therefore make women victims of the same social prejudice as men. The women's foes were aristocratic snobs, extreme versions of the bluebloods who talked down to Stew Smith (Robert Williams) in *Platinum Blonde* and Dan Brooks (Warner Baxter) in *Broadway Bill*.

Ladies of Leisure, Capra's first collaboration with Swerling, pitted the prostitute-heroine against her lover's straight-laced parents, who, while frowning on such a union, never behaved as monstrously as the mother in *Shopworn* (1932), directed by Nick Grinde, written by Swerling and Riskin, and starring Barbara Stanwyck. *Shopworn* could have been Capraesque; it involved four Capra regulars—Swerling, Riskin, Stanwyck, and Capra's favorite director of photography, Joseph Walker. To the Capra blend of class consciousness and tarnished virtue, the writers added another element: oedipalism, or, in the vernacular, "smother love." The mother, who wants to save her son from Kitty Lane (Stanwyck), is even characterized by her smarmy lawyer as suffering from "mother love," as if it were a disease. Kitty goes even further, branding it a "queer, selfish sort of love." It is also vengeful, since mother has Kitty sent to reform school on a trumped-up morals charge.

For *Shopworn*, Swerling and Riskin wrote a Capra script for a Nick Grinde movie; the result was not an amalgam but a pastiche. When the script allowed, Capra provided a happy ending in the screwball tradition. To Capra, screwball was more flexible than it was to, say, Howard Hawks, who saw as its hallmark the battle of the sexes, where the weapons were wit and deviousness. Although Capra never formulated a definition of the genre to which he contributed, he would have agreed that a screwball comedy was the kind of movie in which barriers that up to the denouement seemed unsurmountable disappeared within the last few minutes, leaving the misunderstood parties exonerated, the skeptics converted, the classes free to marry, and the audience satisfied.[9]

Capra needed actors who could convince audiences, especially those of the Great Depression, that such endings were possible. His emphasis on realistic acting endeared Stanwyck to him, since she had a natural fire and a contempt for pretense. Capra's most believable characters were played by actors who could easily be mistaken for real people—Jean Arthur, James Stewart, Gary Cooper, Thomas Mitchell.

Despite the honesty of Stanwyck's performance in *Shopworn*, which also opted for a happy ending, there was no creative mind behind the camera. Stanwyck had learned enough from Capra to apply her skills to a movie that was a Capra clone but not Capraesque. Capra would have known how much to add to the mix; had he directed *Shopworn*, he would have asked Swerling and Riskin to go easy on the psychology. The plot was getting top-heavy; it was a cross between *Ladies of Leisure* and Sidney Howard's play *The Silver Cord* (1926), which proved that "smotherers" do not go gentle into the night. But unlike Capra's films, *Shopworn* does not build to a natural denouement. The resolution comes from another plot: mother points a gun at Kitty but is too guilt-ridden to pull the trigger. Kitty then goes into musical comedy and, just as she is on the brink of stardom, decides to leave the stage, take back her old beau, and become a doctor's wife.

That a Capra film is unique is evident from the way *Shopworn* was photographed. Walker did not have the same relationship with Grinde that he had with Capra; nor did the editor, Gene Havlick, who joined the Capra stock company in 1933. The panning is jerky. The fluidity that Havlick achieved optically through wipes and dissolves is absent; instead, fades mark the end of the acts—and acts they are, rather than film sequences. Finally, *Ladies of Leisure* broods uneasily over *Shopworn*; while the former is not vintage Capra, the latter is not vintage Stanwyck.

As Capra moved closer to his forte—a blend of screwball, social consciousness, and romantic comedy—his interest in the fallen woman movie waned. His last, *Forbidden* (1932), another Swerling screenplay, combined two familiar figures from popular fiction into a single character: the mother who gives up her child (*Stella Dallas*) and the backstreet mistress (*Back Street*). Again there is Stanwyck, now as Lulu Smith, a librarian on a Caribbean cruise who meets and falls in love with Bob Grover (Adolphe Menjou), a married lawyer with an invalid wife. They become lovers, and even after bearing Grover's child (which he and his wife adopt), Lulu continues as the "other woman."

Forbidden prefigured the kind of film with which Stanwyck became closely identified: film noir (*Double Indemnity, The Strange Love of Martha Ivers, The File on Thelma Jordan*) in which she played a femme fatale. In *Forbidden*, Lulu marries a newspaper editor (Ralph Bellamy) to keep him from destroying Grover's reputation. When her husband learns she is the mother of the Grovers' adopted daughter and threatens a smear campaign, Lulu shoots him in noir fashion: dressed in an evening gown, she stands at the fireplace, holding the pistol at her side. Yet the composition is less self-conscious than it would have been in film noir: Capra makes it more realistic and thus less stylized by showing a patch of dried blood on Lulu's mouth from the blow she received from her husband.

Forbidden is more a woman's than a fallen woman's picture, one in which "the woman—a woman—is at the center of the universe."[10] At the center of a universe marked by privilege and revenge is a woman who determines her own destiny. Lulu's decision to be a backstreet mistress may strike some as unenlightened, but she is not in the *Back Street* tradition, in which the mistress is little more than a camp follower, accompanying her lover (but at a distance), boarding the ship after him, and waiting for his call in a hotel room. Lulu goes to work and becomes a lonely hearts columnist, a position that is ironically fitting.

It is Grover who profits from the affair. While he rises, Lulu falls—from librarian to mistress to murderer to ex-convict. Grover rose because he accepted the leveling ground Lulu gave him, which he transcended at her expense. At the end, when Lulu leaves his deathbed, wandering into the crowd and disappearing into urban anonymity (as Stanwyck would do a few years later at the close of *Stella Dallas*, whose fade-out is strangely similar to *Forbidden*'s), it is also Capra walking away from a genre that he tried to deepen through social awareness and his own brand of humanity, realizing that his gift lay in immortalizing not the problems of mistresses and prostitutes but those affecting a broader section of humanity. Yet the idea of a "fall," whether from grace or position, intrigued Capra, perhaps because he thought of himself as one who had "risen." As he says at the end of his autobiography, "If doors opened for me, they can open for anyone."[11]

In Capra's films, however, success does not necessarily mean celebrity. While Capra rose from obscurity to a *Time* cover in 1938, his characters achieve less spectacular recognition. Having come from the lowly, Capra could only rise; but those already at the top, whether through birth, luck, or both, have to undergo some kind of fall if they are to become human beings instead of sociological clichés.

In the best of Capra's Columbia films, there is always a fall—a descent or a "coming down" from a position of eminence, actual or assumed, to a level that achieves what levels do: uniformity of elevation. Thus anyone belonging to the privileged but desiring one of the unprivileged must "fall down" to the other's level. In terms of human nature, the fall is mutually restorative, uniting the falling with the fallen so they can begin a new life on an equal footing. In *Ladies of Leisure*, Kay gives up being a "party girl," and Jerry, his puritanism. Kay's humanity, previously dormant, resurfaces to humanize Jerry, whose innocence redeems her. In *Forbidden*, Lulu's transformation from bespectacled librarian to fur-draped mistress is accompanied by her lover's gradual realization of her sacrifice and his selfishness, which he acknowledges on his deathbed. These rhythms, narrative and cinematic, where rise and fall diverge, intersect, and meet, give Capra's films their distinctive tempo. Lulu loses her virtue while Grover advances professionally; Lulu relinquishes her daughter while Grover averts scandal; Lulu returns to the work force as Grover campaigns for governor; Grover settles into the governor's mansion while Lulu goes to prison. The final scene, in which Grover's dying confession of love is followed by Lulu's disappearance into the crowd, reduces both of them to non-being: the dead and the vanished.

While the fall concept is implicit in movies like *Ladies of Leisure* and *Forbidden*, it also characterizes Capra's anomalous blend of screwball, romance, and social consciousness, in which those occupying the aerie of privilege must come down to ground level. If Capra's films are truly democratic, it is because they reflect a willingness first to consider, then to adopt a different philosophy of life. Babe Bennett and Clarissa Saunders (both played by Jean Arthur) lose their cynicism once they get to know Longfellow Deeds and Jefferson Smith, respectively. The tycoon father in *Broadway Bill* heads for the open road, leaving his bewildered family to join his daughter and her happy-go-lucky fiancé, whose values he has come to respect and whose insouciance he envies.

One of the reasons *It Happened One Night* is among the best loved movies in Hollywood history is that Ellie Andrews, the Colbert character, discovers the drawbacks of privilege. There is no fun in being an heiress: no bus trips with brash young men, no slaps on the buttocks, no learning how to dunk donuts or eat raw carrots, no playacting at being a plumber's daughter. "I'd change places with a plumber's daughter any day," Ellie finally admits.

It is not merely a matter of Ellie's dropping down to the level of Peter Warne (Clark Gable). Capra has too much respect for his characters to allow anyone, no matter what class he or she comes from, to be a puppet. While Ellie does not manage as well as Peter (who has had more experience in the art of survival), she does surprisingly well for a "brat." Ellie pawns her watch to buy a dress after she dives from her father's yacht; she stops a car by hiking up her dress; she fakes a lower-class accent convincingly enough to fool detectives. Ellie is one of Capra's People; she is also a woman who wants a man as a friend as well as a lover. That Peter feels similarly about women makes him one of Capra's People, too.

Purity of relationship is part of Capra's signature, which was rewritten in Columbia's romances of the decade. Capra achieved that purity even in his pre-Code movies. Thus, to insist that Capra's depiction of men and women as friends was Code-dictated is to ignore the pivotal scene in *Ladies of Leisure* in which a rainstorm forces Kay to spend the night in Jerry's apartment. When Jerry provides her with her own bed, she is puzzled; accustomed to a totally different kind of male, Kay stares at him, wondering why he expects her to sleep alone. Kay says nothing, but the look on Stanwyck's face is enough. Her expression, partly quizzical, partly wounded, is juxtaposed with rain lashing the window. Rain, that cleansing symbol in Capra, often appears in a sexual context. Jerry is not oblivious to the possibilities of the occasion, but his ability to suppress his desires transfigures himself and Kay, whose sexuality seems to dissipate, leaving her unfulfilled and lying alone—but, from Capra's point of view, a better person.

Similarly, in *It Happened One Night*, Ellie and Peter, separated by the "walls of Jericho," lie silently in their beds. As the rain beats against the window panes, each longs for the other, or at least for the other's affection. But there is a barrier stronger than the blanket Peter has strung between their beds: propriety.

Being at Columbia and functioning as Harry's alter ego made it possible for Capra to create a microcosm of haves and have-nots; of men who learn from women and vice versa—in short, a Capracosm. Capra not only introduced types with whom audiences could identify; he also made it possible for those types to appear in other Columbia films.

While all the studios made their share of musicals, crime movies, comedies, melodramas, and programmers in the 1930s—even combining genres (comedy mysteries like MGM's *The Thin Man* [1934], socially conscious musicals like Warners' *Gold Diggers of 1933*)—Columbia did more than darken the bright. If class consciousness could be added to a romantic triangle (*Platinum Blonde*); if screwball could be amalgamated with racetrack drama (*Broadway Bill*), urban romance (*Mr. Deeds*), and muckraking (*Mr. Smith*), other unions were also possible.

At the Big Five—MGM, Warners, Fox, Paramount, and RKO—there was great respect for genre. For pure social consciousness, one could single out Warners' *Wild Boys of the Road* (1933), which focused solely on the children of the Great Depression. For unalloyed screwball, there was RKO's *Bringing Up Baby* (1938), in which no world exists but the world of madcap.

Except for *Twentieth Century* (1934) and *The Awful Truth* (1937), Columbia never made pure screwball. Yet even these two films, studied within the context of Columbia's romantic comedies of the 1930s, are consistent with studio policy, which was based partly on Harry's vision of what movies should be and partly on the way that vision was implemented by directors and writers.

In *Twentieth Century*, there was little Ben Hecht and Charles Mac-Arthur could change about their 1932 play except to provide a kind of prologue before the action moves aboard the Twentieth Century on a Chicago–New York run. Oscar Jaffe (John Barrymore) and Lily Garland (Carole Lombard), temperamental director and self-dramatizing star, are doubles. The casting of Lombard opposite Barrymore enhanced the doubling; each had a distinctive profile—a fact that director Howard Hawks emphasized, at one point even having them appear in profile together. That Lily and Oscar are mirror images is more apparent from the way Lily adopts Oscar's mannerisms once she becomes a star: she poses rather than sits, delivers lines rather than speaks, and turns every space she occupies, including a train compartment, into a stage.

The way Oscar undermines Lily's marital plans is more typical of what men do to each other than of what men do to women, as one might expect from the authors of *The Front Page* (1928), in which editor Walter Burns resorts to an outright lie (a charge of theft) to keep his star reporter, Hildy Johnson, from marrying Peggy Grant. Oscar and Walter are machiavels, not monsters; their deceptions are intended for the good of the deceived. Oscar has to make Lily realize she is meant not for the bland George Smith but for himself; and that both of them are meant for the theatre. Since Hildy is ready to give up the newspaper business for an advertising job, Walter must show him, however treacherously, that he is a born reporter.

For *Twentieth Century*, Hecht and MacArthur reworked the plot device they had used four years earlier, so that what Walter does to Hildy in *The Front Page* became what Oscar does to Lily in *Twentieth Century*. When *The Front Page* was transformed into *His Girl Friday* (1940), with Hildy Johnson now a female instead of a male, Walter Burns can still do what he does in the stage play: keep Hildy from marrying the wrong person—this time the wrong man.

In *The Awful Truth*, the audience is encouraged to regard Jerry and Lucy Warriner as a couple who have flirted with, and perhaps succumbed to, infidelity. As played by Cary Grant and Irene Dunne, the Warriners are friends whose temporary lapse into enmity makes them even more aware of their need for each other. That each tries to sabotage the other's romantic prospects does not suggest a divorcing couple so much as it does competing friends, whose tactics derive not from sexual rivalry but from emulation. Ultimately, all is forgiven as both realize, to paraphrase the Irving Berlin song from *Call Me Madam* (1950), that the best thing for each of them is the other. One thinks of Shakespeare's *Two Gentlemen of Verona*, in which Valentine forgives his friend Proteus, although the latter nearly wrecks his love life: "'Twere pity two such friends should be long foes" (act 5, 4).

While *Twentieth Century* and *The Awful Truth* are too sophisticated to be Capraesque, they depict couples who are distant relatives of Capra's lover-friends, who keep battling and outwitting each other until both realize that no one ever wins the war of the sexes; if there seems to be a loser, it is through choice. *His Girl Friday*, on the other hand, is quite Capralike, mainly because Charles Lederer's script retained *The Front Page's* subplot about anarchist Earl Williams, who has been sentenced to death (as a high shot of the gallows in the courtyard reminds us) and the prostitute Mollie Malloy, who jumps from a window rather than reveal Earl's hiding place. The result is a film that mixes politics, class, and romance—and one that Capra himself might have made—but earlier in his career when he knew the art of restraint.

When Howard Hawks, whose direction would be hard to improve, felt that Hildy's dialogue in *The Front Page* would work better if the character were female,[12] the sexual metamorphosis that resulted confirms Columbia's interest in adding to its growing number of screwballs, which by 1940 included *Twentieth Century, She Married Her Boss* (1935), *If You Could Only Cook* (1936), *Theodora Goes Wild* (1936), *More Than a Secretary* (1936), *The Awful Truth,* and *You Can't Take It with You* (1938). Lederer and Hawks not only made Hildy female (Rosalind Russell); they also made Walter Burns (Cary Grant) her ex-husband. *His Girl Friday*, then, became a comedy of remarriage.[13] While these may seem like radical changes, they were consistent with the basic themes of *The Front Page*.

Men can become wedded to each other in an employer-employee union that involves the same commitment as marriage. When Hildy of *The Front Page* decides to "divorce" Walter by marrying Peggy, Walter feels free to use any means he can to prevent it. When Hildy becomes a woman in *His Girl Friday*, there is no difference between Walter Burns's attempt to win her back and similar efforts by Oscar Jaffe in *Twentieth Century* and Jerry Warriner in *The Awful Truth*.

What makes *His Girl Friday* Capraesque is not just the portrayal of a couple who discover that what they have in common is each other; it is also the Earl Williams subplot. Capra's humanity softens screwball's brittleness, so that even if one insists on calling *It Happened One Night* screwball, it is screwball with warmth and feeling. Hawks, who in his previous screwballs, *Twentieth Century* and *Bringing Up Baby*, was dealing with material that militated against compassion, showed great sympathy for Earl and his Mollie. When Hildy interviews Earl, she does not speak to him as a convict but as another human being; when Mollie delivers her diatribe against journalists who are more interested in a scoop than in a person's life, a moviegoer who had seen *Mr. Smith Goes to Washington* in 1939 might have wondered if Mollie had seen it, too.

While Capra's signature was unique, another's hovered over it, dissolving into it so that the two hands became one. If Columbia made movies that commingled styles and themes, it was because Harry wanted them and found someone like Capra who wanted to make them. Even before CBC became Columbia, the films were Harry's—films he thought would appeal to audiences because of the characters (unfaithful spouses, prostitutes, murderers, shopgirls). He understood this milieu; he did not understand families like the Hardys or the Minivers; they were MGM's creations. Nor did he understand epics; they were DeMille's province. What he envisioned for Columbia reflected his years in New York, where he developed a talent for survival by applying the art of the hustle to whatever enterprise seemed promising—hustling pool and then hustling songs. When *Traffic in Souls* became a hit, Harry hustled that; when he became a production head, he hustled product.

Since Harry could apply the techniques of street salesmanship to any venture, the idea of a movie mix appealed to him, as it did to Capra, on the principle that the more ingredients in the film, the broader the appeal and, in the case of films with a political or social thrust, the less likelihood of categorization in terms of left/right, New Deal/Republican.

By the mid 1930s, audiences had grown accustomed to movies about women marrying their bosses. More of a cycle than a genre, movies such as Warners' *Beauty and the Boss* (1932) and *Goodbye Again* (1933), and RKO's *Behind Office Doors* (1931) and *The Office Girl* (1932) were romantic fluff. But they were not screwball, which pits man and woman against each other in a contest where the goal is more than winning a mate; it is winning a mate by using the weapons of wit and ingenuity.

When Sidney Buchman came to Columbia in 1934, he quickly learned Harry's formula for a successful movie: genre plus—the "plus" being whatever the genre could sustain. Being a left-wing radical at the time, Buchman was able to add even more to the mix. In *She Married Her Boss*, directed by Gregory LaCava, an executive secretary (Claudette Colbert) not only marries her boss, a department store tycoon (Melvyn Douglas); she also inherits his brat of a daughter by his first wife and his snooty sister, whose interest in her brother borders on the unhealthy. Buchman's contempt for privilege is evident in the way Julia (Colbert) transforms the household; she thinks nothing of insulting her stepdaughter, even calling her "stupid"; nor is she intimidated by her sister-in-law. And once she has set her husband's house in order, she starts on his business.

But Julia cannot be superwoman; 1935 audiences would not accept a woman without flaws. Although she is superior to her husband, there must be at least one scene showing her with feet of clay. So Buchman has Julia drink too much champagne, thereby causing a minor scandal. Buchman, however, was too far to the left to allow a man who was little more than a corporate cipher to emerge as his wife's better, especially after the audience has seen her talking and working circles around him. Thus, in a moment of totally unmotivated merriment, Julia and her husband hurl bricks through the window of his department store. Perhaps Buchman's comrades would have gotten the anticapitalist message, but it was an unfortunate resolution to a film that, if allowed to reach its natural conclusion, would have advanced the cause of feminism.

In *More Than a Secretary* (1936), directed by Alfred E. Green, a quintet of writers (Matt Taylor, Dale Van Every, Ethel Hill, Aben Kandel, and Lynn Starling) worked two themes from *She Married Her Boss* (employer-secretary romance, secretary's superiority) into a new plot that also blended screwball and feminism. The co-founder of a business school (Jean Arthur) masquerades as a secretary to improve her institution's reputation. Although her employer (George Brent), the publisher of a fitness magazine, promotes her to associate editor, he is still oblivious to her talents, which outstrip his. Again the secretary's superior ability, evidenced by her increasing the magazine's circulation, cannot go unchallenged. Audiences in 1936 may not have appreciated the ambivalent ending, in which the publisher wins back his ex-secretary by placing ads in his own magazine that are really declarations of love. Yet he could not have done it if she had not turned the magazine around and given it a wider readership.

The Cohn/Capra concept of film as potpourri is also apparent in two Columbia movies, *Cocktail Hour* (1933) and *Virtue* (1932), in which women break out of their restrictive molds and men reveal a tenderness they had been taught to suppress. While these may seem to be woman's films, they are a special kind—the Capra kind. *Ladies of Leisure* and *Forbidden* dramatized the folly of class by making integrity the common denominator of love. *Cocktail Hour*, written by Gertrude Purcell and Richard Schayer, features a commercial artist (Bebe Daniels in her early thirties, but looking older), courted by two unmarried young men and one middle-aged married man during a cruise. Director Victor Schertzinger, who was so attuned to the world of operetta that he treated nonmusicals as if they were libretti, even managed to work in a shipboard song for Daniels.

Schertzinger, however, could not deviate from Columbia's melange philosophy; just as the froth is about to spill over, the champagne turns bitter and reality intrudes when one of the younger suitors accidentally sends his older rival crashing out of a hotel window. In the early 1930s, audiences would have expected a man to cover for a woman, but in

Cocktail Hour it is the reverse. The artist and her sidekick, a Kansas pianist masquerading as a White Russian, are emancipated, pre-Code women who believe life is for living and expect men to feel the same. *Cocktail Hour* is not a double-standard movie any more than Capra's woman's films are; the artist and her friend are women who believe in paying their way and who assume that men do, too. If men traditionally take the rap for women, perhaps it is time for role reversal. While the writers opted for the happy ending (the fall is not fatal), their choice is the only false note in a movie that rings amazingly true.

Virtue is the opposite of *Cocktail Hour*; here a husband comes to the aid of his wife, who has been unjustly accused of murder. Traditionally, in the fallen woman's film the heroine is vindicated only after great suffering on her part (*Madame X, The Old Maid*), often when she is too old to enjoy her victory. The other extreme is death without vindication (*Back Street*). Midway is the kind of film (such as *That Certain Woman* [1937] or *To Each His Own* [1946] in which the man finally realizes the woman's worth and starts venerating her (which for her may be even worse than not being exonerated).

What gives *Virtue* its special character is its refusal to conform to type. In the woman's film, man and woman usually belong to different classes; in *Virtue*, they belong to the same class: the wife (Carole Lombard) is an ex-prostitute, her husband (Pat O'Brien), a taxi driver. The plot does not revolve around the woman's attempt to hide her past *à la Waterloo Bridge* (in both 1931 and 1940 versions) because the man already knows about it. Thus there is no question of her being abandoned. Again, the spirit of Capra broods over *Virtue* for reasons other than the writer's being Capra's favorite, Robert Riskin. *Virtue* argues, perhaps naively, that a working-class husband will come to his wife's defense sooner than an upper-class husband whose wife has been charged with a serious crime, and that there is greater trust between blue-collar couples than white-collar ones.

If Capra had been production head at Columbia, like Thalberg at MGM or Zanuck at Fox, he could not have had a greater effect on the studio's image. That Harry sanctioned the Capra touch attests to his appreciation of the special kind of movie Capra was capable of making.

In September 1932, when *No More Orchids* (1933) went before the cameras, Capra's *American Madness*, with its unsettling recreation of a bank run, had already opened. The subject matter was sadly familiar: by 1932 more than 5,000 bank failures had occurred. Since Capra made Columbia sensitive to topicality, the beleaguered bank plot was repeated in *No More Orchids*, whose characters include a banker in financial straits (Walter Connolly); his daughter (Carole Lombard), whose class-conscious grandfather expects her to marry a count; and the daughter's "common man" lover (Lyle Talbot), who cannot afford her favorite flower. "Then there'll be no more orchids," she replies.

No More Orchids could have been a combined *Platinum Blonde* and *American Madness.* But in 1932 Carole Lombard, two years away from becoming a screwball heroine, was still known as a serious actress and continued as such despite her roles in *Twentieth Century, My Man Godfrey* (1936), *Nothing Sacred* (1937), and *Mr. and Mrs. Smith* (1941). *No More Orchids* explains Lombard's later identification with screwball: the movie begins as a screwball comedy. The same quartet of playboy suitor, doting father, pampered daughter, and middle-class lover appeared a year later in *It Happened One Night,* with Walter Connolly playing Claudette Colbert's father, as he had Carole Lombard's.

But a bank failure is no laughing matter, so *No More Orchids* might better be called screwball tragedy. Although the banker succeeds in saving his daughter from a loveless marriage, he does so by defying the wishes of his father-in-law, who only agrees to bail out the bank if his granddaughter marries into royalty. One could easily imagine Ellie Andrews in a similar predicament, except that in *It Happened One Night* there is no wicked grandfather. Instead, there is a car waiting to whisk Ellie and Peter away for the nuptials planned for Ellie and King Westley. The writers of *No More Orchids,* Gertrude Purcell and Keene Thompson, did not provide a *deus ex machina*: The banker commits suicide by crashing his plane, and his daughter and her lover, unaware of his death, drive on to a new future. What begins as a screwball comedy, with a madcap heroine on a cruise (not unlike the opening of *It Happened One Night*), darkens progressively until the emphasis shifts from the heroine to her father, whose sacrificial act resolves the plot.

Brief Moment (1933), another Capraesque movie, affirmed the Capra doctrine that the affluent must emulate the working class if they want to be anything other than objects of derision. And they were precisely that in *Brief Moment,* in which a family of bluebloods is shocked when one of its own (Gene Raymond) marries a nightclub singer (Carole Lombard). But the bride, instead of being awed by the ways of her in-laws (rendered in a stunning montage of carousal over which is superimposed her censorious face), is merely bored. When she leaves her husband because he cannot hold a job, she vindicates her class by proving that the work ethic is superior to hedonism.

Brief Moment also illustrates another Capra principle: the time-honored offend and mend. If the rich are targeted for censure, they must redeem themselves before the fade-out. Thus, if the upper-class husband is to win the respect of his working-class wife, he must get a job and hold it, as he eventually does. Rarely in a 1930s movie was there such contrast between the indolence of the privileged and the industriousness of the masses. If Capra saw *Brief Moment,* he had the last laugh: the husband's conversion to the dignity-of-work philosophy would convince only well-heeled moviegoers wanting an ending that did not demean their way of life but forgetting (or failing to remember) that most of the movie mocked it.

Although Capra never directed Carole Lombard, she appeared in enough Capra-inspired films to qualify for admission to his populist pantheon. A year after Capra's *Lady for a Day* opened, the similarly titled *Lady by Choice* (1934), directed by David Burton, *Brief Moment's* director, premiered; the film capitalized on the success of its predecessor, even to the extent of having May Robson reprise her "Apple Annie" role in *Lady for a Day* as a derelict transformed into a *grande dame.* This time, the metamorphosis is not the result of a mother's attempt to fool her daughter, but of the desire of a fan dancer (Carole Lombard) for publicity. *Lady by Choice,* which combines class consciousness and romance, could easily have taken a serious turn when the dancer confronts an implacable judge and a sanctimonious mother who threatens to disinherit her son if he marries an "exhibitionist." For the screenplay, Jo Swerling drew on characters from two earlier Columbia movies; one was a movie he had written; the other, one of Robert Riskin's. If the meddlesome mother and the transformed vagrant seem familiar, it is because they had appeared, respectively, in *Shopworn* and *Lady for a Day.* But while the mother in *Shopworn* has the heroine sent to jail, the dancer gets a reprieve from the judge (Walter Connolly again), who relents, leaving her free to marry her disinherited lover.

With Columbia's writers repeating popular themes and successful formulas, and the Great Depression calling attention to the gulf between the classes, the studio continued to turn out films with the Capra touch, which was soon felt throughout the industry.[14] But it was at Columbia where Capracorn—or, to be more accurate, CapraCohn—originated; and it was at Columbia that Capra thrived. Capra's eagerness to exploit his immigrant roots enabled him to connect with the American experience in a way that Harry, who ignored his origins along with his religion, could not. Capra did for Harry what Harry could not do alone: Capra recreated America as a promised land that keeps its promises. Capra and Harry were doubles; each lived in the other's shadow for more than a decade. But while Capra needed a studio to give him some degree of latitude, Harry needed Capra to give his studio an identity.

That identity had become so apparent that "Capra movie" and "Columbia product" were almost synonymous, as Harry knew when he allowed *If You Could Only Cook* (1935), directed by William A. Seiter, to be advertised in Britain as a "Frank Capra production" in 1937.

It is easy to see how Harry could play such a trick on British audiences and why they would fall for it. For that matter, Americans seeing *If You Could Only Cook* on the heels of *It Happened One Night* would have reacted similarly. "Capraesque" the film certainly is. The screenplay is by Howard J. Green (*The Younger Generation, The Donovan Affair, Submarine*) and Gertrude Purcell, who did the Capra clone *No More Orchids*; Robert Riskin's brother, Everett, was associate producer; and Gene Havlick, who cut all of Capra's Columbia films since *Lady for a Day*, was the editor.

Although *If You Could Only Cook* reverses the classes of *It Happened One Night* (rich boy/poor girl), the film begins and ends the same way: a millionaire enters the world of the working class and is so changed by the experience that he marries into it. An automobile designer, James Buchanan (Herbert Marshall) leaves his thriving business to find some relief from the social whirl. He strikes up an acquaintance with the unemployed Joan (Jean Arthur), who is perusing the classifieds on a park bench. Assuming Buchanan is also looking for work, Joan talks him into pretending to be her husband so they can apply for a butler-and-cook position at what turns out to be a bootlegger's home. Like Ellie and Peter at the motor court, Joan and Buchanan must deal with their accommodations: a room with a double bed. Since the "walls of Jericho" technique only works with twin beds, Buchanan retires to the porch.

While the underworld subplot causes the film's middle to go off in a different direction, *If You Could Only Cook* returns to its screwball origin in time for the resolution. Since class distinctions have been leveled, Buchanan's wedding to a socialite must be stopped—and is, thanks to the bootlegger (sympathetically played by Leo Carrillo), who stands in for Alexander Andrews of *It Happened One Night* and does for Buchanan what Andrews did for Ellie by making sure Buchanan marries Joan. If Capra had made *If You Could Only Cook*, it would have had greater warmth, a more provocative title, and a different Buchanan, Herbert Marshall being too arch for the role. Nevertheless, the movie attests to Capra's influence.

That influence was not restricted to comedy; it can be seen in two vastly dissimilar cases: *Whirlpool* (1934) and Columbia's Grace Moore films (1934-37).

Whirlpool occupies a special place in Columbia's 1930s releases. When it opened, Harry, who had been president of the studio for two years, had stopped using "Produced by Harry Cohn" as part of the main title. But he did not give up his seal: he simply changed it to "Harry Cohn, President," which he continued to use for the rest of the decade except on films whose directors were important enough to merit their own. The movies Howard

Hawks made for Columbia (*The Criminal Code, Twentieth Century, Only Angels Have Wings, His Girl Friday*) were "Howard Hawks Productions"; *The Whole Town's Talking* (1935) was a "John Ford Production." Harry's name was absent, as it was in Capra's movies after 1932. Even Harry had to accede to *auteurs*.

As a 1934 film, *Whirlpool* should have borne the "Harry Cohn, President" seal; instead it was a "Harry Cohn Production." *Whirlpool* obviously had special meaning for Harry: it was his personal bid for respectability in a year that saw the release of two films over which he could never exercise the control he wished, films that redeemed Columbia when they won a total of seven Oscars: *It Happened One Night* and Grace Moore's best known film, *One Night of Love*. With *Whirlpool*, Harry had to deal not with Capra, Hawks, or Ford but with Roy William Neill, a talented director who never became more than a cult figure; nor did Harry have to humor an opera star like Grace Moore, who had her own ideas about her first Columbia movie. But Harry did have Capra's Dorothy Howell (*Say It with Sables, Submarine, The Donovan Affair, Rain or Shine*) as one of the writers.

Whirlpool had the greatest number of plot devices of any Columbia movie of the 1930s: assumed identity (as in *Lady for a Day*), the newspaper world (*Power of the Press, Platinum Blonde*), the Enoch Arden syndrome (remarriage on the assumption a spouse is dead, a theme that Columbia explored comically in *Too Many Husbands* [1940] and that D.W. Griffith treated seriously in several films beginning with *After Many Years* [1908]); and an intense father-daughter relationship that ends when the father sacrifices his life for his daughter's happiness (as in *No More Orchids*).

From a purely visual standpoint, *Whirlpool* deserves attention. The opening montage rivals anything Warners could have achieved: fifteen years (1914-29) are condensed into less than a minute as World War I battle scenes, the spinning hands of a clock, and newspaper headlines wipe each other away in the Capra fashion: one shot begins with a wipe moving right to left; the next, with the wipe going in the opposite direction.

Whirlpool is unusual in its depiction of an incestuous attraction that was not repeated in a prison film until *White Heat* (1949), when the characters were mother and son. But *Whirlpool* is only nominally a prison movie. A criminal's wife, assuming her husband is dead, remarries; their daughter, believing the same about her father, becomes a reporter. When father (Jack Holt) and daughter (Jean Arthur) discover each other, they head out for a night on the town, rendered in a montage of clubs, neon signs, and clinking champagne glasses and ending in a kiss that is far from paternal. Since the father has no chance of a pardon, he commits suicide rather than ruin his daughter's life. It was not merely the presence of Holt and Arthur that raised *Whirlpool* above the B level; it was the production itself. But it was not any production; it was a Harry Cohn Production.

Grace Moore was Harry's inspiration. Always conscious of other studios, particularly MGM, Harry was delighted when Louis Mayer could not make a movie star out of Moore. Harry, who had seen Moore on Broadway before she became a Metropolitan Opera diva, believed he could succeed where Mayer had failed.

Each of Moore's MGM films, *A Lady's Morals* and *New Moon* (both 1930), was a failure. Soon MGM would find its resident soprano in Jeanette MacDonald, whose *New Moon* (1940) eclipsed Moore's. In the meantime, Harry wanted an opera star on his roster if for no other reason than to show Mayer—and Hollywood—that a diva could be one of the people. Actually, Moore fared better in Hollywood than her other Met colleagues, Rise Stevens, Lawrence Tibbett, Gladys Swarthout, and Lily Pons. She appeared in as many movies as Mario Lanza.

There was something wrong with the properties MGM selected for Moore: a biopic loosely based on the life of Jenny Lind (*A Lady's Morals*) and a Sigmund Romberg operetta (*New Moon*). Since Moore could sing both opera and operetta, each movie should have been a natural. But what Moore needed was a script that portrayed her not just as an opera star but as a small-town American who dreamed the American dream and awakened to an international career.

Moore's Columbia debut, *One Night of Love*, was carefully planned to evoke—and surpass—*A Lady's Morals* and to suggest similarities between Moore's character in the film and the singer herself. In *A Lady's Morals*, Lind, in a display of temperament, stages an "I won't go on" scene—and of course goes on. If Moore could play a character who indulged in such histrionics once in an MGM picture, she could do it twice in *One Night of Love*—first as Carmen, then as Madama Butterfly. *One Night of Love* was also intended to recall Moore's life, a success story epitomizing the kind of transformation film that had become a Columbia staple. Just as Tennessee-born Moore went from obscurity to fame, so did her character, winning acclaim first in Europe, then in America.

Love Me Forever (1935) was even more adventuresome in its amalgamation of opera with the underworld and social consciousness as a nightclub owner (Leo Carrillo) falls in love with a singer (Moore) whom he makes into an opera star. Since Sidney Buchman wrote the script, *Love Me Forever* went more deeply into human relationships than one would expect in a movie about an operatic soprano. Carrillo is genuinely moving, as is Moore in the scene in which she declines his subtle invitation to be his mistress in return for an elegantly furnished apartment.

While Robert Riskin, unlike Buchman, was never a Communist party member, his liberalism was often misinterpreted as Communism, when in fact it was egalitarianism, which made him an ideal collaborator for Capra. Riskin, who wrote and directed *When You're in Love* (1937), retailored *It Happened One Night* for Moore, showing just how flexible "Capriskin" was. Here the couple are a diva and a nature lover (Cary Grant), who teaches the jaded soprano to sing for the joy of song and not for money. *When You're in Love* recalls *It Happened One Night* in other ways: a low-key landscape evokes the haystacks where Ellie and Peter nearly make love; the couple are again mistaken for husband and wife. But Riskin could not repeat his walls of Jericho; instead Moore and Grant must contend with a double bed, which they barely escape having to share.

By the time Moore made her last Columbia film, *I'll Take Romance* (1937), the studio had developed a reputation for screwball comedy. Thus Moore's swan song was a cross between romantic comedy and screwball. Now the couple are a theatrical agent (Melvyn Douglas) and an opera star (Moore); when the star overhears the agent planning to kidnap her to keep her from breaking a singing engagement, she goes along with the scheme and ends up falling in love with him.

What is noteworthy about Moore's Columbia films is their total lack of condescension to the audience. At MGM, opera excerpts were worked into the script, frequently without any concern for accuracy. In *The Great Caruso* (1951), the tenor dies at the end of *Martha* because the opera ends with "The Last Rose of Summer," which the studio apparently considered an upbeat requiem. While Marjorie Lawrence did perform Isolde, she did not make her comeback in that taxing part but in the less demanding role of Venus in *Tannhäuser*. Her return as Isolde in *Interrupted Melody* (1955), based on Lawrence's autobiography, is certainly more dramatic, but MGM was taking no risks: this Isolde was not going to die at the end of the Liebestod.

In Moore's films, opera was part of the action, and the excerpts were longer than in other movies about the opera world. In *Love Me Forever*, the nightclub owner stages Act 2 of *La Bohème* at his establishment for Moore; when his protégée reaches the Met, she performs excerpts from Act 1, including "Mi chiamano Mimi," which Moore makes more provocative than it was probably intended to be. And just as *One Night of Love* ends with "Un bel di" from the second act of *Madama Butterfly*, *I'll Take Romance* concludes with the first-act love duet from the same work.

In 1937, Massenet's *Manon* was not standard repertoire, yet in *I'll Take Romance*, when Moore gives Douglas a tour of the Met, the *Manon* sets are up and she obliges him with the famous Gavotte, whose context is deftly worked into the dialogue. Interestingly, the one film in which Moore sings nothing operatic—*The King Steps Out* (1936), which was partly based on an operetta and had a score by Fritz Kreisler—is her least enjoyable.

Yet even there her charm was evident; it was Moore's charm, coupled with her lack of affectation, that explains her appeal. She may have been a diva, but she was also a person; when Moore sings "Minnie the Moocher" in *When You're in Love*, she does it with the zest of a small-town American who has not forgotten her origins.

Moore, however, was not meant for a long movie career. As it was, she lasted longer than other opera stars who were wooed to Hollywood. Lauritz Melchior may have made the same number of films, but he never played leads; Moore, on the other hand, never played supporting roles. To her credit, she did not feel she was slumming on Gower Street and was grateful to get an intelligent property like *One Night of Love*.[15] She was also well compensated—$50,000 a picture. Like any star, she measured her worth in terms of salary. When Moore agreed to stay on at Columbia after *I'll Take Romance* if her salary were doubled, Harry contacted New York, which questioned offering her $100,000 a picture: "Cannot tell how long Moore will last" (7 January 1937) was New York's response.

Moore was also obsessed with making a movie of Charpentier's *Louise*, which she had performed in Paris and which had become her favorite work. *Louise* was to have been a British production, directed by Abel Gance, with Columbia as worldwide distributor. But New York balked at the percentage arrangement she proposed and by spring 1938 decided Columbia could do without Grace Moore: "We feel the time and effort wasted on this girl can be better expended," New York informed Harry on 18 April 1938.

On 25 April Frank Capra began shooting *You Can't Take It with You*, which would win him his third Oscar as best director. Initially, Harry was loath to buy the screen rights, especially for $200,000, despite Capra's eagerness to do the picture. Eventually, Harry yielded, primarily to keep Capra at the studio, despite the estrangement between them.

Harry had indulged Capra on *Lost Horizon*, even authorizing a $1.25 million budget that sent New York into shock. Harry was unprepared for Capra's exceeding that budget and, in his judgment, committing an even greater sin: making a movie that ran close to three and a half hours at its first preview. When Harry had it cut to 132 minutes, Capra, whose ego increased with each film, found the emasculation intolerable. Frankly, *Lost Horizon* could have used even more pruning; eventually it received it: the 1952 rerelease ran around 95 minutes.

This was the beginning of the end of CapraCohn. Capra could never forgive Harry, who felt similarly about him—not because of Capra's oversized ego (he understood megalomania) but because Capra went public. When Columbia would not come through with the $100,000 Capra claimed was owed him, Capra sued. Harry was not in the giving vein, at least not in the period between March and November 1937. Harry's motto was "Whoever eats my bread sings my song," and Capra was off-key. But the unkindest cut of all was Capra's suit over the false advertising of *If You Could Only Cook* in Britain. While Capra's motives had more to do with the reediting of *Lost Horizon* than with the misuse of his name, he had done something that was as disloyal as Jack Cohn's attempt to win "Doc" Giannini's support in deposing Harry. It was one thing to sue for money; eventually Capra got his $100,000 and a new contract. But by engaging in litigation over what Harry considered a trivial matter, Capra was, in effect, blowing the whistle on his boss.

Legally, Capra was within his rights to sue. But what Capra in his stubbornness failed to realize was that Harry's calling *If You Could Only Cook* a Frank Capra production was a testimonial to Capra's influence; it was also an indirect confirmation of Harry's image of Capra: a shadow self—the assistant (or, better, associate) production head that New York wanted for the studio and that Harry would never admit was necessary. Capra was necessary to Columbia, but synergy is mutual.

Since the salary dispute and the false advertising charge were separate issues, there is no way of knowing if Harry's resolving the former led to Capra's abandoning the latter. As usual, there are two versions. According to Capra, Harry appeared at his home in November 1937 begging him to return to the studio; otherwise New York would use the loss of Columbia's star director as grounds for firing him.[16] According to Capra's biographer, Capra came to Harry at Columbia, realizing that his whistle-blowing could blacklist him at other studios.[17]

The truth may lie somewhere in between: Harry probably sought out Capra, who repaid the visit. The result was Harry's purchasing *You Can't Take It with You* for Capra. While the film won Oscars for both Capra and Columbia (it was judged best picture), it was not a great moneymaker. The Capra touch had become smudged; what had once been featherlight had grown heavy, then weighty. As if in revenge for *Lost Horizon*, Capra allowed *Mr. Smith* to run 130 minutes, knowing that Harry would be displeased but would do nothing about it.

By the time *Mr. Smith* was released, Capra was no longer at Columbia. If Harry never said goodbye on that October day in 1939 when Capra left the studio, it was because he had said it two years earlier when he felt the same pang of betrayal as he did when his brother and Abe Schneider conspired to remove him.

In the fall of 1939, Capra's value to Columbia was questionable. *Lost Horizon* and *You Can't Take It with You* caused the studio's net profits to drop from $1,318,000 in 1937 to $184,000 in 1938 and $2,000 in 1939. The World War II years saw an upswing as net profits increased from $512,000 in 1940 to $3,451,000 in 1946. By 1939 Harry had gotten the best from

Capra; by defining the Columbia product as a blend of different strains, Capra had made it possible for Columbia to continue making melange movies, combining screwball with reincarnation (*Here Comes Mr. Jordan*), politics (*The Talk of the Town*), and bedroom comedy (*Too Many Husbands* and the Rosalind Russell films of the 1940s); film noir with homoeroticism (*Gilda*), male bonding (*Dead Reckoning*), the oedipus complex (*The Dark Past*), and lesbianism (*In a Lonely Place*); the western with sadism atypical of the period (hand-smashing and cattle-burning in *Coroner Creek* [1948], a deceived male's persecution of a duplicitious female in *Lust for Gold* [1949]); the backstage musical with the unhappy ending (a bombardment that kills two of the principals in *Tonight and Every Night* [1944], a wife who leaves her husband in *The Jolson Story* [1946]).

While Columbia could adjust to a new generation of moviegoers, Capra could only recycle old themes. He had lost his gift of restraint, of knowing how long he could sustain a mood without breaking or changing it. As his self-importance grew, so did his budgets;[18] the growing threat of world war gave politics precedence over narrative. The languid pace of *Lost Horizon* and the overlong filibuster in *Mr. Smith Goes to Washington* obscured the drama at the heart of each. If 1939 audiences loved *Mr. Smith*, it was because in that year democracy could not be defended enough, even though the defense was redundant.

But Capra at his finest—the Capra who constructed drama out of simple truths—had no peer. Among the many classic moments in his films, there are two that have never received their due: the tenderness that Stew (Robert Williams) shows Gallagher (Loretta Young) at the end of *Platinum Blonde*, when he finally acknowledges her worth, and the unexpected death of the race horse in *Broadway Bill*, which would have elicited a crescendo at Warners or a scream at MGM. Capra chose utter silence, as if the spectators were too stunned to speak and too respectful to vulgarize the death of a champion.

Even Capra's detractors, who called his moviemaking style "Capracorn," would have to admit it is distinctive. Some directors' names end up as adjectives; few become nouns; "Capra" became both. But "Capracorn" is not entirely accurate; his special brand of film would have been impossible without Harry. So, perhaps, "CapraCohn" is more precise; or, if one is a deconstructionist and enjoys playing with brackets and virgules, "CapraCo[h/r]n."

7

Harry's Three P's

Traditionally, a production chief's primary interest was product—the studio's films; the president's, profit. As Columbia's production head and president, Harry had to be concerned with both. A dual commitment to quality and cost effectiveness led to personalized contracts and tailor-made deals. In Hollywood, it has always been a matter of who one is and where one is on the ladder of success; the location of the rung determines the nature of the arrangement. With independent producers, there was a third consideration: what percentage of the profits would accrue to the studio and how soon they would be realized.

If Columbia was never in the red during Harry's tenure, it was because of his concentration on product, profit, and percentage, as budgets and salaries attest. At Columbia, a movie could be made for less than what Fox spent on sets, which often averaged between 10 and 12 percent of the total budget.[1] Even in the early 1930s, when Columbia was struggling to become one of the majors, budgets were uncommonly low. Although *It Happened One Night* turned out to be a classic, it cost only $333,000, yet it does not look as if it had been made on the cheap. A movie about a runaway heiress traveling north from Florida does not require an elaborate wardrobe. Still, audiences expecting to see Claudette Colbert stunningly attired, at least once, had the chance; for the final scene she donned a wedding gown. The predominantly low-key lighting (for example, the field where Ellie and Peter are about to make love until his scruples intervene; the motor court where the pelting rain underscores the restraint they practice by sleeping apart)—cost Columbia little while imparting an eroticism that cannot be measured monetarily.

Conversely, another screwball comedy, Universal's *My Man Godfrey* (1936), cost $575,375, less than one-fourth of which went to the salaries of William Powell ($87,500) and Carole Lombard ($45,645).[2] Columbia paid half as much ($50,000 for Colbert, a paltry $10,000 for Gable, whose home studio, MGM, thought he was slipping), yet made a movie of greater appeal as well as one that, a year later, won what in 1935 was an unprecedented number of Oscars.

During the 1930s and 1940s, Columbia made three kinds of movies: the AA, costing around $1 million (*The Talk of the Town*, for instance); the Nervous A, not quite in the AA category but expected to perform as such at the box office (such as *The Awful Truth*, which cost about $600,000, thus falling within the Nervous A range of $500,000-750,000); and the B movies or programmers, which averaged $250,000. There were even movies that could be made for less, such as Charles Starrett's series westerns. If Harry could authorize a $1.25 million budget for *Lost Horizon*, which eventually cost $2 million, it was because in the 1930s only one-tenth of Columbia's movies in any given year cost over $500,000, with most coming in around $250,000—and some (such as the "oaters," as the low-budget westerns were called) at $100,000.[3] By contrast, MGM's idea of a B movie was one costing $400,000.[4]

Historically, studio salaries have rarely been consistent. In 1929, Paramount stars were reportedly getting $2,500 a week; featured players, $750.[5] That same year, Universal's *All Quiet on the Western Front* (1930) was about to go into production. Compared to Paramount, Universal was then considered the lesser studio, yet Carl Laemmle spared no expense in making what became one of the greatest antiwar movies in history. It cost $1.5 million, but the salary figures are revealing. Newcomer Lew Ayres in the leading role of Paul Baumer earned $200 a week for thirteen weeks, thus making $2,600. While Louis Wolheim was a fine actor, the role of Sergeant Katczinsky was really a supporting one. But Wolheim, who had been in the business since 1919, made $3,500 a week, working only seven weeks (all his part required of him).

All Quiet was not even Universal's first million-dollar movie; there had been others—*Foolish Wives* (1922), *Uncle Tom's Cabin* (1927), and *Broadway* (1929). Columbia, by contrast, would not be moving into seven-digit budgets until mid-decade.

While longevity and experience were factors in determining actors' salaries, they were not the only ones, as Jean Arthur discovered when she concluded that her salary had remained the same for three years. Arthur was a Columbia contract player, one of its best known, and contract players do not necessarily get the same salary as freelancers, even when both appear in the same picture. Usually, "outside talent" received better pay than contract talent. For *The Talk of the Town*, Ronald Colman and Cary Grant, the outside talent, earned $100,000 and $106,250, respectively, while Arthur got $50,000, even though she worked forty-seven days, in contrast to Grant's thirty-three and Colman's forty-five. In Arthur's next Columbia movie, *The More the Merrier*, Joel McCrea was the outside talent; he made $75,000, while Arthur was given her usual $50,000.[6]

The same situation prevailed throughout the industry. In 1940, Ida

Lupino was not yet a Warners regular when she was signed for *They Drive by Night*. Humphrey Bogart and Ann Sheridan, however, were members of the Warners stock company. Lupino made $10,000; Bogart a little more ($11,200); Sheridan received only $6,000. When Charles Coburn was hired for Warners' *In This Our Life* (1942), he was considered "borrowed talent," yet he made $20,000 in a featured role, while Olivia DeHavilland, contract talent, received $19,905 for a costarring part.

Freelancers could do extremely well for themselves, as Claudette Colbert and Barbara Stanwyck discovered. Both of them avoided long-term contracts, preferring at the most multiple-picture deals. Nor did a film have to be a major one for stars to receive high salaries. When Myrna Loy and Don Ameche, who had been associated with MGM and Fox, respectively, went over to Universal for the forgettable *So Goes My Love* (1945), the studio felt honored and compensated them handsomely—$150,000 for Loy, $100,000 for Ameche. *Casbah* (1948) is not an especially memorable Universal title, but in 1948 Tony Martin was a major recording artist who had also done a few pictures; for his services he was paid $50,000, while his costar, Yvonne DeCarlo, then under contract to the studio, received about half that amount.

In 1948 Universal was also delighted to sign Fredric March for two pictures: *An Act of Murder* and *Another Part of the Forest*. As important a role as Marcus Hubbard is in *Forest*, that of his daughter Regina is its equal. Regina, in fact, was the role that brought Patricia Neal to Hollywood after she scored such a success in the 1946 stage production. Yet Ann Blyth, who played Regina in the film (and had been at Universal since 1944), received $25,000 in contrast to March's $100,000.

Columbia's philosophy of compensation conformed to the industry's; it also worked to Columbia's advantage. A preponderance of movies with stars of lesser magnitude, balanced by AA pictures with Hollywood's elite, kept the studio in the black. What Columbia did was not much different from what regional theaters and opera houses often do: hire guest artists at a salary higher than what they pay company regulars. But if a guest artist or soloist can sell out the house, the result is worth it.

Certainly it was worth paying Claudette Colbert twice her Paramount salary ($25,000 in 1934) to get her for *It Happened One Night*. Hoping Columbia would find her demand unreasonable, she discovered the studio was willing to meet it. What Colbert did not know was that at the same time Columbia was negotiating with her, it was about to sign Grace Moore for *One Night of Love* for the same figure, $50,000.

The salaries paid to Colbert and Moore were justified. Colbert imparted sophistication as well as vulnerability to the role of Ellie; Jean Arthur, who was also considered for the part, might have done the same, although it is hard to imagine Arthur, the quintessential working woman, as an heiress. As for *One Night of Love*, it represents an unusually intelligent—for Hollywood—integration of opera and plot.

With Jean Arthur salary was an obsession. When she came to Columbia in 1934, she showed the kind of versatility associated with stock company performers. She could do drama (*Whirlpool, Only Angels Have Wings*), but her forte was romantic comedy, for which the 1930s were famous. When she was cast in a comedy that was a bit screwball, she could be wacky yet irrepressibly feminine. But what was so appealing about Arthur was her naturalness. One had the feeling she spoke the same way off the screen as she did on. As the 1940s began, Arthur was getting Colbert's 1934 salary ($50,000), which, comparatively, was not low. Of Columbia's contract players, she was one of the highest paid. Had Arthur known what stars were getting elsewhere, she might not have been so disappointed. Even at MGM there were disparities. If one was an MGM newcomer, as Janet Leigh was when she did *Hills of Home* (1948), the paycheck would reflect it: $3,200 for Leigh as opposed to $54,933 for the movie's true star, Lassie.

The other extreme at MGM was the movie costarring its regulars, one or two of whom might not be the box office draws they had been earlier. When Van Johnson, Elizabeth Taylor, and Walter Pidgeon made *The Last Time I Saw Paris* (1956), only Taylor could truly be called a star. Yet all three made about the same: $104,000 (Johnson), $100,714 (Taylor), and $98,831 (Pidgeon in a supporting role).

If Arthur yearned to belong to the MGM family, she might have considered that MGM did not make her kind of picture. And if she wanted to make Colbert's salary, she should have adopted Colbert's philosophy. Arthur spent most of her career at Columbia. While Colbert favored Paramount, she had a flexible enough arrangement with the studio to allow her to accept other offers. Thus, in 1934, the same year Colbert did *It Happened One Night* for Columbia, she starred in Universal's *Imitation of Life*, working 8⅓ weeks on a film that cost twice as much as *It Happened One Night* and netted her almost twice what she got for the Capra film: $90,277.75. If 1934 was a very good year for Colbert, 1935 was even better. One of the five Oscars for *It Happened One Night* went to her for best actress.

Ordinarily stars made more money on a freelance basis than they could as contract players. In the 1950s, Colbert's last decade on the big screen, she made a couple of pictures for Universal. No longer able to command her old salary (at her peak in 1944 she received $265,000 for *Since You Went Away*[7]), she managed to get $75,000 for *Thunder on the Hill* (1951). Her costar was Ann Blyth, still a Universal contract player and getting less than the outside talent. Blyth, in fact, was getting only $2,000

Above: Joan Perry, a Columbia contract player and Harry's second wife, in a pose reminiscent of the logo that became standard by 1936. Below, the most familiar form of the Columbia logo, which was periodically modified but never discarded. Both from Academy of Motion Picture Arts and Sciences.

Frank Capra going over the script of *It Happened One Night* (1934) with
Claudette Colbert and Clark Gable. Museum of Modern Art Film Stills
Archive.

Left: Rosalind Russell on the set of *This Thing Called Love* (1941) with legendary cinematographer Joseph Walker, and director Alexander Hall looking dapper in a pin-stripe suit. Private collection.

Below: Russell with her hairdresser and maid on the set of *My Sister Eileen* (1942), as Hall looks on. Private collection.

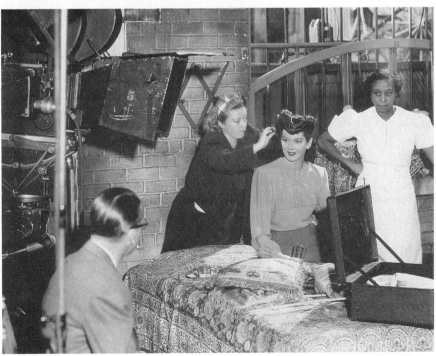

Right: Harry on the set of *You Were Never Lovelier* (1942) with Rita Hayworth and Fred Astaire. Courtesy of Paul Lazarus.

Below: The stars and director of *The Desperadoes* (1943) at Columbia's Burbank Ranch, where westerns were filmed; left to right, Randolph Scott, Evelyn Keyes, director Charles Vidor, Glenn Ford, and Edgar Buchanan. Private collection.

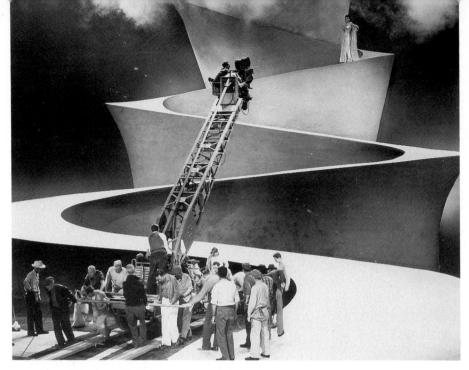

Above: Shooting the production number in *Cover Girl* (1944) that required Rita Hayworth to rush down a winding ramp. Below: Broderick Crawford (left), William Holden, and Judy Holliday rehearsing the stage version of *Born Yesterday* (1950), which Harry insisted be performed before a live audience at the studio prior to filming. Both from Museum of Modern Art Film Stills Archive.

Four of Columbia's best known contract players were Rosalind Russell, Marguerite Chapman, Evelyn Keyes, and Kim Novak.

Russell (above) made some of her best comedies for Harry, a man she described in her autobiography, *Life Is a Banquet*, as having "quite remarkable taste." Marguerite Chapman (right) was a talented actress who worked mainly in Columbia's B unit in the 1940s. Both from private collections.

Evelyn Keyes (above) spent a decade at the studio (1940-51) until Harry's obsessiveness drove her to break her contract. Although the publicity still below is from MGM's *The Legend of Lylah Clare* (1968), Kim Novak made her best films at Columbia between 1954 and 1962, thanks to Harry's belief in her star quality. Both from private collections.

Harry's official studio portrait, with the subject appropriately spotlighted. Museum of Modern Art Film Stills Archive.

more than she had in 1948—$27,000, although her part was equal to Colbert's.

If Jean Arthur was getting $50,000 a picture in the early 1940s, she was not doing badly. In fact, she was making almost as much as Bette Davis at Warners. Davis is an interesting example of a star one would have thought earned more than she actually did; but then, seventeen years (1932-49) of her career were spent at Warners. For her Oscar-winning performance in *Dangerous* (1935), admittedly a consolation prize for losing the previous year for *Of Human Bondage*, Davis received a paltry $13,616, while her director, Alfred E. Green, made twice that amount. In 1934, over at Universal, Chester Morris and Wynne Gibson made more for two forgettable flicks: $15,000 each for *Let's Talk It Over* and *I Give My Love*, respectively. In 1939 when Davis played Elizabeth to Errol Flynn's Essex (*Private Lives of Elizabeth and Essex*), the budget breakdown identifies Flynn as the star, and his salary shows it—$41,300 compared to Davis's $35,000. While Davis's salary had been increasing, it was not very different from Arthur's.

If Davis made more in 1941 than she had in previous years, it was because Warners was so eager to get Gary Cooper for *Sergeant York* that they loaned Davis to Goldwyn for *The Little Foxes* in return for Cooper, who was under contract to Goldwyn. Cooper won an Oscar for his performance; Davis received a nomination, losing to Joan Fontaine for *Suspicion*. Yet Regina Giddens is one of Davis's greatest roles; it also earned her three times her Warners salary.

By 1955, Jean Arthur had retired from the screen. Bette Davis had not and, in fact, would continue to act well into the 1980s despite a mastectomy and a stroke. Still, among the many ironies for which the film industry is famous is Davis's failure to repeat her success in *All about Eve* (1950). In 1955 she returned to Columbia, having not been there since 1932 when she did *The Menace*. She was replacing Mary Pickford in *Storm Center* (1956) at Jean Arthur's 1942-43 salary, $50,000.

In 1942, the only Columbia contract player who did better than Jean Arthur was Rita Hayworth, and that was the result of her appearing on a *Life* cover in March 1941 in a pose that would soon rival Betty Grable's in her white bathing suit and over-the-shoulder beckoning glance. Before Hayworth became a pinup, she was getting $300 a week at Columbia—$100 more than she had made at Republic in 1938.[8] Once Hayworth became a celebrity, her salary was raised to $800 a week for *You'll Never Get Rich* (1941) and *You Were Never Lovelier* (1942), both with Fred Astaire and requiring eight and twelve weeks, respectively, to film. Ten years later, Hayworth was averaging around $12,500 a week—or $150,000 a picture—at a time when her fame was ebbing.

Like the other studio heads, Harry knew there could never be a uniform pay scale; to get outside talent, he would not only have to pay more but sometimes even offer an additional sum that could go as high as 75 percent of the star's salary. But Harry could do the same to his competitors: by loaning out Hayworth to Warners for *Affectionately Yours* and *The Strawberry Blonde* (both 1941), and to Fox for *Blood and Sand* (1941) and *My Gal Sal* (1942), he did as well as Jack Warner when he exchanged Bette Davis for Gary Cooper. When Kim Novak became one of Columbia's last contract players, Harry did to her what he had done to Hayworth: he loaned her to Otto Preminger for *The Man with the Golden Arm* (1955) and to Alfred Hitchcock for *Vertigo* (1958). At the time Novak did *The Man with the Golden Arm*, she was making $750 a week at Columbia; Harry agreed to loan her to Preminger for $100,000.[9] Naturally, not all of it went to Novak, who was still under contract to Columbia at her 1955 salary. After all, she had been in the business only since 1954.

As soon as Harry became head of production, he knew there would have to be a broad range of contracts—from no frills to all the amenities (and then some).[10] The most basic Columbia contract—the kind Jacqueline Logan was offered in 1927—called for the actor to (1) furnish his/her wardrobe except in the case of a period film, for which the studio would provide the appropriate costumes; (2) accede to Columbia's right to "make alterations, changes, substitutions, additions and eliminations in the scenario or picture"; (3) return to work at the same salary for retakes or additional scenes, if necessary; (4) accept the policy of employment "subject to cancellation . . . or termination . . . if production is stopped or postponed"; (5) realize that if location shooting is necessary, "salary is not paid for time consumed in travel unless artist or employee has actually started work on the picture before leaving"; (6) understand that a week is defined as "seven actual working days," and that, if engaged for only one picture, salary commences the day one begins working and ends the day one's part is finished.

Logan, who was never much of a star, made four films for Columbia at $2,000 a week, each film taking about two weeks to make. Priscilla Dean did better: a four-picture contract at $6,500 a picture. The same year Bert Lytell was given a two-film deal with a guarantee of at least two weeks for each film; his weekly salary was higher than Logan's, $2,500. In 1928 Helene Chadwick got less than Logan or Lytell: $1,200 a week for three pictures. Chadwick, however, received other concessions. Columbia provided "all wardrobe necessary for any parts" and, because "her talents and abilities . . . are rare, excellent, unique, uncommon and . . . extraordinary," the studio also paid her traveling and living expenses when she went on location.

Among Hollywood's apocrypha is the making of *The Blood Ship* (1927),

Columbia's first film to play New York's Roxy, "the cathedral of motion pictures" and the grandest venue in Manhattan until Radio City Music Hall opened six years later. Supposedly, a once-successful-now-washed-up actor, Hobart Bosworth, bought the rights to the novel and, after failing to interest other studios in it, turned to Columbia, offering the property free on the condition that he play the lead. Bosworth did play the lead, but he was compensated for it—doubly, in fact. Columbia did not do badly, either, in acquiring both a property and a performer. Columbia paid $11,250 for the rights, but that amount also included Bosworth's salary.

Before Fay Wray became the bride of Kong, she was worth only $1,200 a week—a "week" defined as six working days, one less for her because she had already appeared in a few leads before she did *King Kong* (1933) at RKO. Unlike Jacqueline Logan, who had to come up with her own wardrobe, and Billie Dove, whose 1926 contract required her to furnish "one evening gown, one evening wrap, one negligee, and one street dress" (with the studio providing the rest), Fay had to worry only about "shoes, stockings and undergarments." Since *Kong* was due to open when she signed her 9 March 1933 contract, Fay considered herself important enough to strike out "shoes" and "stockings." Underwear was enough. Like other freelancers who returned periodically to Columbia, (Loretta Young, Rosalind Russell, Humphrey Bogart) Fay came back for two more pictures in 1934. By that time she was known as the quintessential screamer, and her salary went up to $1,750 a week.

In 1933, Irene Dunne's reputation did not rest on a single film, as Fay Wray's did, but on several illustrating a talent versatile enough to encompass comedy (*Bachelor Apartment* [1931]) and drama (*Back Street* and *Symphony of Six Million* [1932], *The Silver Cord* [1933]); two years later, she would add musical comedy to her list of accomplishments with *Roberta* (1935). Since Dunne was another star without a home studio, preferring multipicture arrangements with RKO and later Universal, Columbia offered her a three-picture deal (13 June 1935) at a graduated salary: $65,000 for the first, $75,000 for the second, and $85,000 for the third, payable in seven equal weekly installments.[11]

At first Dunne was pleased with the setup. Columbia offered her more than she got that year at Universal, where she made *Magnificent Obsession*, for which she was paid $42,000. Before coming to Columbia, however, she made another film for Universal, the legendary *Show Boat* (1936), for which she received more than twice that amount, over $94,000. Still, she signed with Columbia and satisfied two-thirds of her contract with *Theodora Goes Wild* (1936) and *The Awful Truth* (1937). The last was to have been *First Woman Doctor*, which was never made because Dunne did not like the script—or by now Columbia. When she went back to RKO for

Joy of Living (1938) and *My Favorite Wife* (1940), Sam Briskin reminded her that she owed Columbia another movie. She returned for *Penny Serenade* (1941), for which she received $85,000 and for which Cary Grant, her *Awful Truth* costar, got $100,000. *Penny Serenade* proved to be less painful than she thought, and Dunne returned a few years later for *Together Again* (1944) and *Over 21* (1945).

The films Irene Dunne made for Columbia were well worth her salary. *Theodora Goes Wild* and *The Awful Truth* are acknowledged screwball classics, and *Penny Serenade*, a television perennial, has been known to make optimists of cynics.

Clara Bow, on the other hand, would not have been worth the $100,000 Harry offered her in 1931 when her career was two movies short of ending.[12] Harry was no doubt influenced by a trial that year that revealed intimate details of Bow's private life, including her addiction to gambling and alcohol, her expensive gifts to lovers, and her affairs with Clark Gable and Victor Fleming. Unfortunately, Bow entrusted the negotiations to Sam Rork, a former movie executive who had seen better days; Rork ingratiated himself with the actress, persuading her to sign a contract with him that called for a cash advance. Since Rork was courting other studios at the same time, he never delivered the signed contract to Columbia within the prescribed fifteen days. Thus Bow never made a movie for Harry and went off to Fox for her last two films, *Call Her Savage* (1932) and *Hoopla* (1935).

Columbia never lost its sense of insecurity even after its emergence as a major studio. In one way, Harry's brash exterior, which masked an inferiority complex, worked to Columbia's advantage. Columbia would have to work harder to get talent and offer them better deals than they could get elsewhere. In many cases, the pictures that stars from other studios did at Columbia were as important to their careers as any they made on their home lots. While Humphrey Bogart is remembered primarily for his Warners movies, his best performance of the World War II years, except for *Casablanca* (1942), was in Columbia's *Sahara* (1943), released the same year as Warners' *Action in the North Atlantic*, in which Bogart played a merchant seaman. Both had scripts by John Howard Lawson; both had vaguely Marxist overtones (antifascist speeches, paeans to brotherhood). Bogart, miscast in *North Atlantic*, had a role that fitted him perfectly in *Sahara* and allowed him to deepen his persona of the cool yet deeply concerned isolato, whose armorlike jaw and world-weary eyes were his only defense against life's slings and arrows.

If James Stewart returned to Columbia after *Mr. Smith Goes to Washington*, it was for films that allowed him to extend his range in a way that his work with Hitchcock, *Vertigo* excepted, did not. When Stewart came back to Columbia in the 1950s, it was for the superior Anthony Mann western *The Man from Laramie* (1955), the elegant comedy *Bell, Book and Candle* (1958), and one of the best courtroom dramas ever filmed, *Anatomy of a Murder* (1959).

To Harry, getting the right star was more important than what the star cost. If the star cost more than what had been budgeted, the figures could be revised or the money allocated differently to absorb the star's salary. Although New York argued that it would be cheaper to make *Counter-Attack* with Alexander Knox than with Paul Muni, Harry demurred: "Are you thinking of today or . . . the future. I personally only think of the future" (27 January 1944 teletype). To Harry, it was a case of win or lose: win with Muni or lose with Knox. While *Counter-Attack* was released too close to the end of the war to have much impact, it was Muni's performance that gave the film whatever success it had. Knox, ideal as the unregenerate Nazi in *None Shall Escape* (1944), would not have made a good Russian partisan. Although Muni received $120,000 for the film, which cost Columbia $200,000 more to make with him than it would have with Knox (who owed the studio another movie anyway), Harry, notorious for his economizing, would never subscribe to the principle that cheaper is better.

Naturally, Columbia would have had an easier time breaking into the majors if it had had the Warner Bros. stock company or the MGM galaxy, if it had had Universal's acreage in the San Fernando Valley or Paramount's theater chain. But it had none of these assets. Although the absence of a theater circuit meant Columbia was unaffected by the consent decrees that forced studios with theaters to give them up, it made Columbia more dependent on exhibitors than studios with their own theaters. It also meant that in cities where Columbia did not have a branch office (but, say, Warners did), a Columbia movie would have to be screened in a Warners projection room if Columbia wanted the film booked on the Warners circuit. It may not have been a degrading experience, but it certainly was illuminating. The alternative was to arrange a preview at a local theater; that, however, would have been insulting to Warners.

If it was difficult to change CBC's Corned Beef and Cabbage image to Columbia Pictures, it was just as difficult to keep the lady with the torch from falling off her pedestal. One way of keeping her upright was to bring the "indies" to Gower Street.

There were always independent producers in Hollywood; some of them—Carl Laemmle and the Cohns, for example—ended up running studios and thus became part of the establishment, eventually playing landlord to a new generation of indies. Historically, United Artists was the haven for independents wanting to live up to their name and achieve a freedom that would be difficult within the studio system. UA, however, had its dark side: botched distribution deals, disputes with the board, suits and countersuits; thus many independents discovered they could fare better elsewhere, as Walter Wanger did at Universal and Sol Lesser at Fox. While there would be a loss of autonomy and greater risk (a film might never go beyond the draft stage), there would also be cash advances—perhaps not much but enough to begin developing the property—and superior exploitation. And since no one has complete autonomy in the movie business, any diminution of authority was offset by the prospect of shared profits and buyouts if the producer wished to sell his or her interest in the film.

In 1935 Harry added a new category to Columbia's Record of Releases: Outside Productions. No two production deals were exactly the same, if for no other reason than that no two budgets were. Still, none were so personalized as those of the 1980s, when a movie with the Columbia trademark could mean anything from a total financial commitment to a minimal one to a straight distribution deal. At least during Harry's tenure there was one constant: a high overhead. Until the early 1940s, Columbia charged outside producers a 20 percent overhead, which usually—but not always—came out to $2,000 per shooting (i.e., ten-hour) day. Some producers could get the daily rate, as Lester Cowan did for *Ladies in Retirement* (1941), but most accepted, however grudgingly, the 20 percent. Much, of course, depended on such considerations as whether the film would be wholly financed by Columbia or, as was generally the case, whether the producer could secure a bank loan for 50 to 60 percent of the estimated cost; the consequences of the film's going over budget and/or schedule; provisions for indirect charges; the distribution arrangement in terms of domestic and foreign grosses; whether the profits would be realized before or after costs had been recouped; and, very important, whether the profits were gross or net.

Although it is impossible to document every outside production, the teletypes provide enough examples of preliminary deals, and a few final ones, to show how Harry, always eager for product, treated those who could deliver it.

A 3 August 1948 teletype about a possible independent deal with Mickey Rooney makes it clear that Harry's primary consideration was a financial arrangement commensurate with the project or, if a star was involved, the star's stature. While the nature of the Rooney project is unknown, discussions between New York and Los Angeles centered on Rooney's audience appeal, which in 1948 was considerably less than it had been when he was Andy Hardy and young Tom Edison. But what mattered to Harry was that Rooney came from MGM; to get someone from the studio he envied, Harry was prepared to listen.

Harry's preference seems to have been a fifty-fifty deal, with a bank loan covering the independent's share. Such an arrangement might seem equitable on the surface; but, as New York informed Harry, Rooney's last two pictures, *Killer McCoy* (1947) and *Summer Holiday* (1948), were "doing badly or spotty at best." Sensing that Columbia would be taking a chance with Rooney, New York argued for "a deal quite favorable to us." The deal would have required Rooney to put up 59 percent of his 50 percent, thereby minimizing Columbia's risk. If for some reason Rooney could not match Columbia's 50 percent, New York had another suggestion. Suppose the film was budgeted at $1 million; the bank would put up $600,000; Columbia, $250,000; and Rooney, $150,000. While on paper this arrangement seemed to favor Columbia, which would then get 62½ percent (with Rooney and the bank getting 37½ percent), it also meant that Columbia could not recoup its investment until the bank recouped its.

Although Rooney made a few minor films for Columbia in the 1950s (and directed *My True Story* [1951] for the studio), the 1948 deal never materialized. Yet the arrangement New York preferred makes one wonder how many so-called 50-50 deals required an independent to put up 59 percent of his half over and above the bank loan. It was much easier when the production company got just 25 percent of the net profits, as Rita Hayworth's Beckworth Corporation did, or when Columbia's investment was minimal, as with 10 percent in Louis de Rochement's *Walk a Crooked Mile* (1948) and *Whistle at Eaton Falls* (1951) plus a 50-50 share of the profits.

In June 1943, Harry was eager to add Sam Wood's name to Columbia's roster of independents. Wood, who had both produced and directed *For Whom the Bell Tolls* at Paramount, was interested in a similar arrangement at Columbia. It was to have been a two-picture deal, the first being the anti-Nazi drama *Address Unknown* (1944), starring his daughter, K.T. Stevens, and budgeted at $400,000. A bank loan would cover 60 percent of the estimated cost, with Columbia putting up the rest. The distribution terms would be 25 percent domestic, 30 percent British, and 40 percent foreign, with the remaining monies divided 60-40 after costs were recouped.

Although *Address Unknown* was made with Stevens, it was directed by William Cameron Menzies. The Wood deal never materialized, perhaps because it involved not the usual 20 percent but a 23 percent overhead. Columbia wanted to increase the overhead for outside productions to bring it in line with its own overhead, which included direct or staff charges (salaries and expenses of the various departments) that could amount to an additional 10 percent, thereby explaining why Columbia's own overhead was around 31 percent. But billing the independents for expenses Columbia might or might not encounter with its own films, such as writeoffs or abandoned projects, would be illegal.

Always conscious of litigation, New York realized the inequity and proposed a 23 percent overhead exclusive of staff charges. This was essentially the arrangement Columbia made with Pat O'Brien's company, Terneen, for *Secret Command* (1944). Columbia agreed to raise the negative cost from $350,000 to $380,000, allow for $50,000 over budget instead of $35,000, and authorize a 40 percent distribution deal with 50 percent of the net profits. But the tradeoff was 23 percent overhead.

Columbia also wanted a flat 23 percent for consistency's sake. Dealmaking has always involved concessions that, if granted, can undermine studio policy and result in films so personalized that the studio's identity is threatened. It was not coincidental that the 23 percent overhead coincided with Harry's dissatisfaction with Gregory Ratoff, who gave Columbia three outside productions, *The Men in Her Life* (1941), *Something to Shout About* (1943), and *The Heat's On* (1943). The last was Mae West's first film since *My Little Chickadee* (1940); it proved to be a failure.

Although Harry should have realized that the 1940s would not be the era of Mae West (who, after *The Heat's On*, did not appear on the screen again until 1970), Ratoff must have been persuasive enough to get a contract giving him complete control of casting and script, as well as an overhead considerably lower than the (then) 20 percent because he would be making minimal use of Columbia's facilities. "Ratoff shoots his pictures off the cuff," Los Angeles complained to New York (21 September 1943). "You can't even follow him on his costs. In addition he shoves every Russian that's around Hollywood in his pics."

After attending a preview of *The Heat's On*, Harry decided to buy Ratoff out. "The hicks may remember Mae West but the preview houses don't," Harry noted (21 October 1943). "This picture is going to be a bust." The public concurred.

Even with a 23 percent overhead, producers could negotiate in other areas. Harry was often so desperate to get a property, particularly a hit Broadway play, that Los Angeles would make a deal that would infuriate New York—for example, making a financial commitment to George Abbott and F. Hugh Herbert for their second film when they had not even made their first. The first was an adaptation of Herbert's Broadway hit *Kiss and Tell*, which George Abbott had produced on the stage. Because it was such a popular play, New York relented and offered Abbott and Herbert 75 percent of the net profits of the movie version. If they accepted the terms, Columbia would not be obligated to a second film; but if the men wanted a second film, as they did, the arrangement would be the same for both: 50 percent of the net. Even with such a compromise, Columbia was at a disadvantage: the *Kiss and Tell* deal included a provision that allowed Abbott and Herbert to recoup $350,000 before Columbia would realize any profits.

When it came time to consider the second film, the previously discussed *Snafu,* Harry was apprehensive; even though the great George Abbott had directed *Snafu* on Broadway, it was still an inferior play. It was bad enough that the rights alone cost $200,000; but $30,000 for the script was outrageous, especially since the script for *My Sister Eileen* (1942), based on a far better play, had cost only $35,000. When the *Snafu* team would not lower their price, a maximum budget of $500,000 was imposed, with Columbia's investment set at $200,000 and a 50-50 share of the profits—but no recouping provisions. Instead, Columbia would recoup its costs, including overhead and distribution, *before* the net profits were shared. It made little difference; *Snafu* came and went.

Harry's relationship with independent producers was one of caution; it was founded on suspicions (not entirely groundless) that arose even before the contract was signed. The producer was out to work the best deal and gain as much control of the film as possible. Conversely, Harry wanted to limit the producer's authority and financial latitude, the latter being especially important since a carelessly executed contract could entitle a producer to a cash advance before principal photography commenced. Harry adopted an "only passing through" attitude: the studio was permanent; producers were not. Thus Harry tried to get as much out of them as he could, and vice versa.

At first Lester Cowan thought he could have his way at Columbia. Although the credits for *The Whole Town's Talking* (1935) cite Cowan as producer, the film was not an independent production. It was produced and directed by John Ford. Cowan's involvement must have been minimal. Yet Cowan thought of himself as a producer, not someone who sticks to the shooting schedule and keeps to the budget; he also considered himself on a par with Wallis, Selznick, and Goldwyn. "[Cowan] has ideas of grandeur, considering himself as good as Wallis, which naturally is a joke," Harry told New York (6 August 1945) when Cowan was pushing another of his schemes.[13]

Lester Cowan was not Hal B. Wallis, but he was doing what every producer has always done: he was making a pitch. *Ladies in Retirement* was a successful melodrama of the 1939-40 season; it was a single-set play with a thrilling first-act curtain where the main character, to prevent her sisters from being institutionalized, strangles her employer while the employer is playing the piano. Gilbert Miller had produced the play on Broadway, and Cowan wanted to produce it for Columbia. In 1941 Harry knew *Ladies in Retirement* could only enhance Columbia's reputation, and if Cowan could help, there was room for him at the studio. Cowan, however, did not know what lay in store.

At first Harry was obliging; he even agreed to an overhead calculated on a daily basis because that was the arrangement Cowan had had at Benedict Bogeaus's General Service Studios, which the independents considered their special facility. Cowan's overhead would be $2,000 per shooting day covering services and equipment, exclusive of sets and labor, which Columbia provided for its own films.

Since there was always the possibility a project might not reach fruition or that its cost could skyrocket, a penalty clause was added to Cowan's contract, to the effect that if *Ladies in Retirement* went over the proposed $300,000 budget, Cowan's $40,000 stake in the film would be reduced proportionately, dollar-by-dollar, so that, if it ended up costing $340,000, Cowan would not get a producer's fee but only a share of the profits. Cowan agreed to the terms; risk-taking went with the territory. So did a thick skin. In order to put up his share, Cowan had to take out a loan. But the proceeds from the loan were made payable to Columbia; Harry was taking no chances.

As it happened, *Ladies in Retirement*, a fine blend of gothic and noir, was respectably viewed. Encouraged, Cowan went ahead with *Commandos Strike at Dawn* (1942). Again he had to scramble for funds to put the package together: $500,000 budget with deferred compensation for himself and the star, Paul Muni, who agreed to $75,000 plus 50 percent of Cowan's profits. This time Cowan was treated like any other independent: he was given a flat 20 percent overhead instead of the $2,000-a-day that he would have preferred.

Like any producer, Cowan took a personal interest in his film, so much so that he devised his own advertising campaign for *Commandos*, thereby antagonizing New York, which bluntly informed him he was inadequate to the task. He was also denied the right of final cut; his jurisdiction over the editing ended, he was told, after the second preview. Moreover, he could not get the writer he wanted, Dudley Nichols. Why pay Nichols $75,000 when Irwin Shaw was available for $18,000?

Cowan regarded *Commandos* as his bid for the big time: a war epic with exteriors shot in British Columbia doubling as occupied Norway, where the action is set. Originally, Cowan planned to do most of the filming on location, thereby avoiding Columbia's overhead by shooting some interiors at General Service Studios; he assumed that Columbia, always short of space and frequently renting it elsewhere, would not object. While Harry sanctioned the location shooting, he was able to find Cowan a soundstage on Gower Street, having no intention of losing the overhead.

It was Cowan's great dream to produce a musical. In 1942, the trades carried an announcement, which surprised Jack Cohn, that Columbia had bought the rights to *Best Foot Forward*, the next Lester Cowan production for the studio. The idea was not that far-fetched; Cowan thought of the 1941 show as a vehicle for Rita Hayworth, who had already made two musicals for Columbia with Fred Astaire and was the studio's only musical comedy star. Harry was interested enough to offer $100,000 for the rights, but MGM, the logical studio to do the movie version, bid $125,000. Cowan began to wheel and deal, enlisting the support of George Abbott, whom he had apparently talked into being the movie's executive producer if the deal went through. When New York got wind of a possible kickback if Columbia went to $125,000 (Abbott would compensate Cowan, who swore that whatever he received would go to Columbia), New York did not equivocate: it had no intention of getting involved in Cowan's financial convolutions. Furthermore, the play's producers were less than impressed with Cowan, and the film ended up an Arthur Freed production at MGM, where it belonged, and with Lucille Ball in a role more suited to her talents than to Hayworth's. But there was a happy ending: in a rare gesture of magnanimity, MGM agreed to loan Gene Kelly out for *Cover Girl* so Columbia would not feel it had lost face.

Cowan was not giving up. He found a play (*Heart of a City*) about London's Windmill Theatre, which had remained open during the Blitz. He was given a paltry $7,500 to develop the property, which eventually became *Tonight and Every Night* (1945). Harry turned down all of Cowan's suggestions, especially his choice of Groucho Marx and Gracie Fields in the leads. He then decided to remove Cowan from the project completely, buying out his interests in *Ladies in Retirement* and *Commandos Strike at Dawn* and encouraging him to use the money to set up his own company, perhaps even releasing through Columbia. "With [Cowan] out I would make [the film] with Hayworth," Harry told New York. And that is exactly what he did.

When one realizes how little money was at stake with *Heart of the City* and how determined Harry was to get it back, one can easily see why Columbia stayed in the black, even during the Great Depression. Wresting the property from Cowan cost the studio $13,250, but it also cost Cowan $2,500. He was allowed to keep his piddling $7,500, the same amount that had been paid to Seton I. Miller for his work on the script. But since Cowan had involved Miller in the project, Cowan owed Columbia $2,500 for Miller's services—the $2,500 coming out of Cowan's $7,500. Thus Miller, who got no screen credit for *Tonight and Every Night*, made out better than Cowan.

Harry was delighted to see the end of Lester Cowan: "Does it mean he is finished with our company as far as any future productions are concerned?" Harry asked New York (1 February 1943). When New York responded in the affirmative, Harry added: "Advise me minute deal is concluded so we can toss that mob out of his offices and use them."

But Cowan would not give up on Columbia. Although he never

worked there again, he kept coming up with ideas. Harry, always the gambler, was willing to listen, and by 1945 they were talking overhead again. Cowan, still obsessed with producing a musical, had his eyes on a song-and-dance version of *Theodora Goes Wild*. But Harry, knowing Cowan's habit of pitting New York against Los Angeles, informed the New York office that all it was to say to Lester Cowan was "hello." New York obeyed.

No two independent producers at Columbia were accorded the same treatment. How one fared depended on two factors: the deal one was able to cut and the product one was able to deliver. Sam Katzman encountered few of Lester Cowan's problems. Born on New York's Lower East Side, Katzman began in the business when it was still centered in the East and when Fort Lee, New Jersey, was America's film capital, with studios on Main Street and Linwood Avenue in an area where dusty roads doubled as western trails and the Hudson Palisades provided the perfect setting for cliffhangers.

Perhaps it was Katzman's background that made it easier for him to negotiate with Harry; perhaps, too, it was the kind of film Katzman made. He had no pretensions about making important movies when he arrived at Columbia in 1943. His forte was the serial and the programmer: entertainment for the Saturday matinee crowd at the local Bijou. For serials, Katzman would invest a total of $50,000, in return for which he would receive a producer's fee (ranging from $3,000 to $6,000 and in some cases $8,000, depending on the serial) before the profits were split—but not before production. He was also given studio space as well as an office. At first Katzman could select his own properties, but by 1948, when some of his movies were grossing poorly (the 1948 releases *I Surrender Dear, Mary Lou,* and *Racing Luck*), Columbia insisted on script approval as well as a different arrangement, similar to the kind it had with Rita Hayworth's Beckworth Corporation: Columbia would do the financing and Katzman would get 25 percent of the profits.

Even though Katzman's movies did nothing to elevate Columbia's stature, he was a favorite son. "We have no desire to hurt him," Los Angeles informed New York (30 September 1948). So Katzman continued releasing through Columbia for two more decades.

The end of World War II saw a number of stars, writers, and directors forming their own production companies. "Going Inc." is not the same as "going hyphenate," where a writer, say, becomes a writer-director to gain greater control of his or her material, as Preston Sturges and Billy Wilder did at Paramount and Joseph L. Mankiewicz did at Fox, or as Alan Alda and Woody Allen did less characteristically by becoming actor-writer-directors. Nor is forming a production company the same as turning producer. When Wilder and Mankiewicz wrote, directed, and produced, they did it within the studio system. Neither formed his own production company; each produced for a studio, the advantage to which was getting an office on the lot (as Wilder did when he made *The Front Page* [1974] for Universal). A writer-director producing for a studio has no distribution worries; those are the studio's concern. Yet distribution has always been one of the main reasons independents link up with a studio. Product, once created, must be delivered.

But product must yield profit. The independents' goal, apart from securing studio space, was not just to have a say in the film but to share its profits. One of the reasons Edward Small enjoyed a long relationship with Columbia (eleven films over seven years), in contrast to Stanley Kramer (twelve over three years, with one hit), was that his films never put a dent in Columbia's coffers.[14] When Small came to Columbia in 1946, he had been an independent producer since the early 1930s, when he cofounded Reliance Productions with Harry M. Goetz, releasing through United Artists. When he went solo with Edward Small Productions, he continued to release through United Artists; but after the war, like other independents, he was eager for a studio affiliation.

In 1946, Columbia offered him an arrangement that allowed for profit-sharing after the studio had recouped its investment. Small's Columbia releases were not as distinguished as those he did for United Artists (*The Count of Monte Cristo* [1934], *The Last of the Mochicans* [1936]) because he was trying to repeat the success of his earlier films by making less expensive equivalents (such as *The Return of Monte Cristo, The Black Arrow, The Brigand*). Casting played a major role in keeping costs down: a male whose name meant something at the box office was paired with a lesser known female, whose salary was commensurate with her drawing power. For *The Return of Monte Cristo* (1946), Louis Hayward received $35,000, while Barbara Britton, whose career had begun three years earlier, got only $7,500. Similarly, for *The Texas Rangers* (1951), George Montgomery's salary was $27,500; Gale Storm's, $4,000. Anthony Dexter's sex appeal netted him $43,000 for *The Brigand* (1951), while Jody Lawrence's merited a mere $5,000. In the case of *Lorna Doone* (1951), Richard Greene and Barbara Hale were more or less on equal footing. Greene had started in pictures in the late 1930s and had now moved to television; Hale's movie work was consistent without being spectacular. Thus he received $20,000; she, $16,500.

Small's films were mostly B films that at least did not look as if they had been made on a shoestring. Although Columbia mistakenly labelled *The Return of Monte Cristo* an AA production, it was really an upgraded B movie that cost $658,284, including overhead, which, in Small's case, was

25 percent. Otherwise, the total direct cost would have been $526,627—less than the $600,000 that had been budgeted. *The Yellow Cab Man* (1948), even with Red Skelton getting $150,000, cost around $900,000, less than it would have if it had been made at Skelton's home studio, MGM.

Small's producer's salary varied from none (*Valentino* [1951]) to $50,000 (*The Fuller Brush Man*); sometimes, it would be deducted from the total cost. There were even greater discrepancies in directors' salaries. As Columbia regulars, Henry Levin and Ray Nazarro received $6,033 and $3,200 for *The Return of Monte Cristo* and *Indian Uprising* (1952), respectively. Phil Karlson, less of a Columbia regular, made a little more—$7,500 for *Lorna Doone*, $9,533 for *The Brigand*. Lewis Allen, associated primarily with Paramount, received a whopping $60,000 for *Valentino*, which brought the total cost to $1.3 million—Small's most expensive movie for Columbia and one of his few failures.

A typical Small film ran around $600,000 with above-the-line costs (script, cast, director) being considerably less than production costs. *The Return of Monte Cristo*, for example, exclusive of overhead, cost $526,627, of which $108,853 went for script, cast, and direction, and the rest for production. Thus, Columbia may not have gotten a film on the order of the classic *Count of Monte Cristo*, but neither did it end up with an embarrassment.

Columbia did well by Small, but not vice versa. When Columbia released some of his films to television in 1957, he voiced his objections, and Columbia bought him out, removing his name from *Valentino*, *The Brigand*, and *Cripple Creek* (1952).

There were independents who were untouchables—admittedly few, but they existed: Sam Katzman for one, Sam Spiegel for another. When Harry began negotiating with Spiegel in 1948, the producer's name was "S.P. Eagle." "Sam Spiegel" did not emerge until 1954. An illegal alien, Spiegel adopted the pseudonym to avoid deportation to his native Poland at the start of World War II. By the end of the war, he had enough connections to circumvent the immigration laws and apply for citizenship.[15] While Spiegel claimed to be apolitical, he had a soft spot for radicals, perhaps because he had known impoverishment and saw the contrast between Hollywood's highlife and Poland's pogroms. On the other hand, Spiegel was never so sympathetic to radicals as to jeopardize his position in the movie business. While in the 1950s it may have seemed noble of him to hire blacklisted writers such as Dalton Trumbo and Michael Wilson, he also got them cheap. Still, his interest in radicalism explains the first film of Horizon Productions, the company he formed with John Huston: *We Were Strangers* (1949), which portrays the events leading to the overthrow of the Machado regime in Cuba in 1933.

When Spiegel failed to interest MGM in the property (his pitch was too streetwise for Louis Mayer), Harry was willing to listen. It would be a coup to have a movie directed by John Huston, who had not yet worked for the studio, nor had the leads, Jennifer Jones and John Garfield. The revolutionary theme did not bother Harry, nor did the rumors that Garfield was a Communist (he was not), which began circulating when the House Committee on un-American Activities began investigating Hollywood politics in the fall of 1947. Harry was also sympathetic to radicals, as long as he did not have to defend them. They may have reminded him of the scrapper in himself. He also knew that the man who functioned as his shadow self, Sidney Buchman, had been a Communist.

Harry, therefore, had no objection to the script, although he loathed the title *China Valdes*, the name of the heroine. It would be *We Were Strangers*, he informed Spiegel and Huston. While neither seemed to care, David O. Selznick did—badly. Jennifer Jones, who was Mrs. Selznick, was playing China.

Any film with Mrs. Selznick that was not a David O. Selznick production was treated as if it were. Selznick, with his mania for memos, fired off his share to Spiegel and Huston, accusing them, among other things, of not having the "guts" to fight for the title of their own movie—a title Selznick dismissed as the inspiration of the "wife of the assistant sales manager in the Buffalo exchange," not knowing its true origin.[16]

Having failed to get the title he wanted, Selznick appealed to Huston's professionalism; he begged him to show more interest in the film, whose rough cut was confusing, overlong, and poorly edited, with misplaced close-ups and inconsistencies in Jones's accent. But Selznick's plea ("You owe it to me and Jennifer") went unheeded. Not only was Huston indifferent to the title; he was also indifferent to the film, which he shot in less than two months, completing it on 26 October 1948. Although *We Were Strangers* was not released until May 1949, by the beginning of February of that year Huston was at MGM making *The Asphalt Jungle* (1950), a more prestigious film at a more prestigious studio.

Harry, who simply wanted the movie to open, dismissed Selznick's eleven-page list of suggestions. Selznick, whose standards made him one of Hollywood's greatest producers, berated Harry for his lack of them, reminding Harry that "any studio that is indifferent . . . pays the price of being discriminated against, in the choice of assignments by stars and directors, who have some integrity of endeavor, and some standards in relation to their own work." Standards were not the point; *We Were Strangers* was unsalvageable. For all its antifascist fervor, the film did not even identify the freedom fighters' politics, which were obvious enough for right-wingers to call the movie Marxist propaganda.

David O. Selznick Productions had no releases in 1949. Columbia had more than fifty; one was *We Were Strangers,* a movie Harry disliked, a view shared by audiences and critics.

Horizon fared much better in the 1950s when it provided Columbia with two of its greatest films, *On the Waterfront* (1954) and *The Bridge on the River Kwai* (1957), both of which Harry disliked because he had no control over them. To Spiegel, whose pockets got progressively deeper, Columbia was merely Horizon's distributor.

Other production companies gave Columbia films that varied in quality: Sidney Buchman Enterprises, Beckworth Corporation, and Phoenix, for example. Since these three can be discussed with some degree of accuracy, they are used as examples.

When Sidney Buchman decided to become a producer in 1944, he had already been assistant head of production. The teletypes of 1942-43 show that when New York called Los Angeles, Buchman was often at the other end. When New York complained to Buchman about the Rosalind Russell film *What a Woman!* (1943), criticizing the excessive close-ups of Russell and suggesting a dissolve at a certain point, Buchman, who shared New York's belief that "the success of the pic . . . depends on the speed which it is cut to" (16 November 1943), argued against the dissolve; it would only be "dead feet." As a former playwright, Buchman thought in acts and knew how they should be cut so the movie could "go like a shot." He had inherited Harry's sense of pace, which was the result of effective editing. But Buchman also knew moviemaking; when New York suggested how a scene in *What a Woman!* could be improved through a close-up and a wild line, Buchman did it in place of Irving Cummings, the director.

As Buchman moved closer to production, first becoming associate producer of *A Song to Remember* (1944), then forming his own company, it was more like a son's entering his father's business than an outsider's adding to Columbia's output. Since Buchman enjoyed a special relationship with Harry, Sidney Buchman Enterprises would really be an extension of Columbia, without the studio's encountering the problems it had with Cowan and Ratoff. Still, a grown son living at home cannot be a financial drain on the parents. Thus Harry pressed for Buchman's owning 100 percent of his company so Columbia could have its share of the profits without paying a second tax on dividends; in turn, Buchman could make the kinds of movies he wanted.

Sidney Buchman Enterprises may not have given Columbia internationally renowned films like Horizon's *On the Waterfront,* but they were certainly respectable. Buchman's films reflected his politics, which had been radical when he belonged to the Communist party but by the mid-1940s had become merely egalitarian. Yet in his first independent production, *Over 21,* for which he also wrote the screenplay, Buchman could not resist throwing in a bit of antifascist rhetoric that, by 1945, had become passé. The movie, based on Ruth Gordon's play, was essentially a comedy about a wife's learning to live on an army base when her middle-aged husband is drafted. When the husband graduates first in his class from officers' training school, he gives an address that recalls Jefferson Smith's sincere but simplistic liberalism. The address is the only lugubrious moment in a bright comedy.

While *Jolson Sings Again* (1949) was a weak appendage to *The Jolson Story*, it was financially successful. But by 1949 Buchman's career was about to decline; the witchhunt was on, and two years later he would face the inquisition himself. Perhaps because the times were so tense, he muted his antifascism, returning to the social consciousness movies of the 1930s that were vaguely populist, mildly proletarian, and always on the side of humanity. *Saturday's Hero* (1951) was the antithesis of *The Spirit of West Point* (1947) in its deglamorization of college football, with its central character as a lower-class kid exploited for his athletic ability. *Boots Malone* (1952) was a genial story about horse racing with definable Capra types; while it was not *Broadway Bill*, it had the same charm.

As writer and producer, Buchman served Columbia well, but both he and Harry knew that Sidney Buchman Enterprises would not be part of the studio after 1952.

In 1947, Rita Hayworth, for reasons ranging from financial security for Rebecca, her daughter by Orson Welles (whom she had recently divorced), and the prospect of getting 25 percent of the net profits from her films, formed the Beckworth Corporation. Of the 1,000 Beckworth shares, Hayworth owned 450, Columbia 400, and the William Morris Agency, which represented her, 50. Beckworth's first film, *The Loves of Carmen* (1948), was an anemic version of Prosper Mérimée's novella, with Hayworth playing at being enticing instead of *being* enticing, as she had been in *Gilda*. The public was not convinced, and the concessions that had to be made to sanitize what was never unsavory to begin with failed to pay off at the box office.

Although not a Beckworth production, *The Lady from Shanghai*, which had been completed in 1946,[17] was released the same year as *The Loves of Carmen*. Neither film was successful, although *The Lady from Shanghai* is now considered a masterpiece of film noir. Marriage to Aly Kahn kept Hayworth off the screen until *Affair in Trinidad* (1952), her second Beckworth movie, whose phenomenal success proved audiences were anxious to see her after a five-year absence, even though she and Glenn Ford were too old for their parts. *Salome* (1953) was a more modest hit, memorable only for its ludicrous characterization of the Judean princess as a penitent who embraces Christianity when she discovers Jesus.

Just as *Salome* was given an upbeat ending, so was Maugham's *Rain*, now renamed *Miss Sadie Thompson* (1953) after the main character. Only in one scene is Rita her old self as she does a lusty dance in which she is as uninhibited as she was in *Gilda* when she removed her gloves and asked for volunteers to unzip her.

In 1954 Hayworth filed suit to dissolve Beckworth. She needed money, and her share of the *Miss Sadie Thompson* profits had not come through. Moreover, her fourth husband, Dick Haymes, was fighting a deportation order and owed alimony to his ex-wives. To keep Hayworth, Harry agreed to her demands, which included a $50,000 loan to Haymes, in return for which she dropped her suit. Hayworth signed a new contract with Columbia for two pictures at $150,000 each, and Columbia bought her share of Beckworth for $700,000.[18] None of the Beckworth films even approached the quality of Hayworth's earlier work. All Beckworth provided Columbia with was product.

It was a different situation with Phoenix Productions.[19] Daniel Taradash, who had come to Columbia in 1939 to work on the script of *Golden Boy* (1939), had won an Oscar for his adaptation of James Jones's *From Here to Eternity* in 1954. Thus Harry was well disposed when, in 1955, Taradash and his fellow Harvard alumnus Julian Blaustein, then a producer at Fox, formed Phoenix Productions. The 9 March 1955 production-distribution agreement between Columbia and Phoenix is typical of the way Columbia negotiated with the independents. It is a document running about 100 pages and consisting of thirty-seven articles covering every aspect of the film from title through remake, should that occur. Columbia would approve the leads, and Phoenix would "cooperate" with Columbia in using the studio's contract players for supporting roles. The maximum budget was $1.5 million, and the screenplay was not to exceed 164 pages. The overhead would be 25 percent. Columbia would retain 25 percent of American, 30 percent of Canadian, and 35 percent of foreign gross receipts until distribution costs were recouped, after which the net profits would be split 50-50 with Phoenix. It was, in Taradash's words, "as good as any independent deal that had been made up to that time."[20]

The first Phoenix production was to have been the movie version of James Gould Cozzens's *Guard of Honor* (1948), which was never made. As it turned out, the first Phoenix was *Storm Center* (1956), which Taradash had originally written for Stanley Kramer's company—a logical choice because of Kramer's interest in controversial material. But Kramer's Columbia films, except for *The Caine Mutiny* (1954), had been unsuccessful, and the thirty-picture arrangement he had with the studio ended with not even half of them made.

Taradash was not beyond striking a deal. He had originally been slated to direct *Picnic* (1955), knowing that Harry would have preferred Joshua Logan, who had directed it on the stage. Taradash agreed to limit his role in *Picnic* to screenwriter if Harry would allow him to direct *Storm Center* for Columbia. While Logan created one of the finest evocations of Americana in the Labor Day picnic sequence, Taradash made the first film released by a major studio to portray the right-wing fanatacism the McCarthy era unleashed and to establish an important distinction between anti-Communist liberals and the anti-anti-Communist left. A librarian, played with Yankee determination by Bette Davis, is an anti-Communist liberal; still, she will not remove a book from the shelf simply because it was written by a Communist and espouses Marxism. As a result, she becomes a social pariah but is vindicated after a child, fueled by Cold War hysteria, sets fire to the library.

There were two more Phoenix productions: *Cowboy* (1958), which featured a charming performance by Jack Lemmon, and *Bell, Book and Candle* (1958), the best of the Phoenix trio. *Bell, Book and Candle* was originally to have been the second Phoenix film, according to the 9 March 1955 agreement. Taradash and Blaustein wanted Rex Harrison and Lilli Palmer, who had played the leads on Broadway, to repeat their roles in the film version. Harry vetoed the idea, as he had the right to. He agreed to give them Ernie Kovacs and Jack Lemmon if they would wait a year: Harry wanted Kim Novak for Gillian, a modern-age witch, but Novak was on loan to Paramount for Hitchcock's *Vertigo* (1958). Harry's involvement in the casting resulted in outstanding comic performances by Lemmon and Kovacs and a surprisingly sensitive one by Novak, whose character discovers she is capable of love when she learns she can cry. The shot of a solitary tear trickling down Novak's face added a human dimension to what, on the stage, had been a brittle drawing room comedy about contemporary witchcraft set in an atmosphere in which black magic seemed no different from dry sherry or bridge.

While the plot remained as unrealistic on the screen as it had been on the stage, Taradash at least humanized the main characters, whom the leads, James Stewart and Novak, inhabited so naturally that one could believe in them, if not in the movie. *Bell, Book and Candle*, thanks to Taradash's screenplay and Richard Quine's sympathetic direction, is a film of small but exquisite moments that linger in the memory: Gillian's cat, Pyewacket, perched on the mantle looking for all the world like a totem; Jack Lemmon putting out street lamps simply by an act of the will; and Stewart and Novak in the Empire State Building Observatory, embracing like moonstruck lovers instead of the ill-starred pair they had played in *Vertigo*.

In 1958 Harry dropped Phoenix's option, not because *Storm Center* was unsuccessful (Harry knew it would not make money) but because Taradash, who could do wonders with bestsellers and plays, refused to adapt MacKinlay Kantor's *Andersonville* (1955), which Harry had bought on the assumption that Taradash would do the screenplay. Regardless, the three Phoenixes were respectable films; the book-burning sequence in *Storm Center* inspired the late Nestor Almendros to enter the industry, becoming one of its greatest cinematographers.

It should not be surprising that Columbia's outside productions could mesh with its own films. Columbia had begun as the CBC Film Sales Company, distributing the movies of others until it could make and distribute its own. From the outset diversity was the key—a special kind of diversity, the result of the union of choice and chance. Humphrey Bogart's production company, Santana, ended up at Columbia because Bogart knew and respected Harry, who offered him a good deal. Of Santana's six films, *In a Lonely Place* is the best; it was not intended as part of Columbia's film noir cycle, yet it blends in perfectly with it. Columbia's noirs, for the most part, depict the sexual underside. Murder provides a sexual thrill for the blonde blackmailer in *Night Editor* (1946). A woman threatens a homoerotic relationship in *Gilda*; in *Dead Reckoning*, Rip (Bogart), an ex-paratrooper, goes so far as to masculinize the femme fatale with whom his dead buddy was infatuated by calling her "Mike" instead of by her real name, Coral. In *The Dark Past*, the Oedipus complex results in parricide. Bannister in *The Lady from Shanghai* is impotent, and his colleague, Grisby, may be gay—at least Glenn Anders's wickedly ambiguous interpretation encourages one to think so. Yet none of these films was an outside production; anyone seeing them, and later *In a Lonely Place*, would view the latter within the context of Columbia's earlier noirs. Bogart's extreme masculinity as Dixon Steele in *Lonely Place* creates a tension in his relationship with Laurel (Gloria Grahame) similar to the one between Rip and Coral in *Dead Reckoning*. But while Rip weakens Coral's sexual power by making her into a buddy and introducing her to the paratrooper's vernacular, Steele's irrational rage makes Laurel even more dependent on her masseuse, Hilda, whose antipathy to men is far from subtle, as is her lesbianic attraction to Laurel.

As the 1950s began and Columbia developed an Oscar-winning streak, there was no difference between the outside productions and the studio's own films that were honored by the Academy. What linked them was the presence of major talent, some of which was Columbia's (Judy Holliday), some freelance (Marlon Brando), some borrowed (MGM's Deborah Kerr). Thus it seemed as logical for Columbia to win Oscars for *Waterfront* as for *Eternity*, although Harry had no role in the former. Except for epics like *Kwai*, Columbia's major films and its major outside productions are indistinguishable. The same kind of seamless blend occurred when Harry initiated a policy in 1948 that moved Columbia into the forefront of stage adaptations. Some of them were in-studio—*Born Yesterday; Harriet Craig* [1950], the remake of *Craig's Wife*; *Picnic*; the *My*

Sister Eileen musical remake; *Pal Joey*. Others, however, were outside productions—Kramer's *Death of a Salesman, The Four Poster, The Happy Time*; Phoenix's *Bell, Book and Candle*. While they were all different (tragedy, comedy, melodrama, musical), they had a common bond: their Broadway origin.

By committing Columbia to movies that resisted categorization and by making Capra's notion of crossing genres and combining themes unofficial studio policy, Harry was able to achieve a level of diversity in Columbia's releases, a diversity that enriches rather than impoverishes. Although Harry would have had no idea who Heraclitus was, he would have understood the philosopher's theory of unity in diversity. Harry ran a studio according to the same principle.

8

Harry and the Production Code

Anyone who saw *June Bride* (1948) at the time of its release might have asked, "How did they get away with it?" "They" were the studio—in this case, Warners; "it" was a scene between Bette Davis and Mary Wickes involving a woman's bust that they would like to remove or at least hide. (They would prefer to paint it black, except that the woman is "attached" to it). The woman's husband listens in shock; what he doesn't realize is that they are talking about a bust that his wife keeps on the mantle.

Most moviegoers in 1948—and for the next twenty years until the ratings system was introduced in 1968—would have wondered how the dialogue "slipped by the censors." What they did not know was there were no "censors." While many knew about the Hays Office, they would have said, if asked to explain its function, that it was Hollywood's equivalent of a "watchdog committee." And they would not have been entirely wrong.

There have always been times when currents of moral indignation circulate in America. Often the movies are the reason: Ingrid Bergman's liaison with Roberto Rossellini while making *Stromboli* (1950), the exaggerated rumors of a Communist takeover of the movie industry in the late 1940s, the backlash against Woody Allen's *Husbands and Wives* (1992) because of Allen's romance with his lover's adopted daughter.

It was not that different in the early 1920s, when moviegoers learned that "America's Sweetheart," Mary Pickford, divorced her husband to marry Douglas Fairbanks; that Fatty Arbuckle took part in an orgy that resulted in a woman's death; that Wallace Reid was a drug addict. Hollywood has always had a small-town mentality; while it encourages images of wild parties and bedrooms with glass ceilings, whenever the image seems to be reality, the town runs scared, as it did in 1922 when the morally indignant put enough pressure on the industry to force the censorship issue. Rather than run the risk of external censorship and impositions from moralists who knew nothing about film, the studios opted for self-censorship, forming their own trade organization, the Motion Picture Producers and Distributors of America (MPPDA), headed by Warren Harding's former postmaster general, Will Hays. A well-known Presbyterian, Hays gave Hollywood credibility; he also gave his name to the MPPDA, which soon was called the Hays Office.

By 1927 a rudimentary list of "Don'ts" (no "sex perversion") and "Be Carefuls" (go easy on "passion") was formulated, although it did not stop DeMille and Lubitsch from making films that were by no means sexually anemic. Apparently, the public did not care as long as it knew that Hollywood had some standard to measure film content.

The coming of sound brought other problems: dialogue by writers who came from journalism, fiction, and the stage and found nothing offensive about double entendre, violence, free love, or infidelity. But the Catholic Church did, and Hollywood was in no position to argue. In 1932, the worst year of the Great Depression, RKO had lost $10.7 million; Warners, $14 million; Fox, close to $17 million; Paramount, $15.9 million. There would be no more "Don'ts" and "Be Carefuls," but instead a Production Code and an agency to enforce it, the Production Code Administration (PCA), created in 1934 and headed by Joseph Breen. Henceforth couples would be sleeping in twin beds, bathrooms would be toiletless, and such obscenities as "cripes," "louse," and "pansy" would be forbidden. As for interracial relationships, they were to be "treated within the careful limits of good taste" on the assumption that such relationships were intrinsically tasteless.

Under such a system it would seem that art would wither; yet the 1930s and 1940s were the glory years of the American film. Moviemakers learned how to beat the Code; Harry did it better than most. When Joe Breen became head of PCA, which became known as the Breen Office, his peculiar view of sex—partly puritanical, partly censorious—became the standard he applied to scripts. As Harry discovered, it was possible to outwit Breen, who relished his authority, repeating key phrases ("it is understood," "unacceptable," "thoroughly and completely unacceptable") that reek of self-importance.

The real Joseph Ignatius Breen was a vulgarian, albeit one who had attended (but had not graduated from) Philadelphia's St. Joseph's College. Lurking behind his letters objecting to suggestiveness in everything from costumes to dialogue was a foul-mouthed man who could be as gross in person as he was puritanical in correspondence. "Fuck" was one of his favorite words; it was also one he relished using, perhaps because it had such monosyllabic finality that it would shock those who thought of it as the unspeakable "f" word. Despite Julian Blaustein's insistence that Jennie in *Portrait of Jennie* (1948) was the figment of an artist's imagination (and that her staying over in the artist's apartment could not possibly have sexual overtones), Breen referred Blaustein to a scene in the script in which Jennie and the artist have tea: "If she can drink tea, she can fuck."[1]

On another occasion, when the courtly Josef von Sternberg referred to a couple's having a "romantic interlude," Breen corrected him: "They fucked." Sternberg eventually agreed, but Breen would not relent until he got Sternberg to use his language—in private.

In Harry's case, there was no question of descending to Breen's level; Harry was already there. Thus there was a mock seriousness about Breen's memos to Harry and Harry's formal replies. Breen knew Harry would not jeopardize Columbia's status by making a movie that would be denied the Production Code seal and shunned by exhibitors; nor would Columbia run afoul of the Legion of Decency with a movie that would merit a "C" (Condemned) rating. Since Breen was head of the PCA as well as a friend of the Legion, to violate the Production Code was to alienate the Legion, which also came into existence in 1934.

While other studio heads ran up against this dual force, few had the same rapport with Breen as Harry did, and may have had to concede more frequently. Columbia made two Rosalind Russell movies, *This Thing Called Love* (1941) and *She Wouldn't Say Yes* (1945), that the Legion initially condemned. Yet whatever changes had to be made to switch their ratings from C to B ("Morally Objectionable in Part for All") were purely cosmetic. Even by 1940s standards, both films were "suggestive" (a favorite Legion term)—and more.

Breen and Harry understood the movie business, but from different angles. Breen was a product of Catholic education which, for all its validity, is based on a set of prohibitions that the young perceive as supplements to the Commandments and equally binding. These mandates, which range from discouraging patent leather shoes that "reflect up" to advising boys to do nothing with girls they would not want their mothers to see, entered the back door of Catholic education, along with the Legion of Decency pledge (which was never binding, although it was often interpreted as such), on the second Sunday of December to coincide, more or less, with the Feast of the Immaculate Conception on 8 December. While many Catholics learned to distinguish the teachings of the Church from the homilies of the pulpit, there were still lingering effects, like those of original sin, that could result in anything from a scrupulous conscience to sexual abstinence in the name of religion.

With Breen, it was the usual mixture of belief and pragmatism. While in theory Breen accepted what he had been taught, in practice he revealed what the system had created: a dirty mind. But Harry was no different. His prurience did not come from the theoretical contemplation of sex but 'from the practice of it. Basically, what Joe Breen was trying to prevent was a generation of Harry Cohns who would not stop at an innocent kiss and would do with women what they would not do in their mothers' presence.

Breen and Harry shared a fascination with things sexual. When Columbia was about to remake *Blind Alley* (1939) as *The Dark Past* (1949), Harry, apparently forgetting the plot, asked writer Malvin Wald to explain the main character's problem, which happened to be an oedipus complex resulting from his guilt for his father's death and his own attraction to his mother. Since Harry did not understand the oedipus complex, Wald explained it to him in terms of the myth. Harry then understood the film: it was about a potential "motherfucker."[2]

Harry and Breen were in the industry when sexual references had to be veiled, and each accepted the principle for different reasons: Breen, to maintain his credibility as a Catholic layman; Harry, to concede to a form of moral blackmail, to which all the studios fell victim, that made the PCA an ally of the Legion of Decency. Ironically, Harry and Breen probably believed in one of the indirect effects of the Code: double entendres so subtly expressed that all that remained of them was the secondary meaning. Thus Harry and Breen played their game: Harry submitted the script, and Breen responded. What Harry proposed, Breen often failed to dispose.

As early as 1937, Columbia was interested in making *Our Wife* (1941), a comedy about a woman's attempt to keep her ex-husband from remarrying. At that time Breen advised that the title not be registered, a suggestion Columbia did not heed. When Columbia submitted a script in 1938, Breen called it "a travesty on marriage."[3] Two years later the script was acceptable except for language ("sex appeal," "horizontal," "vertical," "wrath of God") and excessive drinking. Although the final script was available by February 1941, Breen received it two months later, recording his objections in imperial style: "We have received the final script dated February 20, 1941. . . . On reading it over we note that *none* of the changes requested in our previous letter . . . have been made." The references were to sexual innuendo and Scotch; they were retained, along with "stinking" for "drunk."

Harry had wanted to make *Born Yesterday* almost immediately after Garson Kanin's comedy opened in 1946. By August 1947 Breen, who had responded favorably (perhaps because Harry Brock, modeled after Harry Cohn, was also not unlike himself), said, unbelievably, "This basic material appears to us to be acceptable," even though there was no way of glossing over the fact that Billie Dawn was Harry Brock's mistress. Since so much of the action takes place in a hotel suite, even the suggestion that they have separate bedrooms would not solve the problem. Yet what Breen wanted, it seems, were just some word changes, notably a substitution for "broad." "Broad" was retained, although it was cut in Australia and British Columbia.

Breen made no distinction between the teachings of the Church and religion, the latter being a subject like English or history where information, some of it factual, some questionable, was imparted. Theology says nothing about the female breast, although Breen probably heard a good deal about it from the clergy, who presented it as an occasion of sin and therefore one of the untouchables for young men. Thus he was disturbed by Columbia's *Under Age* (1941), which capitalized on the public's fascination with prostitution. The film used the familiar "hostess" for "prostitute," yet it did not shrink from showing the unhealthiest form of sexual violence—violence by suggestion. Breen, however, was more concerned with "sweater shots [with] the breasts of a number of the girls, clearly and unmistakeably outlined." He wrote to Will Hays about it on 29 March 1941, citing not only films made by Columbia and Universal, but also *The Outlaw* (1941), which he had just seen and whose "breast shots . . . outdo anything we have ever seen on the motion picture screen." While Columbia made some concessions to Breen in *Under Age*, they did not include deletion of the "sweater shots." Even so, it is, by 1940s standards, a daring and highly unsavory film.

Just as Harry regarded New York as something to confront, rage at, and if necessary concede to, he considered the Breen office in a similar light, except that with Breen he was more circumspect. With Breen he could not repeat the sort of shouting matches that left Jack Cohn soaked in sweat and eventually caused him to keep his private phone behind a fake wooden panel so that when Harry called he could rush into the bathroom. With Breen, Harry used the tricks he had learned on the streets of New York; the goal was not to win every battle but to score on as broad a scale as possible by outwitting the opposition.

Harry knew local censors would catch details Breen didn't. Thus there was no point in conceding to Breen if Pennsylvania would eliminate a line of dialogue acceptable to Massachusetts, which might want something else cut. Had Harry yielded to Breen on every matter, Columbia would have ceased production before World War II, since its movies would have become so innocuous they would have bored even the naive. Harry thought the sight of Rosalind Russell fumbling for her keys in her bosom in *Woman of Distinction* (1950) was funny. Breen did not, nor did Pennsylvania, which cut it, but most states agreed with Harry. In the same film, Breen wanted the line "One night he asked her for something, and she gave it to him" deleted. It was deleted—not by Harry, but by Massachusetts.

Harry realized as early as 1936 that there was nothing one could do about state censorship boards and local exhibitors. In that year, Radio City Music Hall deleted two lines from *More Than a Secretary* ("take care of my body" and "lean on me") although Breen had raised no objections to them. Ten years later, Harry remained firm about Rita Hayworth's line in

Gilda: "If I had been a ranch, they would have named me 'The Bar Nothing.'" Originally, the Pennsylvania censors had wanted it cut, but after debating the matter they decided to retain it. It is amazing the number of films Columbia made that the Legion of Decency classified as "Objectionable in Part for All" because Harry would not cave in to Breen when all he had to do was bend a little. If "They Do It in Paris" is too risqué a title, then change it to *He Stayed for Breakfast* (1940), which was still suggestive but apparently not to Breen.

Equally amazing was Harry's ability to succeed where other studio heads failed. Philip Yordan's 1944 play *Anna Lucasta* appealed to a number of studios despite its prostitution theme; nor was the fact that it had originally been performed by a black cast considered a deterrent. It had also been performed by whites, with Anna's being Polish. In the fall of 1944, Hal B. Wallis, who had left Warners to go into independent production, releasing through Paramount, wrote to Breen about *Anna Lucasta*, only to be informed that "the material was thoroughly and completely unacceptable." Breen sent the same letter, verbatim, to Mark Hellinger at Universal. Three years later, Jack Warner, Fox's Robert Kane, Republic's Steve Goodman, and Harry received similar letters. Since Breen was on cordial terms with Kane, he amended what had evolved into a form letter, adding that what mattered more than race was the play's morality; he would raise the same objections if the characters were white.

Yordan was desperate to see his play on the screen; he virtually groveled before Breen, blaming the play's director for the "smut and cheap hokum" and promising to "eliminate these unwholesome elements from the screenplay." Breen was satisfied with the revisions, and *Anna Lucasta* (1949) became one of Columbia's outside productions. With Paulette Goddard as Anna, the character's profession did not have to be decoded.

One could hardly imagine a Shirley Temple movie and a fantasy about Aladdin's magic lamp causing censorship problems, but they did. And in each case, Harry won.

Kiss and Tell was a 1942 Broadway hit by F. Hugh Herbert that introduced Americans to Corliss Archer, whose teenage escapades became the basis of the radio show *Meet Corliss Archer*. Like most Broadway successes, it was destined for the screen. It was no *Anna Lucasta*, but it was mildly risqué: a gossip sees Corliss accompanying her pregnant friend to an obstetrician and assumes Corliss is pregnant. The fact that Mildred, Corliss's friend, is secretly married to Corliss's brother should have lowered any raised eyebrows in the Breen office. But the situation was complicated by the gossip's assumption that the father was Corliss's boyfriend, Dexter Franklin, whose reaction to everything is "Holy cow!" Finally, everything is resolved, and the movie fades out with Mrs. Archer saying, "But I know Dexter couldn't do a thing like that," followed by a close-up of Dexter saying, "Holy cow!" Depending on how one's mind works, "thing" could mean either marriage or intercourse, and Dexter's reaction is either his signature exclamation or his annoyance at a slight to his virility. It was Mrs. Archer's line, actually the play's curtain line, that became a *cause célèbre*.

Shortly after *Kiss and Tell* opened on Broadway, the studios began expressing interest in the rights. Paramount thought of it as a vehicle for Diana Lynn, but Breen warned the studio that "alleged illicit sex and presumed illegitimacy" would have to be "removed entirely from any script." The same letter was sent to Louis Mayer when he inquired about the play. When Columbia bought the rights in November 1944, Breen tried the same approach until he received a script that he apparently accepted.

Whatever script Breen approved was either altered en route to the screen or, more likely, never struck him as controversial. Like *Junior Miss*, and later *Dear Ruth* and *John Loves Mary*, *Kiss and Tell* was mostly fluff with a little spice and double entendres so mild that the secondary meaning was as innocent as the primary. Although Breen warned Paramount about the "alleged illicit sex and presumed illegitimacy," that was exactly what the play was about. There was no way *Kiss and Tell* could be filmed without the mistaken pregnancy that triggers the action.

Less than a month before the bombing of Hiroshima, and at a time when one would think there were more serious matters than a line of dialogue, Dorothy Kilgallen noted in her "Voice of Broadway" column (19 July 1945) that friends who had attended a preview of *Kiss and Tell* wondered how it had passed the censors (the New York censors, that is). On 24 July, Hal Hode, Jack Cohn's executive assistant, wired Harry about Kilgallen's statement and the impending screening that was scheduled for the New York State Board of Regents, whose acting chairman, Dr. Irwin Conroe, was decidedly less liberal than his predecessor. Harry was determined that Conroe not see the film: "You let yourself open so they can attack other parts of the pic," he wired back. The problem was the final line, and Harry knew how it could be solved: with Mrs. Archer's line spoken off screen juxtaposed with a close-up of Dexter's face.

Harry was fortunate in having Hode, who ran interference between Columbia and the local censors. Hode accused both Conroe and vice chairperson Mary Ferrell of undermining the board's "previous intelligent policy," thereby getting them to back down. But once Illinois, Maryland, and Ohio got wind of the board's reaction, they threatened to ban the film unless cuts were made. Hode then traveled to Chicago, Baltimore, and Columbus, explaining the situation and placating the boards with minor eliminations—and only minor ones were made. The film still ends with Dexter's exclaiming, "Holy cow!" in response to Mrs. Archer's line.

Throughout the entire fracas, Breen stood behind Columbia, although initially he would have preferred that the film not be made. Yet if local boards were able to override a PCA decision, the rationale behind the Production Code, which was to prevent external censorship, would be undermined.

The situation might never have arisen if someone other than Shirley Temple were playing Corliss. Harry obviously knew that *Kiss and Tell* was not another *Heidi* (1937). When Mrs. Archer tells her husband that Corliss has been selling kisses to soldiers, he replies, "How did she make out?" When questioned about his behavior toward Corliss, Dexter, thinking it is in reference to an argument they have had, says, "It was all in fun." "Make out" and "all in fun" apparently were not suggestive; "thing" was.

With *A Thousand and One Nights* (1945), Harry had to fight his own battle. The film, an Arabian Nights fantasy spiked with slapstick humor, chiefly through the machinations of Evelyn Keyes as a sexy genie and Phil Silvers as Cornel Wilde's zany sidekick, contained a taboo word: louse, used as a verb in the vernacular ("louse up"). The line occurred in a gin rummy sequence (the film was highly anachronistic) in which Silvers said, "Don't play that card. You'll louse up your hand."

"Louse" was prohibited by the Production Code; it was also an expression Breen abhorred, even though it had no anatomical or sexual associations like "nuts" (testicles) and "nance" (effeminate male); at worst it suggested lice-infestation and delousing.

When Jack Cohn called Harry on 19 April 1945 and read him Will Hays's wire requiring the deletion of the line, Harry, never one to speak cordially to his brother, replied: "I could have gotten that kind of a wire by going direct to Hays myself. . . . What is the next move?" Jack then explained that other studios had similar problems, and with stronger language (such as "hell"). Harry was not persuaded: "louse up" is not "hell." Harry also accused Jack of being acquiescent: "We had a title with the word 'affair' in it. You lost your battle. Paramount comes along and uses 'affairs.' They win their battle. Where does that put you?" When Jack recommended rushing a print to New York and screening it for the Association, Harry refused: it was a Technicolor movie, and Columbia had been making color pictures for only two years. Deadlines had to be met, and a delay could affect shipping the prints.

Harry had made up his mind: "We are going to . . . resign from the Hays office. . . . The gin rummy . . . is the biggest thing in our pic and to have this scene taken out or part of it is too tough for us to take lying down." Unnerved by the prospect of resigning from the Association, Jack suggested that just the gin rummy sequence be shipped to New York.

"That might be your method but not mine," replied Harry. "If you can't fight this thing out and want me to do it from this end, then let's take the pic out of release for the time being."

Finally, Jack agreed to call Hays with the news of Columbia's resignation. This may have been the only time Harry ever complimented his brother: "That's the way I like to hear you talk." It was a gamble, of course, but it came at a time when the industry was affected by a strike that began in March 1945 and lasted for eight months.[4] Hays also knew that his days as MPPDA president were ending (that September). He wanted his pension and counted on Jack Cohn's support. So on 1 May 1945 Joe Breen received the following letter from Hays: "We find . . . 'louse up' . . . in violation of the Code. However, because of certain conditions in the Industry . . . we are prepared to permit the use of it on this particular occasion, but on the distinct understanding that it is not to be considered a precedent. No approval by the Production Code Administration shall hereafter be given to the use of the word 'louse' in any form whatsoever." The film was released in June.

What Betty Grable was to Fox, Rita Hayworth was to Columbia—not only its leading musical star of the 1940s but the one whose movies frequently drew a B rating from the Legion of Decency for "suggestive costuming," "suggestive dancing," or both. When it came to Columbia's musicals, one can see what Harry would have produced if he had stayed in New York and graduated from Tin Pan Alley to Broadway. They might well have been on the order of *Down to Earth* (1947), which mingled erotic ballet with razzle-dazzle, featuring beautiful women in whatever dress— or undress—current standards allowed. And if dress was the norm, undress could be suggested by sheer costumes and body stockings.

What bothered the Breen office about *Down to Earth* was not the song Hayworth, Larry Parks, and Marc Platt sang about the joys of living *ménage à trois* but a ballet in which Hayworth, looking vaguely Grecian, wore chiffon so diaphanous that she seemed to be wearing nothing under it. Geoffrey Shurlock of the Breen office filed a transcript of his 5 November 1946 meeting with Harry and Nate Spingold in which he informed both of them that "several scenes of the exposure of Miss Hayworth's breasts were unacceptable."

Harry preferred to discuss the matter with Breen personally. At the end of January 1947, he finally met with Breen, arguing that he was being discriminated against. He cited *Duel in the Sun* (1947), which contained some of the steamiest sex on film, making *Down to Earth* tame by comparison. Harry used a tactic that had worked a decade earlier when Breen had objected to Jane Wyatt's swiming scene in *Lost Horizon* (1937), claiming that she looked nude. Harry had agreed to cut a scene in which some children go skinny-dipping if he could keep the swimming scene. All that were lost were three frames; Jane Wyatt took her swim, and what one saw depended on the state of one's imagination. Similarly, Harry made some cuts in *Down to Earth*, but Hayworth's breasts still bob under her flesh-colored body stocking that artfully suggests the absence of a bra.

Harry had a special fondness for sex comedy, a hybrid of screwball and romantic and/or drawing room comedy. That he made three of the raciest comedies of the 1940s—*Too Many Husbands* (1940), *This Thing Called Love* (1941), and *She Wouldn't Say Yes* (1945), the last two initially receiving C ratings from the Legion—suggests that he had learned how to break the Code.

Because Capra inspired a kind of comedy that mingled screwball with other elements, *Too Many Husbands*, in which a wife remarries after her husband has been declared dead, only to discover he is alive, seemed like a perfect property for the studio. Naturally, Breen found the subject matter "unacceptable" (18 October 1939). But a month later, when he received the script, he found what he read "very excellent." Still, there had to be changes, notably the deletion of the heroine's being "impatient to indulge in her marital privilege" (the choice of words speaks volumes about Breen).

As usual, Harry had decided on how much he would give; in this case, nothing. With Jean Arthur paired with two handsome men, Fred MacMurray and Melvyn Douglas, the audience would be equally split on its decision as to which of the two would make the best spouse for her, a choice influenced by physical considerations as well as acting ability. The conclusion is open-ended—and subversively immoral, implying the possibility of a *ménage à trois*. While the first husband (MacMurray) is the legal husband, the second (Douglas) clearly plans to stay around. The movie ends with the three celebrating in a nightclub, although what they are celebrating is another matter.

It seems uncharacteristic of Rosalind Russell to have made a series of comedies at Columbia during the 1940s, all of which had problems with the Breen office. Harry was advised against showing "goosing actions" in *Tell It to the Judge* (1949) when Robert Cummings lifts Russell into a row boat. Exactly what Cummings does to get her into the boat is unknown; at any rate it is a wildly funny scene. Because Russell was playing a college dean in *Woman of Distinction* (1950), "suspicion of illicit sex and bastardy" had to be removed from the script. Thus, the dean's child is said to be adopted, and no doubt there were those who believed it. With *My Sister Eileen* (1942), the problem was not the Russell character, Ruth Sherwood, but Violet, the prostitute. Yet Violet hands out calling cards, which suggests that she belongs to a profession (the world's oldest).

Rosalind Russell's dual persona of movie star and devout Catholic has prevented film historians from assessing the person, perhaps because the person was concealed behind the double facade. Only in her dramatic roles (such as Rosemary in *Picnic* or Rose in *Gypsy*) does one see another Russell, possibly the real one, releasing emotions ranging from anger to ruthless determination to, finally, stoic resolve. Rosemary may come closest to the true Russell: a self-mocker who masked her vulnerability behind a body whose height, ideal for sophisticated comedy, never revealed the depth within. That could only be seen when she wore a dress rather than a Jean Louis gown; when she was forced to use her hands instead of a cigarette holder, and to act with her body instead of her face.

But the Russell of the Columbia comedies was a glamorous screwball who, for all her elegant costumes, was never sexy. The better she dressed, in fact, the less sensual she seemed. That was part of the characterization: because she exuded an aura of sophistication, she could hint at unfulfilled desires that wardrobe and wit could not hide. Thus, in a Russell comedy, the plot had to involve some mockery of sex, which implied that she mocked it because she couldn't, or wouldn't, have it.

Harry wanted to remake the 1929 Pathé comedy *This Thing Called Love* in 1938 as a vehicle for Russell and Melvyn Douglas. Until 26 April 1940, Breen had rejected every draft, claiming that the plot was a travesty of marriage because it portrayed a couple who initially agree to a platonic relationship, only to decide otherwise at the fade-out. To Breen, *This Thing Called Love* was a sex comedy that mocked sex. What he did not realize was that the film was a combination sex and screwball comedy, and that the Columbia screwballs tended to mock sex, even when the couples were heading toward it or reconstituting themselves to do it. Sex was never presented as the panacea. What brought men and women together was a serendipitous mix of attraction and affection. Sex came later.

There was another problem with the film: bedroom farce, to be effective, requires bedroom attire. Bra n' panties was not an acceptable combination in 1941, but the script required it. Although the Breen office (9 February 1940) believed "it is understood that the shot showing Binnie Barnes in her panties and brassiere . . . has been deleted from the picture," it wasn't. Yet there was nothing sexy about Barnes's lingerie: her panties looked like overly starched boxer shorts.

While Harry had to make one concession in *She Wouldn't Say Yes*, it occurred at the end, and so rapidly that it hardly detracted from anyone's enjoyment of the film. Russell plays a psychiatrist who refuses to admit her attraction to cartoonist Lee Bowman. Her father (Harry Davenport) knows they are meant for each other and tricks her into what is only a mock marriage. Originally, the film was to have ended with Russell and Bowman in a sleeper en route to the West Coast. Since the Breen office objected to the "marriage," noting that it was invalid because the Russell character was duped into it, the movie had to end with Russell in the upper berth, bending down to tell Bowman in the lower berth that they could get off in Nevada and have a "real" (that is, valid) wedding.

Outwitting Breen may have bolstered Harry's ego, but it did not always result in a commercial success. While Harry won the battle over *The Loves of Carmen*, even getting an A-2 (Morally Unobjectionable for Adults and Adolescents) from the Legion of Decency, he lost the war: the film was not a hit, not so much because the subject matter had been sanitized as because Rita Hayworth and Glenn Ford, as Carmen and Don José, failed to give audiences another *Gilda*. It was a passionless performance, with Hayworth's figure hidden under petticoats and skirts and an off-the-shoulder blouse without décolletage.

There should never have been a problem with *Carmen*; it was based on the Prosper Mérimée novella (which had earlier inspired Bizet's opera) and thus had at least semi-classic status. When Breen asked for some deletions, Harry used his familiar argument: cuts would cause a jump in continuity and require the elimination of an entire scene. Breen was convinced, particularly after Harry played up the film's redeeming moral value: if any film proves that the wages of sin is death, it is *The Loves of Carmen*.

The Legion of Decency also wanted cuts as well as a foreword to the effect that the film was based on the Mérimée work and that Carmen is a gypsy—a fact that supposedly explains her amorality. Columbia obliged, and Carmen was described as "a product of that lawless and unhappy breed." The tradeoff resulted in an A-2 rating that did nothing for the film. The public no longer thought of Hayworth and Ford as a team, and would not for five more years.

When Breen found a script that appealed to his Catholicism, he could be flexible. As he grew older, his flexibility paralleled that of the industry, which, to avoid extinction, had to offer audiences an alternative to television, just as, in the 1930s and 1940s, it had to provide dialogue other than the kind heard on radio. Thus when Breen read the script of *On the Waterfront*, he was delighted. He knew the producer, Sam Spiegel, and when he sent "love and kisses" (4 February 1954) to Spiegel, he was obviously sincere. At last, Breen had evidenced taste; he saw a good script, which he knew would make a great movie.

Yet there were problems—not Eva Marie Saint in a slip but Marlon Brando's saying "You go to hell!" to a priest. Breen wrote to Eric Johnston, Hays's successor and head of the Association (now called the Motion Picture Association of America [MPAA]), arguing that the "line should not be required out [*sic*] of the picture [because] it is used seriously and with intrinsic validity" (23 April 1954). Drawing on his Catholic education, Breen pleaded for the whole over the part. His three-page letter to Johnston resulted in an answer a week later: "The PCA may therefore permit . . . 'Go to hell.' "

There was another reason Breen went to such lengths: director Elia Kazan and writer Budd Schulberg had both purged themselves of their Communist pasts, appearing before HUAC and naming names, thereby endearing themselves to Breen. Their film also featured an activist priest, a type not previously seen on the screen.

The special privilege granted Columbia was not lost on the rest of the industry. Hal Wallis was furious; he wrote to Breen (18 May 1954) that he was "amazed and outraged at the approval of the phrase" when he had been denied its use earlier. Although Wallis wanted no explanation ("as there can be none"), Breen replied in a week, claiming it was not the PCA but the MPAA's board of directors that had approved the line. (Breen did not add that he had petitioned the board to do so.)

Breen also told Wallis he hoped the Code could be "amended so as to obviate these minor conflicts." Minor they were, as Breen realized during his last year as code administrator. His letter to Wallis did not contain the usual Breenisms; it suggested, in fact, that after two decades of acting as America's conscience, he had learned the difference between infractions and exceptions. By the end of the 1960s, the Code would cease to be functional. By then, Harry was long gone. But while he was alive and the Code was enforcible, Harry usually found a way around it.

9

Harry's Hierarchy

By the time the 1930s ended, Harry had established Columbia's priorities in terms of kinds of films and their order of importance. Thus in 1939 he was able to issue a policy statement, indicating that he had a clear image of the studio and its future.[1] Although Capra would be leaving Columbia in the fall of 1939, he had made Harry so conscious of the director's role that it was included in the policy statement: "The company's policy will lay stress, as never before, on the importance of 'director names.'" Readers of fan magazines soon discovered that directors' names in Columbia ads appeared in boldface and lettering larger than that used for the supporting cast. Some even got their names above the title in the Capra tradition. Although George Stevens deserved *auteur* treatment and received it in his three films, Irving Cummings, who seemed not much more than a good craftsman, was also elevated to *auteur*, as moviegoers discovered in 1943 when they saw Rosalind Russell in Cummings's *What a Woman!*

If Columbia's contract directors did not receive authorial status, at least their names were not buried in the ads. These directors had to be versatile, but alternating between melodramas, comedies, films noirs, musicals, and biopics left them little time to develop a signature. Yet if one looks at Columbia's leading contract director of the 1940s, Charles Vidor, it is evident that he made an important contribution to each of these genres. The Hungarian-born Vidor directed *Ladies in Retirement*, a moody recreation of the Broadway thriller; the Chopin biopic, *A Song to Remember*; Rita Hayworth's best musical, *Cover Girl*, as well as her most famous film, *Gilda*; Columbia's first Technicolor venture, *The Desperadoes*; and the Charles Boyer-Irene Dunne romantic comedy *Together Again*.

By Columbia's standards Vidor was well paid for his versatility. By 1946 he was making $3,000 a week, even though he directed only one film that year and none in 1947, and would end his decade-long association with the studio in 1948 with *The Loves of Carmen*.[2] Vidor would have preferred to leave in 1946, either because he thought *Gilda*'s success entitled him to work at a bigger studio or because he could no longer bear

Harry's obscenities. It was the latter explanation he gave a federal judge when he tried to break his contract, at the same time requesting $3,000 for the week he was on suspension. Eventually, Vidor had to pay Columbia $75,000 for release from his contract; as for the alleged obscenities, Harry admitted he spoke that way to everyone and was vindicated for his honesty.

Vidor may have been the best known of Columbia's contract directors, but there were others who could also work in a variety of forms. Henry Levin came to Columbia as a dialogue coach after having been in the theater. He was given a chance to direct in 1943, moving from horror (*Cry of the Werewolf*) to swashbucklers (*The Fighting Guardsman* [1946], *The Gallant Blade* [1948]), to westerns (*The Man from Colorado* [1948]), melodramas (*The Undercover Man* [1949], *Convicted* [1950]), musicals (*Jolson Sings Again* [1949]), and romantic comedy (*The Petty Girl* [1950]).

The most underrated director at the studio was Alexander Hall, who also began as an actor in the theater and played juvenile leads in some silents. Hall came to Columbia in 1937 and stayed a full decade; while he lacked Vidor's range, he had a real instinct for comedy. At a time when death was taking holidays and dream children had become the artist's muse, Hall's *Here Comes Mr. Jordan* (1941), arguably the best fantasy film ever made, took a decidedly offbeat approach to reincarnation, arguing that the soul, representing the person at his or her best, does not die but finds a habitation elsewhere.

In 1947 Harry was looking for a vehicle for Rita Hayworth after her triumph in *Gilda*. The success of the Broadway musical *One Touch of Venus* (1944), in which Mary Martin played the goddess on leave from Olympus, prompted Harry to remake *Mr. Jordan* with Hall as director, along the lines of *One Touch of Venus*. Instead of a reincarnated boxer, the muse Terpsichore descends to earth (hence the title, *Down to Earth*) to help a Broadway producer with his musical and save his life as well. The concept did not work, although Hayworth's dancing, which included ballet, suggested a range that had never been—and would never be—exploited.

The musical was not Alexander Hall's forte; comedy was and, significantly, the three best comedies Rosalind Russell did at Columbia—*This Thing Called Love, My Sister Eileen,* and *She Wouldn't Say Yes*—were directed by Hall. Ironically, in 1953 when Hall returned to Columbia after a six-year absence, it was to direct another musical version of a classic: *Let's Do It Again*, an updating with songs of *The Awful Truth*, with Jane Wyman and Ray Milland exchanging barbs where Irene Dunne and Cary Grant had traded wit. The remake was no substitute for the original, and *Let's Do It Again* was quickly forgotten.

Perhaps the best way to understand Harry's elevation of the director is to look briefly at the way some Columbia directors made the transition from the big to the small screen. Once Columbia's television subsidiary, Screen Gems, was formed in 1948, the studio began behaving like a first-time parent, furnishing the offspring with studio space and performers (Marguerite Chapman, Gloria Henry, Louis Hayward, Ron Randell) who had worked in the B-unit and were used to a tight schedule. Columbia also offered Screen Gems the services of directors who had made pro-grammers and could therefore wrap up a movie in a week, if necessary. If they could finish a movie in a week, they could complete a Ford Theatre episode in a few days.

In 1951 Fred F. Sears directed three Charles Starrett westerns, each of which had a running time of fifty-five minutes. Sears completed each in a week: *Pecos River* (21-29 June), *Smoky Canyon* (12-19 July), and *The Hawk of Wild River* (30 July-7 August). Although his 1954 movies ran a little longer, he finished each in slightly more than a week: *Wyoming Renegades* (21-30 June) and *Cell 2455, Death Row* (28 September-8 October). The same year Sears directed the following half-hour episodes for Ford Theatre, which aired Thursdays on NBC from 9:30 to 10:00 P.M.: "Trouble with Youth" (9-11 June), "Summer Memory" (5-7 August), "Magic Formula" (18-21 August), "Too Old for Dolls" (15-18 October), "Pretend You're Young" (25-27 October), "Letters Marked Personal" (29 November-1 December), and "Second Sight" (15-17 December).[3]

While Screen Gems productions drew on seasoned directors such as Lew Landers, William D. Russell, and Louis King, several who began their careers directing episodes for such Screen Gems series as Dan Raven, Alcoa/Goodyear Theatre, and the Donna Reed Show (Robert Altman, Robert Ellis Miller, Arthur Hiller, Elliott Silverstein, and Stuart Rosenberg) later moved on to film.

Making audiences director-conscious was only one of Harry's goals. More important was his film hierarchy; like most hierarchies, Harry's was not immutable and was, in fact, altered during the next decade. Still, his ability to establish an order of importance in 1939 shows that he under-stood the kinds of movies at which Columbia excelled: the "high-bracket" picture, the western, the serial, short subjects, and the series film—in decreasing order of importance.

Although *Lost Horizon* and *You Can't Take It with You* did not live up to Harry's financial expectations (and *Mr. Smith* completed the trio of Capra disappointments), he had not given up on the prestige picture. But with the advent of World War II there would be fewer of them; perhaps one or two $1 million productions over the next five years but, except for *A Song to Remember*, no $2 million extravaganzas for the duration.

The advantage in having fewer AA movies meant more in other cate-gories. Thus the 1940 budget was increased by $5 million over the 1938-39, resulting in a general upgrading of product. But the "high-bracket" picture (the AA designation does not appear in the policy statement) remained at the top of Harry's hierarchy, with budgets up to $1 million. While Columbia's budgets are less available than those of Fox and Warners, which have donated production files to universities,[4] budgets of the films George Stevens made at Columbia—*Penny Serenade* (1941), *The Talk of the Town* (1942), and *The More the Merrier* (1943)—are obtainable.[5] The three were all budgeted well under $1 million—$630,000, $750,000, and $580,000, respectively. All went over budget. Given the caliber of the stars (Irene Dunne and Cary Grant; Grant, Jean Arthur, and Ronald Colman; Arthur, Joel McCrea, and Charles Coburn), the director, and the writers (Morrie Ryskind for *Serenade*; Irwin Shaw and Sidney Buchman for *Town*; and four for *Merrier*, including Robert Russell; Jean Arthur's husband, Frank Ross; Richard Flournoy; and Lewis R. Foster), the final cost of each film was indicative of its quality: $835,000, $1 million, and $878,000, respectively. *Town* was the best of the three; the budget breakdown reveals that Columbia put its money into what is important: half of it went into script, direction, and acting.[6] The final cost was not unreasonable; in 1942 Columbia could still make movies as cheaply as $150,000.

Although it may seem odd that Harry ranked the western second to the high-bracket picture, westerns played such an important role in Columbia's history that its first Technicolor film was a western, *The Desperadoes* (1943). One would have expected Columbia to make its Technicolor debut with a musical, as Paramount did with *The Vagabond King* (1930). But Columbia's westerns had featured, at various times, many of the genre's best known stars: Buck Jones, Ken Maynard, Tim McCoy, Charles Starrett, "Wild Bill" Elliott, and Gene Autry. Randolph Scott, who starred in *The Desperadoes*, went on to make a number of westerns produced by Harry Joe Brown. Those directed by Joseph H. Lewis (*The Lawless Street* [1955]) and Budd Boetticher (*The Tall T* [1957], *Ride Lonesome* [1959], *Comanche Station* [1960], and others) had enough art in them to escape relegation to the limbo of the "shoot-'em-ups."[7]

In 1939 Harry had no reason to apologize for increasing the number of films in a genre that had great audience appeal. Between 1930 and 1934 Buck Jones had made over twenty westerns for Columbia, many of which had a distinctive style, especially those directed by Roy William Neill, who revealed another facet of his art in the 1940s when he went to Universal for the Basil Rathbone-Nigel Bruce Sherlock Holmes series.[8]

Some of Columbia's early westerns, which dramatized the injustices perpetrated against native Americans (*End of the Trail* [1932] with Tim McCoy, or *White Eagle* [1932] with Buck Jones), anticipated the age of political correctness; so did Gene Autry's post-1947 films.

Autry's Columbia films surpassed those he did at Republic, which never expected him to be anything more than "the singing cowboy." In

1938, when Autry had been in the business only four years, a Republic producer wrote a memo lamenting his lack of talent and recommending darker makeup "to give him the appearance of virility."[9] Luckily, Autry never saw the memo then.

While it was Autry's Republic films that brought him to the attention of moviegoers, they did not represent his best work. When World War II ended, Autry, who had served in the air force, decided to try independent production instead of returning to Republic, whose president, Herbert J. Yates, he had grown to dislike. When Yates held him to his prewar contract, Autry, rather than become embroiled in litigation, agreed to make five more films for Republic before forming Gene Autry Productions, releasing through Columbia.[10] Between 1947 and 1953, Autry made thirty-one pictures for Columbia, many of them drawing on history (the inauguration of the Pony Express, the invention of barbed wire) and portraying the old and new West more realistically than his Republic movies had. Thus a Pony Express rider shoots his disabled horse (*The Last of the Pony Riders* [1953]); native Americans die of malnutrition (*The Cowboy and the Indians* [1949]). Native Americans, in fact, are depicted with a nobility worthy of the later John Ford. The prologue to *The Cowboy and the Indians* states that they were frequently exploited by mercenary whites.

Autry's best Columbia films were those John English directed. Influenced by Ford, English favored poetic landscapes and invested relationships between men and women with a courtly air. When Autry takes leave of Anne Gwynne at the end of *The Blazing Sun* (1949), the source is clearly the parting of Henry Fonda and Cathy Downs in Ford's *My Darling Clementine* (1946), which recalls a knight's farewell to his lady. And just as Ford's films are embellished with familiar songs, so are English's. It was not merely the use of a hit single for a movie title (such as *Mule Train* [1950]); it was also the incorporation of the song into the plot: "Silent Night" at the end of *The Cowboy and the Indians*; "Beautiful Dreamer" at a burial in *Saginaw Trail* (1953).

On a few occasions the songs are anachronistic, such as "Chattanooga Shoe Shine Boy" in *Indian Territory* [1950], but they often do more than supply a title. *Riders in the Sky* (1949) was inspired by Frankie Laine's hit "Ghost Riders in the Sky," which, for copyright reasons, could not be used as the title. It nevertheless becomes the climax of a scene whose emotional impact is rare in a B western (but then, so are flashbacks within a flashback): a cowpoke (superbly played by Tom London) dies, imagining he sees the ghost riders, the shades of the unshriven, who are superimposed over his face as Autry, standing by a rain-splattered window, sings a refrain from "Ghost Riders in the Sky."

If *Mule Train* is in the Museum of Modern Art's film collection, it is because it is an excellent example of a B movie that gave audiences something they never expected. Apart from the fact that the "heroine" (Sheila Ryan) turns out to be the villain, there are other uncharacteristic elements such as long takes, Fordian vistas, and an unusual shot in which the killer turns his back to the camera, facing the victim so that both are in frame.

Of all Columbia's cowboys, none had a longer association with the studio than Charles Starrett, who spent seventeen years there, 1935-52. While his films represented "good stories, efficient productions and above all thumping action sequences,"[11] Starrett never had a director on the order of John English or George Archainbaud, but former editors such as David Selman, Folmer Blangsted, and Leon Barsha. In the late 1940s Starrett was saddled with Gene Autry's old sidekick, Smiley Burnette, whose antics gave the films a folksy quality, making them seem more quaint than realistic. While the formula never varied (voiceover prologue, songs, a mixture of frontier melodrama and low comedy), a few had some unusual twists. The "heroine" of *Phantom Valley* (1948) pulls a knife rather than a pistol on Starrett, boasting that she will even kill her stepfather (whom she has tried to frame) to get the land she feels is hers. *Pecos River* (1951) spoofs the flashback movie, as Smiley Burnette, playing an eyeglass salesman, predicts the inevitable happy ending through glasses with shattered lenses, admitting that the entire film has been a flashback.

Starrett is best remembered for his Durango Kid movies, based on a character he first played in 1940. The premise of these films, which picked up again in 1945 and continued to the end of Starrett's career, was the same sort of transformation that turned the effete Don Diego into Zorro and Clark Kent into Superman. Starrett's character, called Steve (the last name varied from film to film), would don a black hat, mask his face with a black kerchief, and become the crusading Durango Kid, much to the delight of Saturday afternoon audiences, who were responsible for Starrett's being numbered among the top western stars.

The five films Budd Boetticher directed for Randolph Scott and Harry Joe Brown's production company (first known as Producers Actors Corporation, later Ranown) are Columbia's most respected westerns: *The Tall T* (1957), *Decision at Sundown* (1957), *Buchanan Rides Alone* (1958), *Ride Lonesome* (1959), and *Comanche Station* (1960). They are taut narratives (under eighty minutes) in which the West is the backdrop for an exploration of moral issues (revenge, justice, public apathy). Boetticher may lack Ford's mythopoeic vision, and Columbia's Burbank Ranch was no substitute for Monument Valley. Yet within limitations imposed by both budget and setting (often dictated by a script that restricted the action to a single community, as in *Sundown* and *Buchanan*), Boetticher could still create moral fables with formal compositions (a white plain receding into a blue horizon) in place of grand vistas and romanticized landscapes.

Boetticher's world is not without symbols. Wheels, perhaps emblematic of fortune, are ubiquitous; sometimes they jut into the right of the frame, forming an off-center composition with a stretch of road filling in the rest. Symbols are often complementary: a cruciform tree can serve as a grave marker (*Buchanan*) or a natural gallows (*Ride Lonesome*); similarly with plots: Buchanan rides into town and leaves—alone; Bart Allison (*Sundown*) arrives with his friend Sam and leaves, drunk and embittered after Sam's murder, with his friend's now riderless horse.

While *Ride Lonesome* and *Comanche Station* are usually considered Boetticher's best Columbia westerns, *Decision at Sundown* is his most complex. Intended as a response to *High Noon* (1952), it spells out that film's message (the need of the community to take a stand against wrongdoing), but muted because the writer, Carl Foreman, conceived *High Noon* as an attack on McCarthyism at a time when only the most sophisticated moviegoers would draw a parallel between the Old West and contemporary America. While *Decision at Sundown* is politically less subtle than *High Noon*, it is also more ambivalent. The film is not cast in terms of the *High Noon* dichotomy of Marshal = good/Jordan = evil.

The "villain" in *Decision at Sundown*, Tate Kimbrough (John Carroll), merits sympathy. Initially he is the western strongman: a slick gang leader who has taken over the town so completely that the inhabitants have become too apathetic to oust him. On his wedding day the uninvited guest arrives: Bart Allison (Scott), whose wife Kimbrough had apparently seduced and whose suicide he supposedly caused. Within a day, as in a Greek tragedy, Allison rises from intruder to savior, while Kimbrough falls from dictator to outcast. But Allison pays the price for becoming the town's conscience. He loses his best friend, who finally tells him the truth: the wife Kimbrough allegedly stole from him had other lovers—so many that shame drove her to self-destruction.

This is clearly not *High Noon* territory. Kimbrough cannot be killed as Jordan was, although screenwriter Charles Lang, Jr., intended a parallel with the earlier film, in which the marshal's wife shoots the villain. Here, Kimbrough's mistress shoots her lover in the arm to keep him from being killed by Allison.

The real tragedy is Allison's: while Kimbrough and his mistress leave for greener pastures, Allison leaves without his friend and with the knowledge of his wife's infidelity. The ultimate irony is not that of a marshal's throwing his tin star on the ground and rejecting the community that failed to support him, as in *High Noon*, but that of a man who has succeeded in preventing a wedding and, in the process, learned some truths whose pain only liquor can assuage.

Columbia never acquired the reputation for serials that Universal and Republic did, yet it managed to produce *Batman* (1943) and the highest grossing serial in history, *Superman* (1948).[12] Neither, however, was originally slated for the studio. Columbia obtained the rights to *Batman* when DC Comics refused them to Republic, believing it would not be faithful to Bob Kane's concept of the character. By 1943 purism was irrelevant; Columbia scored a hit with the serial by catering to the "slap the Jap" mentality. The villain, Dr. Daka (J. Carrol Naish), was a "shifty-eyed Jap" whose zombies were no match for Bruce Wayne of Gotham City.

Columbia was interested in a Superman serial in 1939 when it seemed certain Republic would get the rights. But negotiations broke down, probably over script control. In 1946 Sam Katzman bought the rights, and once he came to Columbia as an independent producer, he offered them to the studio. Of the two, *Batman* is the better because of the direction of Lambert Hillyer, who never repeated the success of *Dracula's Daughter* (1936) and spent the rest of his career making B movies, most of them westerns.

Since Columbia's true beginning was as Hall Room Boys Photoplays, Inc., it was only natural that the studio would continue making comedy shorts.[13] Columbia could also have staked an early claim on cartoons. Frank Capra, a Walt Disney fan, was so amused by Disney's "Silly Symphony" series, which originated in 1929, that he persuaded Harry to distribute them. No lover of cartoons, Harry thought of them purely as incentives for exhibitors to book the Columbia product. The studio's relationship with Disney ended abruptly in 1932 when Harry would advance only $7,500 per cartoon. Arguing that one cartoon paid for another, Disney wanted $15,000, which Harry refused.[14]

For a studio that gave animation a low priority, Columbia won Oscars for three UPA cartoons it distributed: *Gerald McBoing Boing* (1950), *When Magoo Flew* (1954), and *Mister Magoo's Puddle Jumper* (1956). But cartoons would not enhance the studio's image, nor, for that matter, would shorts, although they were at least something Harry understood. Still, he preferred to remain aloof from the Short Subjects Department, banishing it to the former site of Western Pictures on Beachwood Drive and never inviting anyone from the unit to lunch in the executive dining room. Since the department, run by the Hungarian-born Jules White, had a reputation for pranks and practical jokes, Harry may have thought its members would wreak havoc on his luncheon meetings, which were generally hazing sessions. Given the unit's six-day 9:30 A.M.-5:00 P.M. schedule, lunch was a low priority; a quick bite at the Moviola Grill was sufficient.[15]

When Columbia's shorts—which featured such comics as Andy Clyde, Charlie Chase, Vera Vague, and briefly Buster Keaton—are mentioned, one comedy team comes to mind immediately: the Three Stooges, who worked there from 1934 to 1959. Their background in vaudeville partly explains their reliance on sight gags and physical humor but not their lasting appeal, which spans the decades as each age discovers them on the tube. One reason for that appeal is their speciality, the two-reeler. While the Stooges periodically made features during their long career, they could never dominate a feature as they could a short. And when they were allowed to star in such movies as *Snow White and the Three Stooges* (1961) or *The Three Stooges Meet Hercules* (1963), they became tedious. In a short there is no opportunity for boredom to set in, as often happens in slapstick. If brevity is the soul of wit, it has also been the saving grace of many a short that simply could not have been extended further.

If the Stooges appeal to children (as well as to the child in the adult), it is because, to children, the only difference between what the Stooges and cartoon characters do to each other is the difference between actors and animated figures. Face-slapping and nose-tweaking are on a par with electrifying a cat's tail or turning its head into a mountain of lumps. If Tom of the Tom and Jerry cartoons can recover, so can the Stooge who gets poked between the eyes.

It was not all "Niyuk, Niyuk, Niyuk" with the Stooges. At their best they could handle verbal humor as well as physical. In "You Nazty Spy" (1940), the Stooges impersonate a trio of fascists: Hailstone (Moe), Gallstone (Curly), and Pebble (Larry), representing, very roughly, Hitler, Mussolini/Goering, and Goebbels.[16] 1940 was still early enough to joke about Nazi Germany (called Moronica, which is on Bolonia time) and Nazi anti-Semitism (the Stooges click their heels and say "Sholem Molachem" to a warmonger). That one still laughs at the short is a tribute to both its innocence and comically premature antifascism.

The Three Stooges would never have achieved such popularity if, in 1934, they had signed with a different studio. The reason is not merely Columbia's longstanding interest in comedy shorts but rather the presence of Jules White, whose anarchic sense of humor complemented that of the Stooges. Having relegated Jules and his staff to Beachwood Drive, Harry left them alone to create the same mayhem on the screen they were causing in their unit. Slapstick comics would feel at home there. When one of White's writers defected or broke under the strain of a six-day week, the others would sponge his name off the blackboard, throw the water-soaked sponge at White, and finally toast their departed colleague in paper cups which, when drained, would be hurled at White. It was clearly a case of life imitating if not art, then popular culture.

Columbia had been considering the series film as early as the 1920s, when it made a few Lone Wolf movies, based on the exploits of Louis Joseph Vance's reformed jewel thief. The Lone Wolfs came out sporadically, but once Harry decided to include the series film in the hierarchy, they appeared with greater regularity. By 1951 Columbia had made a total of thirteen series, the best known being Blondie, Ellery Queen, Boston Blackie, Crime Doctor, Jungle Jim, and the Whistler. At first the series film did not figure in Harry's plans for elevating Columbia to major status, but he decided that if MGM could have Nick Carter and Fox could have Charlie Chan, Columbia could have its series characters—but more of them.

Comic strips, radio programs, and detective fiction had proved the appeal of continuing characters. Thus Columbia shamelessly raided radio and the comics for both its series and its serials. Chic Young's comic strip was responsible for Columbia's longest running series, Blondie, which lasted from 1939 to 1950 and always costarred Penny Singleton as the fluttery Blondie and Arthur Lake as her befuddled husband, Dagwood. Since the Bumsteads had been conceived as zanies, there was no limit to what could befall them, from treading the boards to tangling with gangsters.

Columbia was less successful with the series detective.[17] The studio gave up on Nero Wolfe after two movies, *Meet Nero Wolfe* (1936) and *The League of Frightened Men* (1937), convinced Harry there was no future in a detective who is an orchid grower and a gourmand. The Ellery Queen series was also short-lived (1940-42), perhaps because neither Ralph Bellamy, who starred in the first four, nor William Gargan, who did the last three, seemed comfortable as the detective. Bellamy's comic timing was too subtle for the material, and Gargan looked as if he would be more at home in Chandler's Los Angeles or Hammett's San Francisco. Whatever life there was in the series was supplied by Margaret Lindsay, who played Nikki in all the Ellery Queen films. Yet her infectious smile and droll delivery were not enough to carry the series, which had a longer tenure on radio.

Although Boston Blackie lasted almost as long as Blondie (1941-49), it is difficult to understand why. Like the Lone Wolf, Blackie is a reformed crook; but while there were several Lone Wolfs (the last being the dashing Ron Randell in 1949), there was only one Boston Blackie, Chester Morris, who could not sustain an eight-year run. The series suffered from unconvincing disguises and dull magic acts, the latter because Morris was an amateur magician who performed at army bases during World War II. When the series ended with *Boston Blackie's Chinese Venture* (1949), it was evident that whatever potential it had had was exhausted. Unable to take their hero or characters seriously, the writer chose to parody them. A contemporary viewer, conscious of racial stereotypes, might find *Boston Blackie's Chinese Venture* racist. Naive tourists visiting New York's Chinatown are promised a glimpse of the Chinese underworld, which the locals provide. The tourists return to their bus, convinced the days of the Tong

Wars have not passed; meanwhile, the drug traffickers and warlords have doffed their disguises and resumed their card game.

Although the Crime Doctor series, which originated on radio, fared slightly better, it too suffered from casting. At fifty-five, Warner Baxter was not too old for the psychiatrist-sleuth, Dr. Ordway. But when he began the series in 1943, he was only eight years away from his death. The Crime Doctors, the first of which was released in 1943, were among his last films. When the series ended in 1949, he would live only two more years. Ill health, physical and mental, sapped his energy but not his professionalism. Baxter's line readings were always in character; the problem was that Baxter's condition made the character bland.

The first in the series, *Crime Doctor* (1943), explained the meaning of the title, although fans of the similarly named radio program, who had been tuning in since its premiere in 1940, would have had no problem. The Crime Doctor is an amnesiac who has become a successful psychiatrist, not knowing he has formerly been a gangster. He regains his memory when he reenacts a robbery he had engineered. Forced to stand trial for his past crimes, Ordway the criminal is found guilty, but Ordway the psychiatrist, who has been rehabilitating criminals, is not. Since America was at war in 1943, as the judge reminds the jury, the country needs more Ordways—benefactors of humanity, that is.

When a series finds favor with the critics, it is an indication of its worth. While not all eight Whistler films were of the same caliber (the same can be said of most series, including MGM's Thin Man), those directed by William Castle and/or based on Cornell Woolrich stories occasioned favorable reviews for their intelligent plotting and atmospheric settings.[18]

It was impossible for a Whistler movie to be anything less than atmospheric. Just as each episode of the radio show on which the series was based opened with Wilbur Hatch's Whistler theme (whistled to eerie perfection by Dorothy Roberts), followed by the never-changing "I am the Whistler. And I know many things, for I walk by night . . . "), so too did each Whistler film. And since the settings were bars, lighthouses, docks, trains speeding through the darkness, and so forth, the low-key lighting complemented the theme of destiny as a force both unpredictable and inexorable. The Whistler is a less cynical Shadow, a combination conscience and commentator, a presence felt but unseen except for his shadow. Since he announces his prescience at the outset, each film becomes a study in fate, which can be deferred but never avoided.

Each Whistler, except the last, starred Richard Dix, whose career, like Warner Baxter's, was ending when he went into the series. Dix's last film, in fact, was a Whistler: *The Thirteenth Hour* (1947); he died two years later. If Dix was more effective in his series than Chester Morris and

Warner Baxter were in theirs, it was because he was not playing a series character like Boston Blackie or Dr. Ordway. The Whistler is merely a voice; "the strange tales hidden in the hearts of men and women who have stepped into the shadows" could be told of anyone. Thus Dix played a variety of characters: death-obsessed men, dying men, innocent amnesiacs, murderous amnesiacs, detectives, and stranglers. And he was always convincing.

If one wishes to single out a typical Whistler, it would be the first, simply titled *The Whistler* (1944), in which Dix's despondency over his wife's death robs him of the desire to live. Rather than commit suicide, he arranges to have himself murdered by a professional killer, not realizing that his murder has been subcontracted. When Dix's contact is himself killed, the assignment falls to another (J. Carrol Naish). Also unknown to Dix is the fact that the contact's wife has taken over the assignment, making him the target of two killers. As the Whistler observes at the end of the film, each of Dix's would-be murderers has his or her own rendezvous with death: the wife in a car accident, the Naish character with a bullet. And the one who wanted to die, and went so far as to prepay his death, is alive.

There was a category of film known to Hollywood insiders but not included in the 1939 hierarchy: Harry's films. The phrase is not found in film histories, but one hears it from many who were associated with Columbia during the Cohn era: former Columbia story editor Sam Marx, screenwriter Daniel Taradash, Harry's nephew Robert Cohn, and others. These were films in which Harry was personally involved—some of them major productions, others ordinary studio fare. In the absence of complete production files, it is impossible to say how many there were. It is easier, in fact, to list the kinds of films in which Harry had little or no involvement: independent or outside productions; films by directors important enough to enjoy a certain autonomy (Howard Hawks, Rouben Mamoulian, Frank Capra, John Ford, Frank Borzage, George Stevens), most series films (the Ellery Queens, which were Larry Darmour productions shot at the Darmour lot on Santa Monica Boulevard; the Crime Doctors, most of which were produced by Rudolph C. Flothow, who also produced all but one of the Whistlers).

There were also pictures such as *Dead Reckoning* (1947) in which Harry expected to be involved but which were so foreign to him that he could contribute little or nothing to their improvement. Although director John Cromwell was not in the Capra-Ford-Stevens league, he was still able to make *Dead Reckoning* as he planned, despite Harry's objections. As the October 1946 teletypes indicate, Harry was not a fan of film noir; flashback-voiceover narratives obscured clarity of plot. The 3 October preview convinced Harry there was "too much" of everything in the film ("too much in the opening," "too much dialogue"). After the 17 October preview, "throw out" replaced "too much." *Dead Reckoning*, however, was designed as a vehicle for Humphrey Bogart (on loan from Warners) and intended to evoke *The Maltese Falcon* (1941) and *The Big Sleep* (1946); thus narrative logic would be at a premium.

It would be a mistake to conclude that it was only the A movie that merited Harry's attention. Occasionally, there was a B movie that he thought needed improvement. Although it is difficult to imagine Harry's interest in *The Flying Missile* (1950), a tired World War II drama about guided missiles, he was concerned enough about the property to issue detailed notes on the second draft screenplay (16 February 1950), which was so "lousy" that it had to be revised.[19] The revision was no better, with its "bad writing" and "terrible dialogue." Harry became so exasperated by the lack of logic ("WHAT DOES IT MEAN") and motivation ("why" is ubiquitous in his notes) that he finally wrote, "I GIVE UP!"

While *Dead Reckoning* and *The Flying Missile* were clearly not two of Harry's films, *All the King's Men, Born Yesterday*, and *From Here to Eternity* were.

Although it was Nate Spingold's idea to purchase the rights to Robert Penn Warren's *All the King's Men* (1946), once the project got under way Harry became committed to it. There was something about Willie Stark, the bigger-than-life vulgarian who evolved into a populist tragic figure, that struck a responsive chord in him. Harry and Willie were cut from the same cloth: local boys who made good—Harry by going from the streets of New York to Beverly Hills, Stark from a log cabin to the governor's mansion. Each had mastered the art of hucksterism; each had parlayed an instinct into a career.

Robert Rossen, believing the movie version would be his break-through film, desperately wanted to do the adaptation.[20] Rossen had been a successful screenwriter at Warners for ten years (1937-47) before deciding to "go hyphenate" and become a writer-director. Columbia gave him the opportunity in *Johnny O'Clock* (1947), a hard-boiled melodrama of the sort he had written at Warners. Coming to Warners when the studio was in the middle of its proletarian period (which coincided with Rossen's own detour into left-wing politics and eventually the Communist party), Rossen turned out scripts exposing organized crime (*Marked Woman* [1937], *Racket Busters* [1937]), bigotry (*They Won't Forget* [1937]), social injustice (*Dust Be My Destiny* [1939]), and fascism—premature (*The Sea Wolf* [1941]) and otherwise (*Edge of Darkness* [1943]).[21]

Although Rossen was one of the Hollywood Nineteen who were subpoenaed to appear before HUAC in 1947, he had already become disenchanted with the Communist party by the time of the HUAC investigation and left it shortly thereafter, later turning informant.[22] Still, Rossen never lost his commitment to "the people," that anomalous mass that Communism was supposed to benefit. If one wants proof of the integrity of the average American, one need look no further than the faces in the montage sequences in *All the King's Men*. Rossen saw the novel as a vindication of his beliefs, but not of the political path onto which he had briefly strayed. Robert Penn Warren's Huey Long figure, Willie Stark, is the stuff of tragedy. Initially, Willie is motivated by a desire to help the rural poor, but he becomes so corrupted by power and the need to retain it that he degenerates into a dictator, much as Communism, despite its condemnation of Fascism, deteriorated into another form of it.

What happened to Robert Penn Warren's Willie Stark can be explained in three phrases: Columbia Pictures, the story conference, and Harry Cohn.

Since the project originated in New York with Nate Spingold, who arranged for the purchase of the screen rights, Harry at first appeared indifferent. But once *All the King's Men* became a Columbia property, Harry realized, as did Spingold, that it could be not just an AA but a prestige film, a type Columbia had not produced recently. The studio had not made a movie from a Pulitzer Prize winner since *You Can't Take It with You* (1938). While *The Jolson Story* was a huge success, it did not attract the intelligentsia, nor was it the sort of film to win Oscars in the categories of acting and best picture, as *All the King's Men* did on Academy Awards night, 23 March 1950.

Harry, then, wanted Rossen's script to be foolproof before filming began. By August 1948 Rossen had written a detailed story outline with all the major plot points.[23] The outline must have been discussed at a story conference at which Harry was present because the surviving copy incorporates Harry's comments. At this stage, Harry had little to say; later he became quite vocal, subjecting Rossen's script to the same sort of scrutiny that he imposed on *From Here to Eternity*.

Rossen planned to begin the film with the state capitol under martial law, "with people . . . hiding in hotel rooms, etc." At this point Harry interrupted to ask why they were hiding. It was a good question because the film seemed to be starting *in medias res*. Flashback films bothered Harry because they interrupted narrative continuity; flashbacks work best when a fadeout/fadein alerts the viewer to a time change. But a film's beginning cold with a good deal of unexplained activity was too much for Harry, who considered himself the ideal moviegoer; if Harry found the opening confusing, so, he reasoned, would others.

Rossen had his work cut out for him. It took several months before he abandoned the flashback and wrote a sequential narrative; it also took several story conferences with Harry, producers Collier Young and Bill Bloom, and story editor Eve Ettinger.

Every story conference involves give and take—Columbia's more so because Harry would test writers to the limit to see if they believed in what they had written; otherwise he would reduce them to spineless lackeys who were completely at his mercy. Harry knew that an obsequious writer could not produce an AA script; nevertheless, Rossen had to learn that if Harry took a personal interest in a movie (which he had not in the case of *Johnny O'Clock*), he expected to have his say.

First, there was the matter of the novel's length: it had the pace of a tale spun into an epic, complete with digressions. It was also a novel conceived as both a work of serious fiction and a bestseller. Warren's Willie Stark is not just a demagogue who turns into a fascist but the kind of character about whom commercial fiction is written. He is an adulterer, a liar, a cheat, and a blackmailer. While not handsome, Willie attracts women as diverse as Lucy, the teacher he marries, and Anne Stanton, the daughter of a former governor, who becomes his mistress. Also included in the plot are alcoholism, suicide, and assassination, done in an unpretentiously literary style that transforms pulp into art.

The story had to be shortened, and its sensationalism (which appealed to Harry) muted—but not removed. Viewers adept at translating ellipses had no difficulty figuring out that Anne (Joanne Dru) was sleeping with Willie (Broderick Crawford). Disillusioned with Willie, Jack Burden (John Ireland), the novel's and the film's narrator, shouts at Anne, whom he loves: "There's no God but Willie Stark. I'm his prophet and you're his—." Anne's reaction completes the sentence, and the charge. Similarly, Willie's asking Jack, "How much does the Doc [Stanton] know about Anne and me?" was one of those encoded questions—sex by euphemism—that circumvented the Production Code.

The main problem was the structure. Rossen envisioned a frame narrative, beginning with a march on the capitol and ending with Willie's assassination, with the film proper in between. The frame would begin with an anxious populace awaiting news of Willie's impeachment. Then, in a nearby hotel, Anne and Jack would be introduced, their conversation establishing the presence of Anne's brother, Adam, who is lurking about with murder on his mind—Willie's murder. The frame would end with the impeachment proceedings; as they commence, someone would say, "Let me tell you what happened." A dissolve would take the film into the past where the events leading to Willie's impeachment would be chronicled. Presumably, another dissolve would return the action to the trial that would end with Willie's acquittal and subsequent assassination.

"Your audience won't get it," Harry insisted, noting that the prologue ran fourteen pages. "It will take the audience so long to recover [*sic*] to what you are trying to tell them that it becomes impossible. You can't get them to sit in their seats right because you are giving them such a difficult thing to do." Keeping audiences from squirming in their seats was important to Harry, who gauged a movie's effectiveness by the number of times he had to shift positions.

Harry was also irritated by the beginning of the film proper: at a newspaper office, where Jack works as a reporter, someone asks, "Did you ever hear of Willie Stark?" Harry reminded Rossen that after a prologue showing Stark as an object of statewide attention, a line like that was incongruous and could only work without the prologue.

Rossen received enough flack not only from Harry but also from the others to drop the prologue and therefore the frame narrative; instead, the film begins in the newspaper office where Jack is assigned to do a story about Willie Stark, who has acquired a reputation as a rabble rouser.

Even with the elimination of the prologue, Rossen had trouble licking the novel. His only experience adapting serious fiction was the screenplay of Jack London's *The Sea Wolf*. Thus Rossen could not explain why supposedly decent people like Jack and Anne became part of the Stark machine, and why it took them so long to realize their mistake. But Harry was adamant: Rossen "must be ABC as to the relationships of our people."

Rossen's characterizations bothered everybody at the story conferences, particularly Collier Young, who found it difficult to reconcile Jack's educational background and knowledge of American history with his support of Willie. Rossen could only say, "I know the point and the only reason it isn't clear is that I haven't clarified it."

Harry knew what the problem was: "[Rossen] tried to salvage too much from the book and lost the love interest. You keep wanting to see some scene where this guy says, 'I can't.' I know the Huey Long character; a guy who started out honest, became dishonest. But the [other] characters. . . . What's their story? Jack—who says 'I don't care' (whatever his story is) and Anne—who says 'You do that' (whatever her story is)? A swell guy like Adam who lived in the traditions of the judge?"

The viewer is asked to believe that Jack can still love Anne even after she becomes Willie's mistress, and that Anne can remain oblivious to Willie's growing despotism. When Judge Stanton initiates impeachment procedings against Willie, Jack is the one who uncovers evidence of a twenty-year-old peccadillo that Willie can use against Stanton. Confronted with the alternatives of voting against Willie's impeachment and explaining a former indiscretion, Stanton chooses suicide.

Jack may have obtained the incriminating evidence, but it is Anne who puts it in Willie's hands. One can understand Jack's complicity:

Willie's ways have become his. Anne's is the problem. To make her betrayal more reprehensible, Rossen went beyond anything in the novel, turning Warren's Judge Irwin, a friend of the Stantons, into a new character: Judge Stanton, Anne and Adam's uncle.

The only explanation for Anne's betrayal of her uncle is Willie's mesmeric hold on her. Despite Joanne Dru's attempt to combine sensuality and aristocratic coolness, one is still at a loss to explain Willie's appeal to Anne, who no sooner hears him speak about improving society than she turns radical chic, eager to be with the reformer and not just help him implement his program.

When Harry saw a rough cut of the film in February 1949, he wanted two additional scenes: one between Anne and Willie and another between Anne and Adam after the judge's suicide: "We need a scene showing Anne's falling for Stark. What makes her do it? It's pretty unbelievable that she would have an affair with Stark. . . . Why does she turn over the papers . . . which condemn her uncle? Stark's hypnotic influence must have been tremendous. . . . We definitely need a scene after the judge has killed himself, between Anne and her brother, where she at least looks as if she is sorry she was the direct tool to cause her uncle to commit suicide. Perhaps in this scene we can find out what makes her tick. At this stage I don't know."

Nor did the audience. All Anne can say when Jack asks why she became involved with Willie is, "He wasn't like anybody I ever knew before." While the Judge's suicide awakens her from her moral torpor, she says nothing at all to Adam. Harry was right about a scene between brother and sister, particularly since Adam later murders Willie. Instead, Anne merely leaves the house, exiting Bette Davis style—in an arclike sweep with hair falling over one side of her face.

Adam avenges his uncle's death, but whether it is because he knows his sister is Willie's mistress or because Willie is indirectly responsible for the judge's suicide is unclear. Harry liked the idea of Adam's shooting Willie because Willie had been sleeping with Adam's sister. "If [Willie] seduced his sister, there is a reason why Adam would kill him." In the novel, Adam's motive is complicated by his realization that his sister's body has bought him the directorship of the hospital.

Ultimately, it made no difference whether the motivation was clear: *All the King's Men* won Oscars for best film, best actor (Broderick Crawford), and best supporting actress (Mercedes McCambridge as Sadie Burke, Willie's secretary and occasional lover). Sadie is the best realized character in the film; she is Willie's alter ego—cynical, destructive, and driven by self-loathing that she cannot admit is deserved. Sadie transfers her potential for self-destruction to Willie, whom she introduces to alcohol, which furnishes the energy for the Stark machine. Alcohol brings to the surface Willie's feelings of inadequacy, manifest in his constant use of "hick," a term he applies both to the masses that turn out to hear him and to himself. Willie has become the archetypal hick, the chosen destined to lead the chosen. Had a bullet not stopped him, he might have led them down the same lethal path he was traveling.

What is fascinating about the film is not the script so much as Rossen's direction and the performances of Crawford and McCambridge. Rossen got Crawford to project the sincerity that Willie Stark's prototype, Huey Long, must have possessed when, as governor of Louisiana, he abolished poll taxes, reduced illiteracy, provided free textbooks for school children, and paved miles of dirt road. Yet there is a scene early in the film when Jack, who is having dinner with the Starks, agrees to write a series of articles on Willie. Noticing a piece of chicken on his wife's plate, Willie eats it in a close-up implying that he takes as well as gives. In the way Crawford plays Willie, there is nothing intrinsically evil about him. Like "Citizen" Kane, Willie wants to champion the people but ends up exploiting them. Perhaps, as the novel suggests, such self-deception is possible only in a democracy.

Oblivious to the discrepancy between what he hoped to be and what he became, Willie never understands that someone might want to kill him, least of all Adam Stanton, whom he has made director of his hospital. "Why did he do it to me?" are his dying words. The viewer might ask the same question which, ironically, is the one Harry had posed. But even Warren never answered the question satisfactorily. Although Warren made Jack Burden the narrator, Jack is not omniscient; at the end of the novel the author intervenes, reminding the reader that it is his—Robert Penn Warren's—story, also. If Harry had read the novel, he would have received a partial explanation: "As a student of history, Jack Burden could see that Adam Stanton, whom he came to call the man of idea, and Willie Stark, whom he came to call the man of fact, were doomed to destroy each other, just as each was doomed to try to use the other and to yearn toward and try to become the other, because each was incomplete with the terrible division of their age."[24]

Warren's is a literary explanation; it would have meant nothing to Harry, who was a student not of literature but of character as expressed in film. He would never have understood that Adam and Willie are doubles and that in literature either doubles destroy each other or one self destroys the other, rendering the character single. Despite Warren's insistence that Jack knew the reason, one wonders. If Jack did, he should have told the reader himself; he was, after all, the narrator.

Unable to answer the questions posed at the story conferences, Rossen resorted to a visual style with which he was familiar: the style of the Warners social consciousness movie whose frames ran through the projector like a clip of bullets, riddling the screen with one visual barrage after another. Although Rossen discarded the prologue, he used the image of the marching masses as a pictorial background for the opening credits as well as a prefigurative device. To collapse time, Rossen created a montage in which faces dissolved into a kind of WPA mural. These montages are in the style of the antifascist films of the late 1930s and early 1940s, unrelenting in their imagery. The most vivid one—Willie's haranguing a mob, his face framed by blazing torches—evokes Nazi rallies, just as his state police conjure up the storm troopers. Whether 1949 audiences understood Rossen's point, that a homegrown fascist can evolve into a Nazi, is doubtful. What impressed audiences, apart from the performances of Crawford and McCambridge, was the bombardment of images, notably the montages that helped propel *All the King's Men* to heights it might not otherwise have reached. Although Harry was instrumental in Rossen's rethinking the film's structure and abandoning the flashback approach, *All the King's Men* was never one of Harry's favorites. He knew what was lacking when he saw a rough cut: "Whom are you 'rooting' for? There seems to be a confusion in the rambling manner in which the story is told, as to exactly who or *what* the audience is supposed to be 'rooting' for. This is evidently because there are parallel stories in which the dramatic or interesting incidents have been '*dissolved through.*' . . . *The personal story* never seems to really get started until 9500 feet have passed. I think there is too much footage devoted to long shots, boats, piers, people walking, and too little footage devoted to *the people* in the picture. The audience identification with this picture, I think, is through the people, not through the plot development."

Apart from Willie and Sadie, the only real people in the film are the masses in the montages. If one "roots" for anyone, it is for them—the nameless Americans whose faces blaze with an integrity the main characters lack. They are Harry's "*people.*" If Rossen failed to clarify what even Warren could not (except by authorial intrusion), Harry's prodding resulted in a film that was less diffuse than it would have been if Rossen had been given his way. And that prodding was rewarded on Oscar night.

If Columbia did not specialize in stage adaptations in the 1930s and 1940s, it was not because of Harry's lack of interest in Broadway. Harry went to the theater whenever he was in New York. As soon as he saw *Pal Joey* in 1940, he wanted to make the movie version. Unfortunately, he had to wait until a year before his death to achieve his goal. When he did, it bore little resemblance to the cynical masterpiece he had seen seventeen years earlier.

Other studios filmed the stage hits of the 1930s and 1940s: RKO (*Stage Door* [1937]), MGM (*The Philadelphia Story* [1940], *Gaslight* [1944]), Warners

Janie [1944], *The Doughgirls* [1944], *The Voice of the Turtle* [1947]), Paramount (*Dear Ruth* [1947]), Fox (*Junior Miss* [1944]). Columbia's excursions into theater were few: *Holiday, You Can't Take It with You,* and *Ladies in Retirement. Death of a Salesman,* a Stanley Kramer production, was far from successful and is virtually unknown.

Still, Harry's first exposure to show business occurred in New York; thus he never gave up on Broadway. Three years before his death, he even envisioned a Playwrights' Group, with major dramatists like Arthur Miller, Tennessee Williams, William Inge, and Sidney Kingsley writing and producing plays they would later adapt for the screen. Although nothing came of the idea, it is evident that at the end of his life Harry was still thinking theater, as evidenced by Columbia's many stage adaptations of the 1950s: *Born Yesterday, The Member of the Wedding, The Happy Time,* the musical *My Sister Eileen, The Solid Gold Cadillac, Picnic, Pal Joey,* and *Bell, Book and Candle.* If Harry could have afforded it, *Guys and Dolls* would have been a Columbia release instead of a Goldwyn production.

Born Yesterday was to be Columbia's first adaptation of a Broadway smash since *You Can't Take It with You. Kiss and Tell* may have had a good run but it was not major theater, nor was *Ladies in Retirement,* which could only claim to be a superior thriller. Harry wanted to make the movie version of Garson Kanin's comedy as soon as it opened in 1946, going so far as to pay an unprecedented $1 million for the rights. Thus he wanted it done his way, and his way was the way it had been performed on Broadway. It was common knowledge that Kanin's Harry Brock, the millionaire junk dealer, was partly modeled on Harry, although the only ex-junk dealer who ran a studio was Louis Mayer. It did not bother Harry that Brock was a composite of himself and Mayer; he may even have been flattered. All that mattered to Harry, as the August 1948 teletypes show, was that the movie be a replica of the original.

On 11 August 1948 Harry queried producer Max Gordon about filming a performance of *Born Yesterday* directly from the stage to see how it played before an audience: "We could bring the film back here so we could study just where the laughs are and what moods are that would help us in writing continuity." Since laughs can vary from performance to performance (as can a play's rhythm), Harry's was not a practical suggestion. Yet it reveals his obsession with the project as well as his concern about protecting Columbia's investment. Ignoring Gordon's suggestion that he hire the stage manager as a consultant, Harry pressed Gordon to check with Actors Equity about the legality of filming a play in performance.

When Equity agreed provided the entire company was paid a week's salary, Harry wanted to film a performance as cheaply as possible. The quality of the print did not matter ("photo is unimportant"), nor did the expertise of the crew. Anything would do as long as he had something to study. Harry kept hounding Gordon for exact figures, which changed every time they made contact. With Judy Holliday, it would cost around $4,375; with her replacement, Jean Hagen, $1,000 less. When Gordon quoted a higher figure ($6,000-$8,000) at the end of August, Harry, suspecting Gordon was planning to pocket some of the money, had the New York office verify it. As it turned out, Gordon's estimate was accurate.

Still, Gordon cautioned, there were other problems. Cameras in the theater would inconvenience some members of the audience. It would be better to paper the house (distribute free tickets), but that would increase the cost. By December 1948, Harry had modified his plan to the extent of recording a performance instead of filming it. When Gordon realized Harry thought it could be done clandestinely, he warned Harry against it, claiming it would be "bad faith." Although forced to abandon both schemes, Harry was still determined that the movie version be as close to the play as possible.

It may seem difficult, therefore, to understand why he did not immediately sign Judy Holliday, who had scored such a triumph on Broadway as Brock's mistress, Billie Dawn. One reason is that Harry considered Brock, not Billie, the main character. Knowing he would be partially identified with Brock (or perhaps exclusively, since his reputation for vulgarity surpassed Mayer's), Harry wanted a major star for the part. His preference was Humphrey Bogart; his second choice, James Cagney. When neither was available, he briefly considered Brian Donlevy, whose lack of a screen persona might prove interesting and result in a performance that was not in the "tough guy" tradition of Bogart and Cagney.

Another reason for Harry's reluctance to consider Holliday in 1948 was her lack of screen experience; her credits consisted of bits in *Winged Victory, Something for the Boys,* and *Greenwich Village* (all 1944). There were enough actresses at Columbia, Harry believed, who could play the stereotypical "dumb blonde": Lucille Ball, Rita Hayworth (whose possibilities intrigued him), Evelyn Keyes, and others. When Marie McDonald was hired for *Tell It to the Judge* (1949), Harry thought she might make a good foil for Donlevy. It was only after Holliday's scene-stealing performance in *Adam's Rib* (1949) at MGM and Broderick Crawford's success in *All the King's Men* that Harry knew he had his Billie Dawn and Harry Brock. And with William Holden under contract at the studio, he also had his Paul Verall.

Once the leads were set, Harry returned to his plan of replicating the original: he had the cast perform the play before an audience of studio employees so he could get their reaction.

By demanding the celluloid equivalent of the play, Harry deprived

Born Yesterday of much of its spontaneity, forcing director George Cukor, who excelled at stage adaptations, to become a prisoner of the proscenium. Consequently, Judy Holliday repeated her original characterization with a vengeance, forever allying herself with her character. Those who know her only as Billie Dawn have seen just one facet of her art.

Even before *Born Yesterday* went before the cameras on 15 June 1950, the Hays Office had become the Johnston Office. A name change made no difference to Harry. Having won the right to use "louse" in *A Thousand and One Nights*, Harry would not settle for anything less than "broad" in *Born Yesterday*. When Leo Jaffe, then treasurer and vice president (and, being based in New York, the liaison with MPAA), informed Harry the Johnston Office was dubious about the use of "broad" (an important word in the script, despite its sexist overtones), Harry was furious. His reaction was the same as it had been five years earlier: "Then resign from the Johnston office." Always ready to make New York shoulder the blame, Harry berated Jaffe for not doing as he had been told: "I have asked you repeatedly, when you reach a situation . . . in a Johnston meeting, to excuse yourself and call me" (13 April 1950).

Nothing Jaffe could say would convince Harry the situation might change—even that the MPAA was planning to drop certain words, including "broad," from the Code. Instead of feeling relieved, Harry became belligerent, insisting Jaffe had misled him. For a week Jaffe suffered Harry's abuse; then, as if to carve the MPAA decision in stone, Jaffe wired Harry (20 April 1950): "Secured approval for use of word 'Broad' by Columbia."

While one needs access to the teletypes to appreciate the extent of Harry's role in the making of *Born Yesterday*, his involvement in *From Here to Eternity* was evident from the ads: Harry Cohn was "presenting" the film. It was one that he desperately wanted to make, going so far as to pay $82,000 for a first novel considered too controversial to be filmed. Six years earlier, Fox had anticipated a blockbuster with *Forever Amber* (1947), another unfilmable, and encountered such censorship problems that it released a tame period piece with little audience appeal.

Since Hollywood expected an eviscerated *Eternity* as well as a box office fiasco, Harry was determined to prove the industry wrong on both counts. First, he needed a screenwriter who could adapt a novel that dealt with adultery, prostitution, and sadism and that indicted the U.S. Army for its inhumanity and corruption. Daniel Taradash, who specialized in adaptations and had recently adapted Willard Motley's *Knock on Any Door* (1949), was the logical choice, not just for his ability to bring works of fiction to the screen but also because he had spent three years (1941-43) in the Signal Corps, writing and producing training films.[25] Having been in the military, Taradash knew exactly how far he could go and still get the army's cooperation, especially the use of Schofield Barracks.

Taradash did not play down the adultery between Karen (Deborah Kerr) and Warden (Burt Lancaster); it is evident in the lovemaking scene on the beach, which remains one of the most erotic moments in film. Nor did he obscure the fact that Alma (Donna Reed) is a prostitute working in a brothel; by 1953 "hostess" was a well-known euphemism for "whore." Although one never sees what "Fatso" (Ernest Borgnine) does to Maggio (Frank Sinatra) in the stockade, the beatings are not only described but the results are plainly visible: Maggio's battered face makes it evident that he did not die of natural causes.

Taradash preserved the essence of the novel, eliminating and combining characters, transferring the fate of one character to another (Maggio does not die in the novel, but Blues Berry does), and intercutting two ill-fated romances: Warden and Karen, Prewitt (Montgomery Clift) and Alma. His one concession to the army was to administer poetic justice to Karen's unscrupulous husband. In the novel, Captain Holmes's villainy is rewarded: he is promoted to major. In the film he is forced to resign or face a court martial.[26]

The Johnston Office proved as cooperative as the army. Although Joe Breen was still Production Code head, he never had quite the same authority after Eric Johnston replaced Will Hays in 1945.[27] Until then, "Breen Office" was virtually synonymous with "Hays Office." Soon, some studio heads, including Harry, were speaking of the "Johnston Office." Breen still administered the Code, but it was becoming increasingly evident that with the decline of the studio system, the Paramount decision requiring studios with theater chains to divest themselves of them, and the influx of foreign films whose approach to sex posed a challenge to the Code, the days of moral fiat were ending. And so were Breen's days as Production Code head; a year after the release of *Eternity*, Breen resigned from the PCA. Breen's replacement, Geoffrey Shurlock, had been a tempering influence on him for almost twenty years; Shurlock respected Taradash's script and perhaps persuaded Breen to appreciate its merits as well.[28] But even without Shurlock's support, the script met the Code's requirements. As in the novel, both love affairs end unhappily: Warden's true love is the army, not Karen; Prewitt is killed; and with Captain Holmes's forced retirement, justice is done.

Eternity had to be cast properly, and not with Columbia contract players in the leads, since few of them would have been suitable. Just as film historians have wondered whether *Casablanca* would be a perennial favorite with Ronald Reagan, Ann Sheridan, and Dennis Morgan in the leads, they might also ponder an *Eternity* with Edmond O'Brien as Warden, Joan Crawford as Karen, Eli Wallach as Maggio, Aldo Ray as Prewitt, and Julie Harris as Alma. Fortunately, Crawford was more concerned about her wardrobe than her character; Harry vetoed Harris because he disliked *The Member of the Wedding*; Wallach prefered to return to Broadway to play Kilroy in Tennessee Williams's *Camino Real*; and Fred Zinnemann, who had directed Montgomery Clift in *The Search* (1948), refused to make *Eternity* without the only actor (apart from Wallach, whose screen test made him a strong candidate for the role) who could play Prewitt. Finally, signing Deborah Kerr precluded the possibility of O'Brien's playing opposite her. "Perfect casting" has always been an industry cliché; in *Eternity's* case, it was a fact.[29]

That *Eternity* was one of Harry's films is evident from his dealings with Taradash and Zinnemann. At story conferences he played literalist, arguing with Taradash about the difference between "proper" and "respectable." Taradash won with "proper" (the word Alma uses to describe the life she envisions for herself and Prewitt); yet Taradash had to agree with Harry that a scene was needed to show that Prewitt could play the trumpet before he plays Taps after Maggio's death. The "Reenlistment Blues" sequence was the result.

With Zinnemann, it was a matter of casting and running time. Except for Donna Reed, Zinnemann got the leads he wanted; yet even he had to admit that Reed, cast against type (as were Deborah Kerr and Frank Sinatra), deserved her Oscar. If Zinnemann had to sacrifice a few minutes to satisfy Harry, who determined that *Eternity* would not exceed two hours (perhaps recalling Capra's *Lost Horizon* and *Mr. Smith Goes to Washington,* which never met Columbia's expectations), it was not a major loss. *Eternity's* running time is 118 minutes; had *Mr. Smith* been restricted to that length, it would have been a better film.

All the King's Men, Born Yesterday, and *From Here to Eternity* won a total of twelve Oscars in four years. Their success is attributable, to a great extent, to the wisdom of Harry Cohn. Even Zinnemann had to admit that, for all his deficiencies, Harry knew how to make movies: "His taste was quite often awful . . . and he constantly got into our hair checking every line of dialogue, worrying about casting, wardrobe and locations. I wish there were a few studio heads like him today."[30]

10

Death and Transfiguration

By the end of the 1940s, Harry saw Columbia's status as a major studio ensured, even though some of its films had not acquired the cachet of a *Meet Me in St. Louis* (MGM), *Citizen Kane* (RKO), or *Casablanca* (Warners). Still, *Here Comes Mr. Jordan* and *The Talk of the Town* represented a high level of filmmaking; *The Jolson Story* endeared itself to postwar audiences; *Gilda* defined the Rita Hayworth persona for future generations.

If Columbia's films of the 1940s seem minor in comparison to those of, say, Fox or MGM, it is because they are less familiar. That situation, however, began to change at the end of the 1980s when Columbia entered into licensing agreements with such cable channels as Cinemax, the Movie Channel, and Showtime, and with Turner Broadcasting, making titles available to them, (*Whirlpool*, *The Black Arrow*, *Coroner Creek*, Grace Moore's films, the Boston Blackie, Crime Doctor, and Whistler series), some of which had never been telecast before.

Seeing them, one is struck by the unusualness many possessed. Although the main action of *None Shall Escape* was set in 1939, the script written in 1943, and production completed a year before the liberation of Auschwitz, it included a scene of Polish Jews being herded into cattle cars. *Address Unknown* (1944), basically an antifascist film, added the device of the doublecross to the genre: a son knowingly causes the murder of his father, who is responsible for the death of the son's Jewish fiancée.

Anyone who lived during the decade undoubtedly numbers many Columbia releases among his or her favorites. Few movies about classical composers, whatever their inaccuracies, were as popular as *A Song to Remember*; the same cannot be said of MGM's biopic about Robert and Clara Schumann, *Song of Love*, with the improbable casting of Paul Henreid and Katharine Hepburn as the couple and Robert Walker as Brahms. While *Meet Me in St. Louis* is an indisputable classic, the musical that military personnel remember best is *Cover Girl* because Judy Garland's winsomeness was no substitute for Rita Hayworth's glamour.

By the end of the decade, the situation had changed. *All the King's Men*, Columbia's most prestigious film since *Lost Horizon*, won three

Oscars in 1950 for the best picture, best actor (Broderick Crawford), and best supporting actress (Mercedes McCambridge). The following year, *Born Yesterday* followed suit, causing one of the biggest surprises in Academy Awards history when Judy Holliday was named best actress over Gloria Swanson in *Sunset Boulevard* and Bette Davis in *All About Eve*.

Born Yesterday was the first of a number of 1950s films that brought Columbia the highest recognition it had ever known; *From Here to Eternity*, *On the Waterfront*, and *The Bridge on the River Kwai* followed. But there were others that acquired a different, and some might argue greater, importance as film scholars began using them to illustrate movie genres: Nicholas Ray's *In a Lonely Place* and Fritz Lang's *The Big Heat* for film noir; Budd Boetticher's Randolph Scott westerns and Anthony Mann's *The Man from Laramie* with James Stewart; and George Cukor's romantic comedies with Judy Holliday.[1]

Many of Columbia's films that achieved an international reputation were outside productions (Horizon's *Waterfront* and *Kwai*, Santana's *In a Lonely Place*); by the mid-1950s the industry had changed so much that it became increasingly difficult to make in-house films. Except for Sam Katzman, whom Harry could not hurt, Sam Spiegel, whom Harry loathed (but could not ignore after *Waterfront* received eight Oscars), and Harry Joe Brown, who, with Randolph Scott, did for the Burbank Ranch what John Ford did for Monument Valley, independent producers did not last long at Columbia. But that did not stop Harry from courting them.

The wooing of Stanley Kramer was typical of Harry's determination to supplement Columbia's releases with outside productions. In March 1951, Columbia entered into a $25 million agreement with the Stanley Kramer Company calling for thirty films, six a year, with Columbia financing and releasing all of them and sharing the profits. After the first six (*Death of a Salesman*, *Eight Iron Men*, *The Happy Time*, *The Member of the Wedding*, *My Six Convicts*, and *The Sniper*) were unsuccessful, Columbia limited the number to three a year, resulting in a reduction of staff. Finally, after eleven failures, Columbia terminated the agreement on 24 November 1954 even before *The Caine Mutiny*, Kramer's one hit, had a chance to prove itself. To Harry, a single success does not obliterate a rash of failures. It was not until a decade after Harry's death that Kramer returned to Columbia. When he did he gave the studio one of its most profitable (and popular) films, *Guess Who's Coming to Dinner* (1968).

While Harry had no love for Kramer, he had only contempt for Spiegel because he knew he could never claim credit for *Waterfront*; Harry would also never have made *Kwai* because of its all-male cast. Harry's 1957 movie was *Pal Joey*, a dilution of the Broadway original, with a happy ending as well. The Academy decreed otherwise: *Kwai* won seven Oscars, including best picture. *Pal Joey* did not win even in the one category in which it had been nominated, film editing; *Kwai* won that award, also.

Spiegel worked two three-picture deals with Columbia so he could be free to do the same elsewhere, as at United Artists with *The Prowler* and *The African Queen* (both 1951). After *Waterfront*, Spiegel was about to renegotiate his contract when Harry cautioned New York (25 March 1955): "I do not trust Spiegel as a producer and I don't like the deal especially when you are advancing him money. Spiegel is a promoter, not a producer. We should not get hooked on advancing preproduction monies to Spiegel." But a three-picture contract was signed. One of the films, *Kwai*, was a masterpiece; the other two, *The Strange One* and *Suddenly, Last Summer*, are models of stage adaptation.

Even during the last decade of his life, Harry had not given up on finding another Sidney Buchman as assistant production head. In 1952 he began pursuing Jerry Wald, who had been one of Warners' top producers until Howard Hughes enticed him to RKO, where he formed a production company with writer Norman Krasna, Wald-Krasna Productions. Wald soon became disenchanted with Hughes and, anxious to leave RKO, accepted Harry's invitation to come to Columbia. The problem was that Harry wanted only Wald, not Wald-Krasna. So he offered Wald $200,000, $25,000 of which went to Krasna in return for his investment in the company.[2] The title Harry proposed to Wald was vice president, production; at Fox, that would have meant production head. But as Wald discovered, there was only one production head at Columbia: Harry. Wald, in fact, had enjoyed greater autonomy at Warners than he did at Columbia.

Wald tried to please Harry, but he did not understand Harry's mentality. Since Wald was now part of Columbia, he was told he would be involved in *From Here to Eternity*. Yet it was Buddy Adler who became the producer—a meaningless title for that film since it meant being a mere overseer. Wald wanted some role in *Eternity*. He had been at Harry's home on North Crescent Drive the night Ava Gardner offered to make a movie for Columbia if Frank Sinatra, to whom she was then married, played Maggio—the role slated for Eli Wallach, who decided he would rather be Kilroy in Tennessee Williams's *Camino Real* (which had racked up a mere sixty performances in 1953).

Believing that Harry had taken him into his confidence, especially after their weekend meetings to discuss the film, Wald proposed an arrangement allowing him to produce *Eternity* in return for a percentage of the net profits. The weekend discussions, Wald felt, entitled him to 25 percent of *Eternity*. After Harry refused, Wald eventually waived his rights to any share in the film. One must assume, then, that the credits stand: *Eternity* was a Columbia film written by Daniel Taradash and directed by Fred Zinnemann, both of whom deservedly received Oscars for their efforts.

Despite his unsuccessful bid to produce *Eternity*, Wald was determined to act if not like a production head then like an executive producer. But nothing at Warners prepared him for a Columbia story conference with "America's greatest dramatist." Harry would often visualize the script, imagining how it might appear on the screen. He did not exactly go into a trance, but he gave his imagination free rein as he envisaged a character or scene. Harry also thought nothing of interrupting the vice president of production. At the start of a story conference on *Human Desire* (1954), Wald was describing the Glenn Ford character as an "ex-Canadian locomotive engineer" when Harry cut in with "an ex-soldier, highly decorated during the war," at which point Wald continued, "war hero came home. . . ."[3]

Wald had less difficulty with the film's director, Fritz Lang. He was not afraid to criticize the great Lang for the absence of mood lighting or to remind him to make sure the train goes from right to left when it comes into the frame. But Harry also lived up to his responsibilities as Columbia's *real* production head. He scrutinized the script ("Now on page 100 . . ."); he demanded dialogue changes ("The day I got Carl's job back" should be "The day I got Carl his job back"). At one point in his script, Lang wrote, "H.C. is absolutely right."

While Wald had at least some input in *Human Desire*, he had little chance to be at Columbia what he had been at Warners. Writing to Fred Zinnemann (17 November 1961), he explained why he had left the studio: "I quit Columbia because of Harry Cohn's maniacal attitude toward everyone in the studio. If I had an idea for casting, a script change or a story, it always had to be told to Cohn, and no one else. Eventually Cohn would convince everyone that [he] was responsible for all the films made by Columbia and that no one contributed anything at all."

If Harry was behaving maniacally in the mid-1950s, it was probably because he sensed the presence of the eternal footman. His days as studio head, along with his life, were drawing to a close. If he took more credit for his films than he should, it was because he knew that without him they would never have been made—at least not at Columbia. Finally, if Sam Goldwyn could speak of *his* films, why couldn't Harry Cohn?

In March 1954 Harry had his first brush with mortality: a throat operation that revealed a malignancy (although that fact may not have been made known to him). While, internally, Harry knew he would not live out his threescore and ten, he behaved as if he were immortal. On the eve of his surgery he was more interested in hearing about Kim Novak's screen test for *Pushover* (1954). When Paul Lazarus told him it was brilliant, Harry scowled, finding it difficult to accept another's being on the verge of stardom while he was going under the knife.

And Novak went on to stardom, progressing from female fatale (*Pushover*) to girl-next-door (*Picnic*) to alcoholic actress (*Jeanne Eagels*) to younger woman involved with older man (*Middle of the Night*, the film of which she is proudest). Although Harry was never the same after the operation, he monitored Novak's career; to him, she was the embodiment of Hayworth's glamour and Holliday's vulnerability. In more practical terms, Novak came into prominence as Holliday's movie career was ebbing and Hayworth's was going into eclipse. If Harry triggered the end of the Novak-Davis affair, it did not affect Novak's feelings for Harry. On 27 February 1958 she was on the set of *Bell, Book and Candle* when she heard the news of Harry's death; she rushed off in tears.[4] She also attended his memorial service.

While Harry was grooming Novak, he was also planning a biblical epic, *Joseph and His Brothers*. It is curious that Harry, who generally avoided movies with religious themes, chose this particular story. Perhaps he was influenced by the success of *Salome*; perhaps he thought the film would exorcize the demons that estranged him from his brother, effecting the reconciliation of which neither was capable. Ever cautious, he set a $1.7 million minimum budget, knowing it would go higher if, as he intended, Clifford Odets wrote the script, William Dieterle directed, and Rita Hayworth played the female lead, as she had in Dieterle's *Salome*. The only female role Hayworth could have played in *Joseph* was Potiphar's wife. If *Salome* is any indication of Columbia's idea of biblical fidelity, one could imagine a much greater role for Potiphar's wife than the few verses devoted to her in Genesis 39:6-20.[5] Harry also hoped to team Hayworth with Glenn Ford, again to capitalize on their reunion in the successful *Affair in Trinidad*. When New York suggested Susan Hayward (28 July 1955), Harry admitted she was a better actress but that Hayworth "has much bigger box office."

Joseph never came to pass. By 1955 Dieterle was past his prime and Hayworth was married to Dick Haymes, a splendid singer (but no actor) who envisioned himself as Joseph. With Harry's having to renegotiate Hayworth's contract for $150,000, put Haymes on the payroll, and buy out Hayworth's share in Beckworth, *Joseph* became one of the most expensive films never made. Hayworth satisfied her contract with *Fire down Below* and *Pal Joey*, and the public was spared seeing Dick Haymes in a beard.

After Jack's death in 1956, Harry felt the September of his life approaching. The premonition of death at sixty-seven drove him to make one final effort to find an assistant production head, perhaps someone to whom he might pass the scepter. Since Harry had always been envious of

MGM, he picked George Sidney, the director of such MGM musicals as *Anchors Aweigh* (1945), *The Harvey Girls* (1946), and *Annie Get Your Gun* (1950). Harry expected Sidney to help him achieve a lifelong ambition, the film version of the 1940 Rodgers and Hart musical *Pal Joey*, which had had a spectacular revival in 1952. Sidney, who had no feeling for the musical's underlying cynicism, softened the tone and sweetened the brew. While Frank Sinatra and Kim Novak at least came off unscathed, Rita Hayworth as the bored matron with an eye for young men was given the number "Zip," a mock striptease that, in the original, was sung by a minor character. Clearly intended to evoke "Put the Blame on Mame" from *Gilda*, "Zip" became a self-parody, with the World War II goddess mocking her own persona. Sidney did little better with Harry's other pet projects, *The Eddy Duchin Story* (1956) and *Jeanne Eagels* (1957), although the former had a magnificent soundtrack and both offered intelligent performances by Kim Novak as the first Mrs. Duchin and the self-destructive actress, respectively.

Not only did George Sidney come from the Tiffany of studios but so did his wife, Lillian, who had been an acting coach at MGM and had quoted Louis Mayer's accolade to her so often ("Lillian Sidney is the only woman I have ever met who could run a studio") that Harry began to believe it.[6] He would sit in his bedroom while Lillian Sidney synopsized scripts for him, arguing for those she liked and against those she did not. Yet all Harry ever got from the Sidneys were some social contacts: the films they gave him were negligible.

On 14 February 1958, Harry's will was ready to be signed; on 7 March it was filed for probate. Like its maker, the will was generous and frugal, simple in bequest and complex in execution. On one matter Harry did not equivocate: there was to be no funeral service. If "service" is restricted to a religious ceremony conducted in a place of worship (a church or temple), there was none in that sense. What one wishes to call the event that took place on 2 March (which will be described shortly) is a matter of semantics.

Harry left his Beverly Hills home on North Crescent Drive—with its $129,000 projection room, galleria, dining room, bar, library, oval card room, four bedroom suites, sitting room, and quarters for six servants—to his wife; his jewelry to his sons, John and Harry, Jr.; $10,000 to his niece Judith, Max Cohn's daughter; $10,000 to his sister Anna; $1,000 each to two servants, mentioned by name, if they were still employed at the time of his death; and $500 to any servant who had been in his employ for at least four years prior to his death.

Harry's will was consistent; since he had never acquired a reputation for philanthropy during his lifetime, he saw no reason to acquire one posthumously; "I give no gifts to charity by this will for the reason that I have made substantial transfers during my lifetime to the Harry Cohn Foundation." Louis Mayer may have tried to convince the world, and perhaps himself, that MGM was a family; but Harry knew the difference between the workplace and the home, professional bonds and blood lines. Harry's family was not on North Gower Street but on North Crescent Drive. It was for them that, in 1954, shortly after his throat surgery made him sensitive to his mortality, he established the Harry Cohn Foundation, whose assets included 220,000 shares of Columbia stock—one-ninth of the shares outstanding. Since John and Harry, Jr., were fourteen and twelve, respectively, in 1958, Harry left detailed instructions as to how they would receive their shares of the trust in the event of their mother's death or if one of them died before the other, and how the remaining principal of the trust would be distributed once the beneficiaries were dead. Although the Cohns had lost their daughter, Jobella, who died almost immediately after she was born in 1943, they had later adopted a girl, Catherine Perry Cohn, who was also included in the trust. Harry, however, expected fidelity to the Cohn name; as one journalist remarked, Catherine Perry Cohn's initials were the same as Columbia Pictures Corporation's. This was no doubt coincidental, but, as a Cohn, her financial future was shaped by Harry's Columbia stock. Harry specified that if Catherine chose not to consider herself a member of the Cohn family, her trust would be discontinued.

Should further proof be needed that George and Lillian Burns Sidney would have played an active role at Columbia if Harry had lived, the will provides it: Lillian was a witness and George was named a trustee of the estate (which was valued at between $10 and $14 million).

Within two weeks of his signing the will, Harry was dead; his conviction that he would die at the same age as his brother was borne out on 27 February 1958. While vacationing in one of his favorite cities, Phoenix, he suffered a fatal heart attack. Although he had died before the ambulance reached St. Joseph's Hospital, Joan Perry Cohn, a Catholic convert, informed a priest that before Harry died he had uttered the name of Christ, whereupon the corpse of Harry Cohn was baptized.[7]

If Mrs. Cohn actually believed Harry spoke the name of Christ reverentially, one must assume either that she understood subtlety of inflection or knew how to decode her husband's exclamations and expletives. In Flannery O'Connor's short story "A Good Man Is Hard to Find," a woman who prides herself on being an exemplary Christian begins saying "Jesus" in a far from respectful manner when she encounters a mass murderer. The ultimate joke, of course, would have been Harry's invoking Christ's name in anger at the prospect of death. Yet Mrs. Cohn was determined to have as Catholic a memorial service as possible; Harry's being a Christian—at least in his next mode of existence—would simplify matters. It would also facilitate their reunion in the hereafter.

Harry, who prided himself on being unique, became the only studio head who was both bar mitzvahed and baptized. If Harry's "baptism" seems sacrilegious, Canon Law can be interpreted in such a way as to sanction it.[8] While the Code of Canon Law in force in 1958 suggests that the sacrament can be administered only to one who is alive and not yet baptized, theologians have also distinguished between *valid* baptism (requiring the intention to be baptized) and *licit* baptism (requiring instruction in the faith and repentance of past sins). Although Harry never seems to have evidenced any interest in Catholicism, Mrs. Cohn must have convinced the priest that he did. While not a licit baptism, it was at least valid; that is, it "took." Even if its validity seems questionable, Harry's baptism can be considered *conditional*: baptism is administered conditionally if there is any doubt about the intention of one in danger of death.

Harry was, of course, out of danger of death; he *was* dead. Still, there are arguments to justify his baptism. The Catholic Church has always considered some form of baptism, traditionally called the first sacrament, a prerequisite for salvation. While baptism by water is the most common form, it is not the only one; there are other kinds: the unbaptized, for example, can die for a faith into which they have not been formally initiated, thereby receiving baptism of blood. And what of the desire to be baptized? If a priest were convinced that such a desire existed—evidenced, for example, by the invocation of Christ's name at the moment of death—there would be no reason to withhold baptism, regardless of the physical state of the initiate. Extreme Unction, the last sacrament one can receive (hence its other name, the Final Anointing), can be administered conditionally if a person shows no signs of life; why then cannot the first sacrament be administered under the same circumstances? The emphasis placed on baptism in the 1950s created such a range of possibilities and interpretations that posthumous baptism cannot be ruled out or considered irreconcilable with the teachings of the Church. If the Church taught that baptism in some form (immersion or aspersion, of blood or desire) was the *sine qua non* of salvation, Harry had to be saved. Whether he wanted it or not was irrelevant.

On Friday, 28 February, workmen labored to turn two Columbia soundstages, 12 and 14, into a chapel. Mrs. Cohn chose a Sunday for the memorial, as befitting a new addition to the faith. The weather also suited the occasion. Believers in prodigies might have recalled *Julius Caesar*, Act 2, scene 2 ("When beggars die, there are no comets seen; / The heavens themselves blaze forth the death of princes"), wondering if the reverberating thunder and lightning zigzagging across the sky that set fire to a palm tree were signaling the end of a prince.

The ceremony began at 2:00 P.M.; it was a photo opportunity and an autograph collector's dream. The Hollywood Catholics were represented by Kim Novak, Loretta Young in a black dress and turban, Rosalind Russell in a matronly white hat, Maureen O'Hara, John Ford, and Pat O'Brien, among others. The seventy-four honorary pallbearers included Spencer Tracy, Dick Powell, Tony Curtis, Paul Lazarus, Glenn Ford, Jack Lemmon, and Frank Capra.

The fans did not have a long wait; the service was brief but impressive. The orchid-covered coffin rested on a raised platform resembling an altar, framed by banks of flowers. There was nothing about the service to suggest that the deceased had been born a Jew; but then, he had been reborn a Christian. Gloria Krieger, a Columbia contract player whose career seems to have ended with the service, sang "The Lord's Prayer." Then Danny Kaye delivered the eulogy that Clifford Odets had written (Appendix A). The language of the Church even permeated Odets's text: Columbia was "Harry Cohn's Cathedral"; "God had put a special mark on his forehead"; "from [his] marriage will come his true immortality" (Odets means Harry's children, but Mrs. Cohn no doubt interpreted it differently). Finally, Danny Thomas, a prominent Hollywood Catholic, read the Twenty-third Psalm, after which the cortege proceeded in the rain to the nearby Hollywood Memorial Park Cemetery, where Thomas repeated the psalm alongside the coffin.

Harry's death made the front page of the *Los Angeles Times* on 28 February. The next day an editorial appeared extolling him as "one of the greatest of all individualists in motion pictures" and "a leader in the film industry [who] held that position by his genius, by his inability to recognize the possibility of defeat, and by his incredible ability to develop the ultimate talents of actors, directors and writers that worked for him."

It was an accurate summation. The world's greatest dramatist could not write drama but could get it on the screen; the artist who could not paint placed film's palette at the disposal of his studio; and the architect who could not build made a rabbit warren on Poverty Row into a cathedral.

Harry Cohn was not a complex man, unless complex is synonymous with multifaceted. Like others who pursued a variety of careers until they found the one best suited to their talents, Harry went through an apprenticeship that started on Broadway and ended in Hollywood with his becoming president of a studio. He was not pursuing the dream job as much as his own dream—one that he could never articulate because it would mean admitting to the same dream that everyone in the arts has in common: recognition. It was not enough merely to surpass his brother and become the Cohn associated with Columbia; it was having the respect of creative people who could accept his street-fighter facade because they knew it was protective coloration and that beneath it was a man who knew his deficiencies and expected them to be remedied by those who had what he lacked.

With Harry, it was not a matter of compensating for the loss of a brother's affection, although he certainly knew the loneliness of life at the top. Thus Harry made it difficult for those he cultivated to plan their evenings until 5:00 P.M., at which time they would learn whether or not they would be dining with Harry. Claiming a previous engagement meant being followed in Harry's car to make sure the engagement was genuine. Harry could live without Jack's love but not with the void left by an unfinished education. Others had to finish it. Thus Harry surrounded himself with men and women of taste who, having come up through the ranks, could interpret vulgarity and arrogance as self-directed rage. Capra, Riskin, Swerling, Buchman, and Van Upp could deal with him, but those he considered privileged, like Buddy Adler and Collier Young, became targets of abuse.

Although the last quality anyone would attribute to Harry is humility, he did possess it; he would not have called it that, but he also could not have come up with a word to characterize his ability to bring international renown to a studio whose longevity even his brother doubted. Harry might have hidden behind "chutzpah," "guts," or "luck," but it was humility, the sort that occurs at that moment of truth when the self confronts its nature, realizing its strengths and limitations, and then deciding to reveal only the former. That act of introspection, one of internal humility, leads to a proud exterior—the only exterior that a studio head, unsure of himself, can adopt.

Accepting one's limitations is only the beginning; next comes transcendence, so that what is actually limited appears to others as limitless. Those who were on intimate terms with Harry—or as intimate as they could be with a studio head—helped him extend his personal boundaries into a horizon that seemed without end. The company of writers like Swerling, Riskin, and Buchman improved his vocabulary; otherwise, he could never have argued about characterization and motivation at story conferences. Nate Spingold made him sensitive to art and haute cuisine, so that he felt as much at home at Le Pavilon with Spingold as he did at Lindy's with Frank Costello. But it was not merely writers and art collectors whom he courted. Harry was a gambler, and there was as much to learn from a bookie, who could give him tips on a horse, as there was from an intellectual. If Harry's circle was eclectic, so was his studio, and so were its pictures.

The clearest proof that Harry could not achieve his vision of Columbia by himself is his hiring of Capra at a time when the director was without prospects. Harry must have sensed that Capra could give Columbia the tag-defying image he envisioned. Since Capra was as conflicted as Harry, attracted to slapstick and farce as well as to romance and social consciousness, he could shift back and forth between them, even managing to create combinations. Capra's mix-and-match movie became the norm at Columbia, although neither Harry nor Capra thought of it as such; they only knew that a certain kind of movie was being made that evidently pleased the public.

What Capra effected during his twelve years at Columbia, the most crucial years in the studio's history, was the realization of Harry's dream. Harry did not choose the pure strain of film, as Louis Mayer did. A pure strain may be distinctive but it can also become extinct when the prototype can no longer reproduce itself. Harry favored the hybrid on the principle that mixed strains are longer lived and more adaptable. He would have been flattered to learn that Columbia was, to use the current buzzword, a high concept studio whose films resisted simplistic labels such as thriller, youth movie, and dynasty flick. While Harry envied MGM for its twenty-two sound stages and hundred-acre back lot, he was opposed to Columbia's making movies in the MGM tradition, which elevated the grand bourgeois to a way of life. Instead, at Columbia narrative strains and story lines were intertwined, resulting in combinations that undermine the very nature of genre.

To achieve his dream, Harry needed someone who felt similarly, someone who could speak in tongues—Harry's, America's, and the world's. Capra's trilingual ability precluded Columbia's ever becoming like Eliot's Prufrock, pinned to the wall like a butterfly awaiting classification by a prissy lepidopterist.

The Columbia of Harry and Capra was not destined to remain on Gower. Within fifteen years of Harry's death, Columbia moved to Burbank, forming with Warners, which had its home there, the Burbank Studios. When the doomsday prophets started to wail, Columbia countered by claiming it had been a Burbank resident since 1935 when it purchased property there that became known as the Burbank Ranch and provided the exteriors for many Columbia westerns. The studio's next change of address occurred in 1989; after being owned by Coca-Cola (1982-89), Columbia became part of Sony Pictures Entertainment and relocated to Culver City. Although Harry knew by 1950 that the industry would be changing dramatically over the next quarter of a century, he would have considered outside ownership unthinkable and foreign ownership impossible. Eventually, Harry would have yielded to the changing times; having learned to adapt early in life, he would have admitted that the studio could no longer be autonomous. But what would have given him the greatest pleasure was, first, that Columbia was the last of the majors to become the subsidiary of a corporation, and—what was especially meaningful to one who envied MGM—that as part of Sony Pictures Entertainment, Columbia now occupies the old MGM lot on West Washington Boulevard in Culver City.

Although Columbia left Gower Street in 1972, its name has not entirely vanished from the scene. The elegant Columbia Bar and Grill is at 1448 North Gower; next to it is Columbia Stage and Screen Cosmetics; and at Columbia's old address, 1438 North Gower, are the Sunset-Gower Studios, used for television production. On the corner of Sunset and Gower, partially obscured by a Denny's, is another Gower Gulch; it is a far cry from the original, where cowboy actors with gunbelts and ten-gallon hats passed the time while waiting for extra work. The new Gower Gulch is a shopping center that looks like a trading post in a B western. Still, it is gratifying to know that in a town that barely remembers last year's Oscar winners, some vestiges of the past live on, if only in name.

Appendix A

Eulogy for Harry Cohn, by Clifford Odets

[Delivered by Danny Kaye]

How short is the time of man.

We've come here today, dressed in solemnity, both in body and mind, in a final tribute to an unusual and remarkable man named Harry Cohn.

We sit here on this great stage, perhaps very fittingly,—we sit on this great stage of the studio that Harry built,—in itself a monument to some of his more remarkable qualities.

Without irreverence, this was Harry Cohn's Cathedral. This is where he lived, and worked, and dreamed, and this is where his energies, ambitions, and vision gave reality to those dreams. This is where the fierceness of the flame that was within him burned some and warmed others.

The story is well known—even legend—in its way of how Harry Cohn came from the sidewalks of New York and entering some remote back door of Hollywood and with nothing—nothing but his two bare hands—quickly took his part and place in the making of motion picture history.

The pictures he made along the way—the stars he found and developed—these are parts of the legend already familiar to most of us here today.

Harry performed most of what he proposed to perform in life. As tragically brief as life is, he lived nevertheless for two-thirds of a century—he lived long enough to enjoy the fruits of his extraordinary labor. I think few men enjoyed life so fully as Harry did.

His was truly a lust for life. Probably there was not an hour of his life that he did not live deeply and fully with an energy and a zest which, in themselves, are usually the distinguishing marks of a gifted person.

Men cannot be all things to all men.

They cannot, unfortunately, be all things even to themselves—but in this constant battle of man with himself, Harry emerged with a true sense of what you are and let the chips fall where they may.

Harry was always himself—always. He was a large scale business man and if, like most business men, he did not choose to succumb or go under, he was sometimes capable of reacting strongly—even harshly.

We have felt his anger, his defiance, his stubbornness—his pride—but many of us have felt his warmth, his understanding—his gentleness and some of us even his love.

The activity of developing stars, producers and directors, was a matter of immense personal solace to Harry—himself little educated, he admired almost to a fanatic degree, talent. Talent itself was a quality which bred in him a deep respect, almost as though the gifted human being was set aside, as if God had put a special mark on his forehead.

Harry was, in his trade, a master—and a master in business, art—or what-not—is one who masters, and Harry Cohn was not afraid to master.

It doesn't mean that he didn't listen to those who were expert in their field. The attitude of Harry behind his desk—lips pursed—head half bent—listening shrewdly— is a very very familiar one.

We remember, too, his lack of posturing—his frequent self-deprecation—his wry humor—and his sudden flashes to tender concern for others—which he chose to cover with a bulldog gruffness—rather than reveal a strong streak of sentiment in his nature.

Yes, Harry was a complex and gifted man. It was bracing to know him—stimulating—his appetite for anything under the sun quickened yours. It cannot have been easy for a man of Harry Cohn's joy of life to reconcile himself to mortality. It cannot have been easy.

But long ago, sensing man's essential loneliness—man's need—man's need of family—of love,—Harry married a woman he loved and respected and from that marriage will come his true immortality, for from that marriage have come three beautiful children, intelligent and maturing, who will carry some parts of their father and mother wherever they go. This is the legacy that he leaves—far beyond the legacy of wealth and fame. This is the legacy of his immortality.

Harry Cohn's breadth and size were of an older day that we shall not see again. I am glad that I knew Harry Cohn and his brawny vigor—he was an unforgettable man.

Appendix B

The Columbia Empire on the Eve
of Harry Cohn's Death

Figure 1. Columbia Pictures Corporation Board of Directors, May 1957

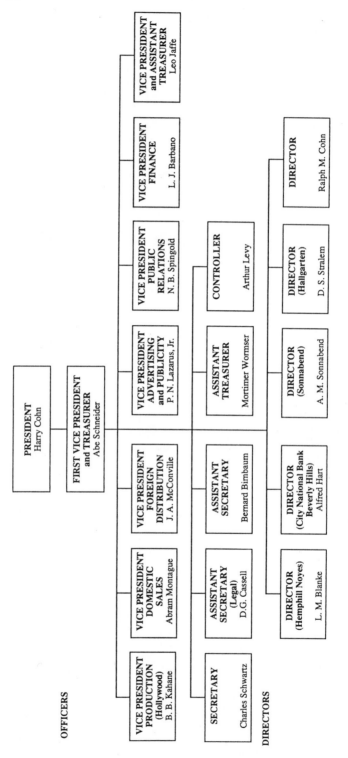

OFFICERS

| PRESIDENT
Harry Cohn |

| FIRST VICE PRESIDENT
and TREASURER
Abe Schneider |

| VICE PRESIDENT
PRODUCTION
(Hollywood)
B. B. Kahane |
| VICE PRESIDENT
DOMESTIC
SALES
Abram Montague |
| VICE PRESIDENT
FOREIGN
DISTRIBUTION
J. A. McConville |
| VICE PRESIDENT
ADVERTISING
and PUBLICITY
P. N. Lazarus, Jr. |
| VICE PRESIDENT
PUBLIC
RELATIONS
N. B. Spingold |
| VICE PRESIDENT
FINANCE
L. J. Barbano |
| VICE PRESIDENT
and ASSISTANT
TREASURER
Leo Jaffe |

| SECRETARY
Charles Schwartz |
| ASSISTANT
SECRETARY
(Legal)
D.G. Cassell |
| ASSISTANT
SECRETARY
Bernard Birnbaum |
| ASSISTANT
TREASURER
Mortimer Wormser |
| CONTROLLER
Arthur Levy |

DIRECTORS

| DIRECTOR
(Hemphill Noyes)
L. M. Blanke |
| DIRECTOR
(City National Bank
Beverly Hills)
Alfred Hart |
| DIRECTOR
(Sonnabend)
A. M. Sonnabend |
| DIRECTOR
(Hallgarten)
D. S. Stralem |
| DIRECTOR
Ralph M. Cohn |

Source: Boyce Nemec Management Consultant

Figure 2. Columbia Pictures Corporation Corporate Management, Divisions, and Subsidiaries, May 1957

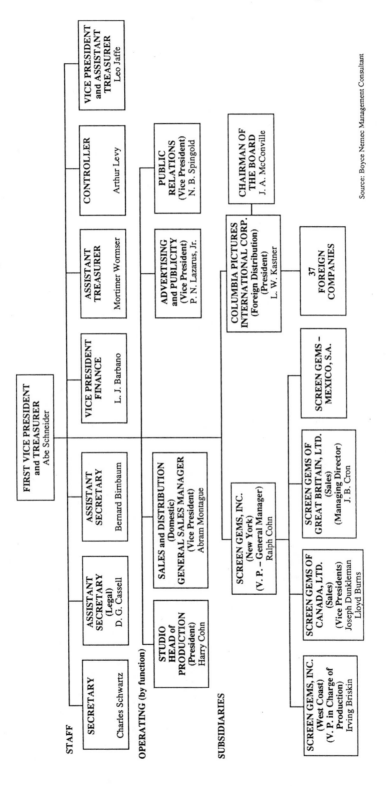

Source: Boyce Nemec Management Consultant

Figure 3. Columbia Pictures Corporation Hollywood Studio, April 1957

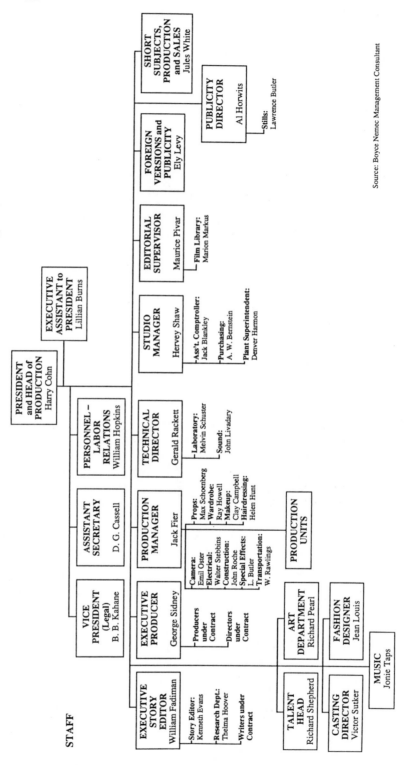

Source: Boyce Nemec Management Consultant

Notes

Introduction

1. A. Scott Berg, *Goldwyn: A Biography* (New York: Ballantine, 1989), 5.
2. Thomas Schatz, *The Genius of the System: Hollywood Filmmaking in the Studio Era* (New York: Pantheon, 1988).
3. Letter to author, 4 May 1988.
4. Gene M. Gressley to author, 4 April 1990: "We purchased [the Columbia Pictures Collection] via lot. Some of it was given to us by a young man who acquired it in Los Angeles. . . . I have forgotten the man's name."

1. Two Persons in One God

1. On these and other stories, see Norman Zierold, *The Moguls* (New York: Avon, 1972), 186-211; also Bob Thomas, *King Cohn: The Life and Times of Harry Cohn* (New York: McGraw-Hill, 1990 rpt.), *passim*.
2. The reference is to the subtitle of Neal Gabler's *An Empire of Their Own: How the Jews Invented Hollywood* (New York: Crown, 1988); on Harry Cohn see 151-83.
3. Schulberg described his wife's experience in his *King Cohn* review in *Life*, 3 March 1967.
4. Interview with author, 10 June 1989, Los Angeles.
5. Two years before he died, Harry held the same views, as he told the *New York Herald Tribune*, 28 Feb. 1956: "We believe here that writers are more important than either star or director because the story is the whole foundation of the film."
6. On these threats see Al Morgan, "Svengali of the Silver Screen," *Playboy*, Oct. 1959, 122; Sammy Davis, Jr., Jane Boyar and Burt Boyar, *Why Me? The Sammy Davis, Jr. Story* (New York: Farrar, Straus and Giroux, 1989), 87.
7. Davis, Boyar, and Boyar, *Why Me?* 99.
8. Sammy Davis, Jr., Jane Boyar, and Burt Boyar, *Yes I Can* (New York: Farrar, Straus and Giroux, 1965), 433: "I was impressed by the glamour of a movie star and she was impressed by my talent, but she hadn't thought about me any more than I had thought about her—until it was forbidden."
9. *New York Law Journal*, 7 Oct. 1952, 2.
10. Bolton recounted the incident in the *Morning Telegraph*, 4 March 1958.

2. From Yorkville to Broadway

1. Marie Jastrow, *A Time to Remember: Growing Up in New York before the Great War* (New York: Norton, 1979), 90; see also Joseph Lovitz, "A History of Yorkville," *Our Town*, 21 March 1975, 26.

2. Bob Thomas has also written *Clown Prince of Hollywood: The Antic Life and Times of Jack L. Warner* (New York: McGraw-Hill, 1990).

3. Letter from Paul Lazarus to author, 4 April 1990.

4. Unlike Columbia University, which at the time had a reputation for being sectarian (in addition to requiring Latin and Greek for admission), New York University was known for its "entrepreneurial and utilitarian emphasis"; see Bayrd Still, "The Founding of New York University: Pioneer in Urban Higher Education," *NAHO*, 13 (Spring-Summer 1981): 28.

5. Interview with Oscar Saul, 10 June 1989.

6. William T. Braun, "Problems of the Operating Room," *Motography*, 6 Nov. 1911, 226.

7. Laurence Bergreen, *As Thousands Cheer: The Life of Irving Berlin* (New York: Viking, 1990), 38. On the myriad duties of songpluggers, see David Ewen, *The Life and Death of Tin Pan Alley: The Golden Age of American Popular Music* (New York: Funk and Wagnalls, 1964), 126-30.

8. On such gimmicks, see David A. Jasen, *Tin Pan Alley: The Composers, the Songs, the Performers and Their Times* (New York: David I. Fine, 1988), 38-40.

9. Siegfried Kracauer, *Theory of Film: The Redemption of Physical Reality* (New York: Oxford Univ. Press/Galaxy Books, 1985), 18.

10. For a description of the 1915 opening, see Richard Koszarski, *An Evening's Entertainment: The Age of the Silent Feature Picture, 1915-1928* (New York: Scribner's, 1990), 5-8.

11. The traditional *Traffic in Souls* story is in Terry Ramsaye, *A Million and One Nights: A History of the Motion Picture through 1925* (New York: Simon and Schuster, 1986 rpt.), 611-16; it is repeated in Charles Drinkwater, *The Life and Adventures of Carl Laemmle* (New York: Putnam's, 1931), 161-64. I.G. Edmonds, *Big U: Universal in the Silent Days* (Cranbury, N.J.: A.S. Barnes, 1977), forcefully argues against Ramsaye's version. Kevin Brownlow, *Behind the Mask of Innocence* (New York: Knopf, 1990), 71-80, demythologizes it, making a strong case for Jack Cohn's role in the film's success.

12. The standard work on the subject is by the dean of early film history, Charles Musser, in collaboration with Carol Nelson, *High-Class Moving Pictures: Lyman H. Howe and the Forgotten Era of Traveling Exhibition, 1880-1920* (Princeton: Princeton Univ. Press, 1991).

13. *Motography*, 23 Nov. 1912, 394, referred to Brandt as "the guy who puts all the bull in the bulletins."

14. *Motography*, 31 Aug. 1912, 166.

15. *Motography*, 9 Jan. 1915, 50.

16. *Motion Picture News*, 4 Jan. 1919, 66.

17. Interview with author, 26 Oct. 1989.

3. From Broadway to Hollywood

1. *Variety*, 1 May 1917, 29.

2. *Motion Picture News*, 27 Dec. 1919, 178, credited the Cohns; an ad in the

10 Jan. 1920 issue gave the 1600 Broadway address but credited the National Film Corporation of America as producer.

3. *Motion Picture News*, 27 Dec. 1919, 178.

4. *Motion Picture News*, 10 March 1920, 3317.

5. *Motion Picture News*, 17 April 1920, 3512.

6. Fred J. Balshofer and Arthur C. Miller, *One Reel a Week* (Berkeley: Univ. of California Press, 1967), 140.

7. Edward Small, "You Don't Have to Be Crazy to Be in Show Business But It Helps!: Autobiography of Edward Small, As Told to Robert E. Kent," 211, in the Edward Small Collection, University of Southern California, Department of Special Collections, hereafter abbreviated as USC-Special Collections.

8. Ibid., 212.

9. On the importance of Herbert J. Miles, see Howard T. Lewis, *The Motion Picture Industry* (New York: Van Nostrand, 1933), 4, 11-12; whether the Miles brothers or Percival Waters's Kinetograph Company was the first to open up a rental exchange is problematical; see Charles Musser, *The Emergence of Cinema: The American Screen to 1907* (New York: Scribner's, 1990), 367.

10. *Motion Picture News*, 2 April 1921, 2243.

11. Brandt did the same with *Life's Greatest Question* in addition to supervising the editing. Brandt thought of himself as a filmmaker, not in the way Mayer, Goldwyn, or even Harry did, but as someone able to provide product for exhibitors, even if it meant creating a company to do so. Thus in April 1921 Brandt, still fascinated by serials, became president of the Star Serial Corporation with the idea of making serials for Eddie Polo, whose career he had tried to promote at Universal. Brandt had no success with that company, either.

12. *Motion Picture News*, 13 Jan. 1923, 216.

13. Small, "You Don't Have to Be Crazy," 212.

14. Robert Grau, "The Growth of Universal," in *The First Tycoons*, ed. Richard Dyer MacCann (Metuchen, N.J.: Scarecrow, 1987), 55.

15. *Motion Picture News*, 12 Jan. 1924, 143.

16. "C.B.C. Starts Independent Exchanges," *Motion Picture News*, 16 Feb. 1924, 732.

17. Her story is recounted in *People*, 9 Feb. 1987, 49.

18. *Motion Picture News*, 5 Sept. 1925, 1142.

19. *Motion Picture News*, 10 Oct. 1925, 1684.

20. Bruce Torrence, *Hollywood: The First Hundred Years* (New York: Zoetrope, 1982), 87.

21. Columbia's net income for 1931 was $560,292; for 1932, $574,292.

22. The contract is in the Edward Small Collection at USC.

23. Burkan's letter to Wright and Brandt's letter to Harry are in the Jack Oakie Collection, USC-Special Collections. USC archivist Ned Comstock believes the correspondence is there because Loyd Wright was Oakie's lawyer.

24. Lewis, *Motion Picture Industry*, 105.

25. I have reconstructed the encounter from the *Murder on the Roof* teletypes between 10 Jan. and 13 Feb. 1930.

26. Details come from *The Miracle Woman* teletypes of 10 Feb. and 11 Aug. 1930.

27. In his autobiography, *The Name above the Title* (New York: Macmillan, 1971), 131, Capra claims the con man dies at the end, which is not true; Capra's contempt for the film ("a can of claptrap and corn") apparently blinded him to its virtues.

28. Marquis James and Bessie Rowland James, *Biography of a Bank: The Story of Bank of America N.T. & S.A.* (New York: Harper & Brothers, 1954), 245-47.

29. Gerald D. Nash, *A.P. Giannini and the Bank of America* (Norman: Univ. of Oklahoma Press, 1992), 120.

30. Attilio H. Giannini, "The First Loans," in *The First Tycoons*, ed. MacCann, 57-60.

31. Letter to author, 4 April 1992.

32. Thomas, *King Cohn*, 79.

33. Hank Messick, *The Beauties and the Beasts: The Mob in Show Business* (New York: David McKay, 1973), 54.

34. Ibid., 53, 102; Eugene Rosow, *Born to Lose: The Gangster Film in America* (New York: Oxford Univ. Press, 1978), 151, repeats the story of the Roselli connection.

35. *New York World Telegram*, 3 May 1933, sec. 2, 21.

4. The Patriarch

1. On Ralph Cohn's career see "Businessman Who Blends the World of TV and Movies: Ralph Cohn of Screen Gems," *Printers' Ink* 267 (1 May 1959): 60-66; "Screen Gems' Secret Weapon," *Sponsor* 13 (18 April 1959): 36+.

2. *Columbia Pictures Television: The Studio and the Creative Process* (New York: Museum of Broadcasting, 1987), 13.

3. Interview with Robert Cohn, 4 June 1990.

4. Joseph Curtis's son, Bruce Cohn Curtis, attributes his father's death to losing the project, maintaining that Joseph Curtis's production company was the lawful owner of the script since it was Curtis who hired Schulberg to write it; cf. Stephen Farber and Marc Green, *Hollywood Dynasties* (New York: Putnam, 1984), 47.

5. A Scott Berg, *Goldwyn: A Biography* (New York: Ballantine, 1990), 333.

6. Richard B. Jewell, with Vernon Harbin, *The RKO Story* (New York: Arlington House, 1982), 70.

7. Briskin's tenure at RKO was brief and unnoteworthy; in 1938 he was replaced as head of production by the great Pandro S. Berman.

8. Until at least May 1957 Spingold's name remained on the roster as vice president, public relations, alongside Lazarus's as vice president, advertising and publicity; see Appendix B, chart 2, p. 197.

9. On Buchman's involvement in *The Jolson Story*, see Bernard F. Dick, *Radical Innocence: A Critical Study of the Hollywood Ten* (Lexington: Univ. Press of Kentucky, 1988), 62-63.

10. Interview with Evelyn Keyes, 30 May 1990.

11. Information about Audience Research, Inc., is derived from "Gallup Poll Finds How to Sell a Movie," *Look*, 26 Oct. 1948, 54-55; and *What's Happening in Hollywood*, 21 Sept. 1946, n.p.

12. Samuel Marx, *A Gaudy Spree: The Literary Life of Hollywood in the 1930s* (New York: Franklin Watts, 1987), 171.

5. The Boss

1. Interview with Evelyn Keyes, 30 May 1990. Subsequent quotations are from this interview.

2. Evelyn Keyes, *Scarlett O'Hara's Younger Sister: My Lively Life in and Out of Hollywood* (Secaucus, N.J.: Lyle Stuart, 1977), 162.

3. On Giannini's involvement with Italy's fascist government, see Anthony Slide, "Hollywood's Fascist Follies," *Film Comment* 27 (July-Aug. 1991): 64.

4. I am indebted to Paul Lazarus for describing Harry's office in his letter of 4 April 1990.

5. Similar thanks to Malvin Wald for his letter of 3 June 1990 about the executive dining room.

6. Frederick Christian, "Buddy Adler: Hollywood's Last Tycoon," *Los Angeles Examiner*, "The American Weekly," 13 March 1960, 18.

6. CapraCohn

1. Capra, *The Name above the Title*; Joseph McBride, *Frank Capra: The Catastrophe of Success* (New York: Simon & Schuster, 1992).

2. Such is the conclusion, and a valid one, of Raymond Charney, *American Vision: The Films of Frank Capra* (New York: Cambridge Univ. Press, 1986). Robert Sklar, *Movie-Made America: A Cultural History of the Movies* (New York: Vintage, 1975), 214, compares Capra with Disney as filmmakers with "remarkable skill at infusing social myths and dreams with humor, sentiment and a sense of shared moral precepts and responsibilities," a skill that explains their lasting appeal.

3. *The Name above the Title*, 78-80.

4. McBride, *Frank Capra*, 186-87.

5. I am grateful to Terrance McCluskey, director, Records and Archival Management, Sony Pictures Entertainment, who, on 13 March 1991 at Columbia's New York office at 711 Fifth Avenue, showed me copies of Capra's contracts from 1927 to 1932.

6. See Charles Maland, "Frank Capra at Columbia: Necessity and Invention," in *Columbia Pictures: Portrait of a Studio*, ed. Bernard F. Dick (Lexington: Univ. Press of Kentucky, 1992), 74.

7. Raymond Durgnat, in *The Crazy Mirror: Hollywood Comedy and the American Image* (New York: Delta, 1970), 123-34, distinguishes between the Republican self-help film and the New Deal film, noting that *Mr. Deeds* is politically ambiguous. Deeds is self-reliant and a self-employed man (i.e., a Republican), who wishes to help the unfortunate (the starving farmers)—a New Deal philosophy that makes him a Roosevelt Republican.

8. Morris Dickstein, in "It's a Wonderful Life, But . . . ," *American Film* 7 (May 1980): 42-47, has also observed similarities between Chaplin and Capra.

9. Although "screwball comedy" seems to defy definition, Molly Haskell in her Foreword to Ed Sikov, *Screwball: Hollywood's Romantic Comedies* (New York: Crown, 1989), 10, comes closest when she calls it "a sort of existential American version of the French *l'amour fou:* a challenge, in the name of love, to the very precepts on which a sane and civilized society is based." She also notes that these "often anarchic and exhilarating" movies turn the world upside down, thus enabling men and women to release their inhibitions and find themselves as well as each other. Perhaps the best way of summing up screwball is to quote Peter Warne's line in *It Happened One Night*, when Ellie's father asks if Peter really loves his daughter. After giving all the reasons why no one could love her, Peter finally admits he does—and then adds: "But don't hold that against me. I'm a little

screwy myself." Sikov himself (17) rightly calls the world portrayed in screwball "wider" and "more contradictory" than that in other 1930s films.

10. Molly Haskell, *From Reverence to Rape: The Treatment of Women in the Movies* (New York: Holt, Rinehart and Winston, 1974), 15.

11. *The Name above the Title*, 495.

12. On the transformation of *The Front Page* into *His Girl Friday*, and Hildy's change of gender as Hawks's inspiration, see Gerald Mast, *Howard Hawks, Storyteller* (New York: Oxford Univ. Press, 1982), 208-42.

13. On the comedy of remarriage, see Stanley Cavell, *Pursuits of Happiness: The Hollywood Comedy of Remarriage* (Cambridge, Mass.: Harvard Univ. Press, 1981).

14. Elizabeth Kendall, in *The Runaway Bride: Hollywood Romantic Comedy of the 1930s* (New York: Knopf, 1990), has shown that the Capra influence exists in such disparate films as *Swing Time*, *The Awful Truth*, *Make Way for Tomorrow*, *Stage Door*, and *Love Affair* (see especially 103, 168, 192, 200, 221). Sikov, *Screwball*, has detected Capra touches in *Libeled Lady*, *Breakfast for Two*, *Red Salute*, *It's a Wonderful World*, *Ball of Fire*, and *The Bride Came C.O.D.* (see 92, 192, 215).

15. Grace Moore, *You're Only Human Once* (Garden City, N.Y.: Doubleday, 1944), 200: "Disconsolately I went over to Columbia . . . and signed what was to be the most fortunate contract of my career." Since *One Night of Love* was based on incidents from her life, she had a role in shaping the plot and deciding on the music she would sing; see Rowena Rutherford Farrar, *Grace Moore and Her Many Worlds* (New York: Cornwall Books, 1982), 158.

16. *The Name above the Title*, 23.

17. McBride, *Frank Capra*, 373.

18. *Mr. Smith's* budget was $1,674,400. It was a box office disappointment, making *Variety's* "All-Time Rental Champs" list only in 1992, by which time it had grossed a mere $3,500,000; see *Variety*, 22 Feb. 1992, 168.

7. Harry's Three P's

1. Aubrey Solomon, *Twentieth Century-Fox: A Corporate and Financial History* (Metuchen, N.J.: Scarecrow, 1988), 103.

2. Budget and salary information for the Universal, Warners, and MGM pictures discussed in this chapter has been taken from the respective studio collections in USC-Special Collections.

3. See the comparative breakdown in Thomas Schatz, *The Genius of the System: Hollywood Filmmaking in the Studio Era* (New York: Pantheon, 1988), 380.

4. Ibid., 379.

5. Lewis, *Motion Picture Industry*, 118-19.

6. Figures come from the George Stevens Collection, Margaret Herrick Library, Academy of Motion Picture Arts and Sciences, Los Angeles.

7. Schatz, *Genius of the System*, 334.

8. Barbara Leaming, *If This Was Happiness: A Biography of Rita Hayworth* (New York: Viking, 1989), 34-35.

9. Karl Thiede, "Harry Cohn of Columbia," *Views and Reviews*, Spring 1970, 38.

10. See Chapter 6, note 3, above.

11. Information about Irene Dunne's salaries and contracts comes from the Irene Dunne Collection, USC-Special Collections.

12. Harry's attempt to bring Clara Bow to Columbia can be documented from evidence in the Clara Bow Collection, USC-Special Collections.

13. Information about Lester Cowan derives from the Columbia teletypes.

14. Budgets for Edward Small's Columbia features come from the Edward Small Collection, USC-Special Collections.

15. On Spiegel's early years in Hollywood, see Andrew Sinclair, *Spiegel: The Man behind the Pictures* (Boston: Little, Brown, 1987), 42-54.

16. Selznick's correspondence with Huston, Spiegel, and Harry can be found in the John Huston Collection at the Herrick.

17. On the film's turbulent production history, which partly explains Columbia's delay in releasing it, see Charles Higham, *The Films of Orson Welles* (Berkeley: Univ. of California Press, 1971), 111-24.

18. Leaming, *If This Was Happiness*, 303-6.

19. Information about Phoenix comes from the Daniel Taradash Collection in the American Heritage Center at the University of Wyoming at Laramie.

20. Letter to author, 8 April 1990.

8. Harry and the Production Code

1. Jack Vizzard, *See No Evil: Life inside a Hollywood Censor* (New York: Pocket Books, 1971), 76. For a history of the Production Code, including text and amendments, see Leonard J. Leff and Jerold J. Simmons, *The Dame in the Kimono: Hollywood, Censorship and the Production Code from the 1920s to the 1960s* (New York: Grove Weidenfeld, 1990).

2. Letter to author, 5 June 1990.

3. References to the correspondence between the Breen Office and Columbia come from the files of the Motion Picture Association Production Code Administration Collection, sometimes called the Hays Office Collection, in the Herrick.

4. On the Conference of Studio Unions strike, see Larry Ceplair and Steven Englund, *The Inquisition in Hollywood: Politics in the Film Community, 1930-1960* (Garden City, N.Y.: Anchor Press/Doubleday, 1980), 217-25.

9. Harry's Hierarchy

1. *Motion Picture Herald*, 13 May 1939, 49-50.

2. Vidor returned to Columbia for *Song without End* (1960) but died before he could complete it; George Cukor finished the picture.

3. Shooting schedules are given in "Columbia Pictures Productions Information, 1926-73," n.p., n.d., at the Herrick.

4. Both USC and the Wisconsin Center for Film and Theatre Research at Madison have Warners collections; both UCLA and USC have Fox Collections. (USC also has a Universal collection.)

5. They are in the George Stevens Collection at the Herrick.

6. The script of *The Talk of the Town* cost around $96,000, including $5,000 for the rights to Sidney Harmon's story that became the basis of the movie. George Stevens received $100,000 for directing; photography came to around $16,000. Cast salaries came to $314,432, including $50,000 for Jean Arthur, $100,000 for Ronald Colman, and $106,250 for Cary Grant. Set operation (grips, prop men, set

maintenance) came to $24,291; about $82,000 went for the set, including design and construction; surprisingly little (around $16,000) for costumes and makeup; $43,000 for processing, recording, dubbing, and editing; and $22,349 for music. The grand total also included a 20 percent overhead ($169,832) and a "general" category covering wage adjustments, social security, and insurance that added up to $47,672. The final cost of *The Talk of the Town* was approximately $1 million.

7. On Boetticher's westerns, see Jim Kitses, *Horizons West* (Bloomington: Indiana Univ. Press, 1969), 89-130; Stanley J. Solomon, in *Beyond Formula: American Film Genres* (New York: Harcourt Brace Jovanovich, 1976), 48-51, provides a good analysis of Boetticher's *Comanche Station* (1960).

8. On Neill's westerns, see Don Miller, *Hollywood Corral* (New York: Popular Library, 1976), 32.

9. The memo was donated to the Gene Autry Western Heritage Museum in Los Angeles by Republic Pictures chairman Russell Goldsmith in 1991.

10. For details of Autry's screen career, see Gene Autry, with Mickey Herskowitz, *Back in the Saddle Again* (Garden City, N.Y.: Doubleday, 1978).

11. Miller, *Hollywood Corral*, 145.

12. The major Columbia serials are discussed in Ron Kinnard, *Fifty Years of Serial Thrills* (Metuchen, N.J.: Scarecrow, 1983), 101-27.

13. The standard work on Columbia's comedy shorts is Ted Okuda, with Edward Watz, *The Columbia Shorts: Two-Reel Hollywood Film Comedies, 1933-1958* (Jefferson, N.C.: McFarland, 1986).

14. Leonard Mosley, *Disney's World* (New York: Stein and Day, 1985), 128.

15. To understand how the department functioned, Ellwood Ullmann, "A Labor of Laughs at Columbia," *Los Angeles Times*, 11 April 1982, Calendar, 3, is indispensable.

16. For the script and background of "You Nazty Spy," see Joan Howard Mauer, *The Three Stooges Book of Scripts* (Secaucus, N.J.: Citadel Press, 1984), 180-221.

17. Thus far there is only one major source for Columbia's mystery series—Jon Tuska, *The Detective in Hollywood* (Garden City, N.J.: Doubleday, 1978), who discusses the Lone Wolf (264-75), Ellery Queen (209-24), Boston Blackie (289-99), Crime Doctor (250-55), and Whistler (283-88) movies. Tuska repeats much of this information in *In Manors and Alleys: A Casebook on the American Detective Film* (Westport, Conn.: Greenwood, 1988).

18. William Castle's Whistler films comprise *The Whistler* (1944), *The Mark of the Whistler* (1944, original story by Cornell Woolrich), *The Power of the Whistler* (1945), *The Voice of the Whistler* (1945), and *Mysterious Intruder* (1945). The last Whistler, *Return of the Whistler* (1948), was based on a Woolrich original but was directed by D. Ross Lederman.

19. Harry's notes on *The Flying Missile* were included in the (as yet uncatalogued) 1950 Wyoming teletypes.

20. One of America's most famous radio writers, Norman Corwin, was Columbia's first choice for the script; his, however, proved unsatisfactory.

21. For a general discussion of Rossen's films, see Alan Casty, *The Films of Robert Rossen* (New York: Museum of Modern Art, 1969).

22. Rossen named fifty-four names.

23. The outline and conference notes were filed with the 1948-49 Wyoming teletypes.

24. Robert Penn Warren, *All the King's Men* (New York: Modern Library, 1953), 461-62.

25. For the Taradash biography, see Jay Boyer, "Daniel Taradash," *DLB* 44 (1986): 370-77.

26. My knowledge of Taradash's role in *Eternity* derives from an interview published in *Columbia Pictures: Portrait of a Studio*, ed. Dick, 145-51, and a detailed letter of 8 April 1990.

27. Leff and Simmons, *Dame in the Kimono*, 135.

28. Taradash credits Shurlock with minimizing any censorship problems; cf. *Columbia Pictures*, ed. Dick, 150.

29. On the casting and filming of *Eternity*, see Fred Zinnemann, "From Here to Eternity," *Sight and Sound* 57 (Winter 1987/88): 20-25.

30. Ibid., 25.

10. Death and Transfiguration

1. On *In a Lonely Place*, see James W. Palmer, "*In a Lonely Place:* Paranoia in the Dream Factory," *Literature/Film Quarterly*, 13, no. 3 (1985): 200-207; J.P. Telotte, *Voices in the Dark: The Narrative Patterns of Film Noir* (Urbana: Univ. of Illinois Press, 1989), 189-90; Jon Tuska, *Dark Cinema: American Film Noir in Cultural Perspective* (Westport, Conn.: Greenwood, 1989), 208-10. On *The Big Heat*, see Tom Flinn, "*The Big Heat* and *The Big Combo:* Rogue Cops and Mink Coated Girls," *Velvet Light Trap* 11 (1974): 23-28; and Thomas Schatz, *Hollywood Genres: Formulas, Filmmaking and the Studio System* (New York: Random House, 1981), 142-44. On *The Man from Laramie*, see Jeanine Basinger, *Anthony Mann* (Boston: Twayne, 1979), 124-28. *The BFI Companion to the Western*, ed. Edward Buscombe (New York: Atheneum, 1988), notes the merits of Boetticher's *Buchanan Rides Alone* (252), *Decision at Sundown* (258), and *Ride Lonesome* (293), as well as Mann's *The Man from Laramie* (283-84). Patrick McGilligan, *A Double Life: George Cukor* (New York: St. Martin's, 1991), 215, quotes François Truffaut on Holliday's 1954 film *It Should Happen to You* ("a masterpiece"); for an overview of Holliday's Columbia films, see Ruth Prigozy, "Judy Holliday: The Star and the Studio," in *Columbia Pictures*, ed. Dick, 131-44.

2. Financial details of the Wald agreement are taken from the *Hollywod Reporter*, 26 Aug. 1952, 1, 5.

3. My reconstruction of Wald's experiences at Columbia derives from material in the Jerry Wald Collection, USC-Special Collections.

4. Thomas, *King Cohn*, xvii.

5. Clifford Odets was thinking along the same lines; he planned to call the character Zuleika, the Persian name for Potiphar's wife in Byron's "The Bride of Abydos"; cf. Leaming, *If This Was Happiness*, 303-6.

6. Paul Lazarus, letter to author, 14 Sept. 1991. On the April 1957 organizational chart (Appendix B, p. 198), Lillian Burns [Sidney] is listed as executive assistant to the president (Harry), and George Sidney, as executive producer.

7. Thomas, *King Cohn*, 363.

8. I am grateful to Rev. Thomas L. Sheridan, S.J., professor of theology at St. Peter's College in Jersey City, N.J., for explaining to me how complex a matter baptism is. My conclusions on the validity of Harry's baptism are based on a standard text that Roman Catholic priests would have known in 1958 in one of its many editions: Rev. Heribert Jone, *Moral Theology*, trans. Urban Adelman, 15th ed. (Westminster, Md.: Newman Press, 1961).

Bibliographical Essay

Early Film History

Although there are numerous books on the silents, anyone writing about a studio and attempting to place it within the context of Hollywood history must begin with Scribner's History of the American Cinema series, whose first three volumes under Charles Harpole's editorship reflect the highest standards of film scholarship: Charles Musser, *The Emergence of Cinema: The American Screen to 1907* (1990); Eileen Bowser, *The Transformation of Cinema, 1907-1915* (1990); and Richard Koszarski, *An Evening's Entertainment: The Age of the Silent Feature Picture, 1915-1928* (1990).

The dedication of Bowser's volume is significant both for the dedicatee and the inscription: "Dedicated to Richard Griffith, former Curator of the Department of Film of the Museum of Modern Art, who assigned me to read The Moving Picture World in January 1955. I have not finished it yet." These encouraging words from another legendary MOMA curator attest to the importance of the trades, the best known in the silent era being

The Moving Picture World

Since the trades served the industry, they often contained information that was speculative and in need of verification. Nevertheless, it is impossible to trace the whereabouts of the Cohns and Joe Brandt during the critical years 1912-32 without them. While some of the trades may have been promotional media for established film companies, they are reasonably accurate in their accounts of Columbia in its formative stage (Hall Room Boys Photoplays and CBC). The chief problem with the trades is the number of name changes and mergers. A publication might originate under one title and expire under another: *Nickelodeon* becomes *Motography* (1909-18). One reads the *Moving Picture World* from 1907 until 1927, when it is absorbed into *Exhibitor's Herald*, becoming *Exhibitor's Herald-World*. The best (and thus far only) guide through the labyrinth is Anthony Slide, *International Film, Radio, and Television Journals* (Westport, Conn.: Greenwood, 1985), which not only demystifies the renamings and transformations but also lists library locations.

Archives and Special Collections

As Thomas Schatz has shown in *The Genius of the System*, archival research is imperative for studio history. Schatz admits, however, that his decision to concentrate on MGM, Warners, Selznick, and Universal was based on, among other considerations, "the availability of their corporate records in archives around the country" (493). Columbia presents a problem: while there are Universal and MGM collections at the University of Southern California, and Warners collections at USC and the Wisconsin Center for Film and Theatre Research at Madison, there is at present no comparable Columbia collection. What the American Heritage Center at the University of Wyoming at Laramie has called the Columbia Pictures Collection consists of thirty-six boxes of material, largely teletypes between New York and Los Angeles, with occasional story conference notes, summaries of audience responses at previews, and transcripts of post-preview discussions by studio executives, some of whom are named (e.g., S. Sylvan Simon after a *Fuller Brush Girl* preview in Los Angeles in June 1950); but, except for Harry and Jack, it is often difficult to identify the parties. Although there are not a large number of transcripts, those that exist illustrate a thorough knowledge of filmmaking and a commitment to excellence that even extended to B movies. A scene will get a bigger laugh if the dissolve is held longer, or it will move faster if it is reedited. The dialogue will be more audible if the music is softer; conversely, a scene might profit from the addition of music. Tempo was always a major concern: "I worry about the TEMPO of the telephone call—it's much too SLOW," someone (perhaps Harry) complained after a preview of *The Brave Bulls* in September 1950. "Trim" is also a recurring criticism. ("TRIM reactions," "TRIM second insert," "TRIM opening," S. Sylvan Simon ordered after a *Fuller Brush Girl* preview.)

While the Columbia material at the American Heritage Center enhances one's appreciation of the "genius of the system" and figures prominently in this book, it is insufficient for a study of either the studio or Harry Cohn. Even if there were a Columbia collection on the order of the Fox collection at UCLA, it would not answer all the questions a researcher has. No collection could. Many actors, directors, screenwriters, and producers have established their own collections at various centers. While the Margaret Herrick Library in the Center for Motion Picture Study at the Academy of Motion Picture Arts and Sciences in Los Angeles has an excellent Paramount collection, the collection of one of the studio's most famous director-producers, Cecil B. DeMille, is at Brigham Young University. While USC has an MGM collection, the Herrick has the collection of one of MGM's best known directors, George Cukor.

Thus anyone researching a studio must go from the studio collection to the collections of those associated with it. For Columbia, this means the following:

The Frank Capra Archive in the Wesleyan Cinema Archives at Wesleyan University is significant for Capra's replies to the many fans who wrote to him personally. Their letters make it abundantly clear that they regarded him as their spokesperson, expressing their own beliefs about freedom, democracy, justice, and dissent. Interestingly, audiences knew enough about Capra to write to him as if he were the film's "author," suggesting that "Capraesque" was more a way of life than a label.

The John Huston Collection at the Herrick. Although Huston is not a name one associates with Columbia, he directed three films for the studio; the last two, *Fat City* (1972) and *Annie* (1982), have nothing to do with Harry's Columbia, but the first, *We Were Strangers* (1949), does. While there is little in the way of production material on *We Were Strangers*, a memo from David O. Selznick, occasioned by the casting of his wife, Jennifer Jones, as the female lead, confirms Selznick's perfectionism as well as his obsession with the memo form (see p. 137).

The Edward Small Collection at USC. The Small collection is significant for two reasons: Small's unpublished autobiography, "You Don't Have to Be Crazy to Be in Show Business But It Helps!" which attests to the high regard in which Jack Cohn was held and the skepticism that greeted Harry's entrance into film; and the sensible budgets of Small's Columbia films that explain his seven-year relationship with the studio.

The Jerry Wald Collection at USC. Although Wald's tenure at Columbia was brief (1952-55) and frustrating (Malvin Wald believes his brother's early death four years after Harry's was not unrelated to his Columbia stay), Jerry Wald was always the consummate producer, checking scripts for motivation and makeup tests for accuracy. The Wald Collection, which includes production information on such films as *The Long Gray Line, Miss Sadie Thompson, Tight Spot, The Queen Bee,* and *Three for the Show,* is chiefly important for the *Human Desire* material, Wald's 1961 account of his travails to Fred Zinnemann (see p. 184), and Harry's script notes on *Three for the Show,* in which he voiced his objections to musicals lacking integration of score and script ("I have never made a musical that threw music in from nowhere. In addition all the dialogue leading up to the song is terrible").

Other USC Collections. While Irene Dunne and Jack Oakie were not Columbia regulars (Dunne made five films for the studio, Oakie two), their collections are significant for vastly different reasons: Dunne's for her salary and the studio's insistence that she fulfill her three-picture contract; Oakie's for Joe Brandt's 1929 reaction to Harry's fear of being fired (see p. 46). The George Sidney Collection at USC consists of scrapbooks—a disappointment to anyone hoping to find some compelling reason for Harry's faith in Sidney's ability to handle production.

The Daniel Taradash Collection at the American Heritage Center of the University of Wyoming. While the Center has extensive holdings, they range from a handful of clippings and some publicity stills to copies of executed contracts and budgets. The Taradash collection reflects the latter; thus it has been possible to document the arrangement Columbia made with Phoenix, the independent production company Taradash formed with Julian Blaustein (see p. 140).

Eyewitness Accounts

As those who were part of Hollywood's Golden Age decline in number, it becomes increasingly important to record their memories. Admittedly, memory is a finely spun web that unravels with time, yet there is nothing like the firsthand testimony of a true participant as opposed to an onlooker. If one has done enough research (and is a student of human nature), it is not difficult to tell when the subject is embellishing the past or rewriting it. Enough wrong dates, casts, and titles should make one suspicious. But when one enters book-lined apartments like those of Ron Randell and Evelyn Keyes and hears articulate actors speak knowledgeably about their days at Columbia; or when one gets well-documented letters from Betty Garrett and Paul Lazarus and hears Oscar Saul reconstruct encounters with Harry that corroborate what one has heard from others—there is every reason to accept them. Perhaps it was Harry's authoritarianism that sharpened wits and left indelible memories; perhaps the experience of working at an ex-Poverty Row studio makes one less inclined to idealize it. Interviews with and letters from Robert Cohn, Betty Garrett, William N. Graf, Evelyn Keyes, Paul Lazarus, Ron Randell, Oscar Saul, and Daniel Taradash impart an authenticity that no amount of scholarship can duplicate.

The one name that will always be linked with Columbia is Frank Capra. While his autobiography, *The Name above the Title*, is engagingly written, it has been criticized as being more fiction that fact, as Joseph McBride has shown in a spectacular work of humane revisionism, *Frank Capra: The Catastrophe of Success* (New York: Simon & Schuster, 1992). If the autobiography "reads like a script," as Donald C. Willis, *The Films of Frank Capra* (Metuchen, N.J.: Scarecrow, 1974), 207, claims, it is a Capra script offering hope to the world's "little people."

The History of Columbia

Of all the studios, Columbia has attracted the least attention from film historians; even Universal has done better. Perhaps the problem is the "King Cohn/White Fang" syndrome, the Poverty Row stigma, or a general unfamiliarity with Columbia's films. Perhaps, too, it is the unavailability of production files or the absence of a specific location for Columbia material. Since Harry Cohn *was* Columbia, the first book that dealt with the studio was Bob Thomas's 1967 biography, *King Cohn*; interestingly, Bosley Crowther published his history of MGM (*The Lion's Share*) before his biography of Louis Mayer (*Hollywood Rajah*). Harry would have been pleased that he came first. In view of Thomas's longtime association with Hollywood, *King Cohn* cannot be dismissed as mere popular biography. While I have profited from it and cited it several times, the absence of footnotes and sources has in a way proved a blessing, allowing me to go my own way and work from the trades, teletypes, and interviews. The Harry Cohn of the teletypes is a far more intelligent studio head than "King Cohn," who does not seem to have had the slightest idea of narrative structure or character development.

The first serious look at Columbia as a studio was Edward Buscombe's "Notes on Columbia Pictures Corporation, 1926-41," *Screen* 15 (Autumn 1975): 65-82. Although Buscombe modestly writes that his article "amounts to very little in the way of real knowledge" and was "the result of a few hours in the library" (82), he has produced a sketch needing only expansion to be complete. Within seventeen pages, he covers the creation of the studio, the role of A.H. Giannini (whom he carefully distinguishes from his brother, A.P. Giannini, thus rectifying a common mistake), Columbia's tightly-knit family of brothers and brothers-in-law, and an appreciation of the way Columbia's liberal (Robert Riskin) and left-wing writers (Paul Jarrico, Sidney Buchman) perpetuated Capra's populism.

While there have been a number of books on the Hollywood studios, the most scholarly are Douglas Gomery, *The Hollywood Studio System* (New York: St. Martin's, 1986), whose section on Columbia (161-72) is especially valuable for its list of the studio's net profits and assets from 1930 to 1949; and Joel W. Finler, *The Hollywood Story* (New York: Crown, 1988), whose coffee-table appearance belies the wealth of information inside.

Although my primary debt is to the sources acknowledged in this essay, it is not meant to detract from those cited in the notes. To include everyone would result in a list longer than the end credits of a contemporary film.

Index